IMAGES
of America

TOWNS OF THE SACRAMENTO RIVER DELTA

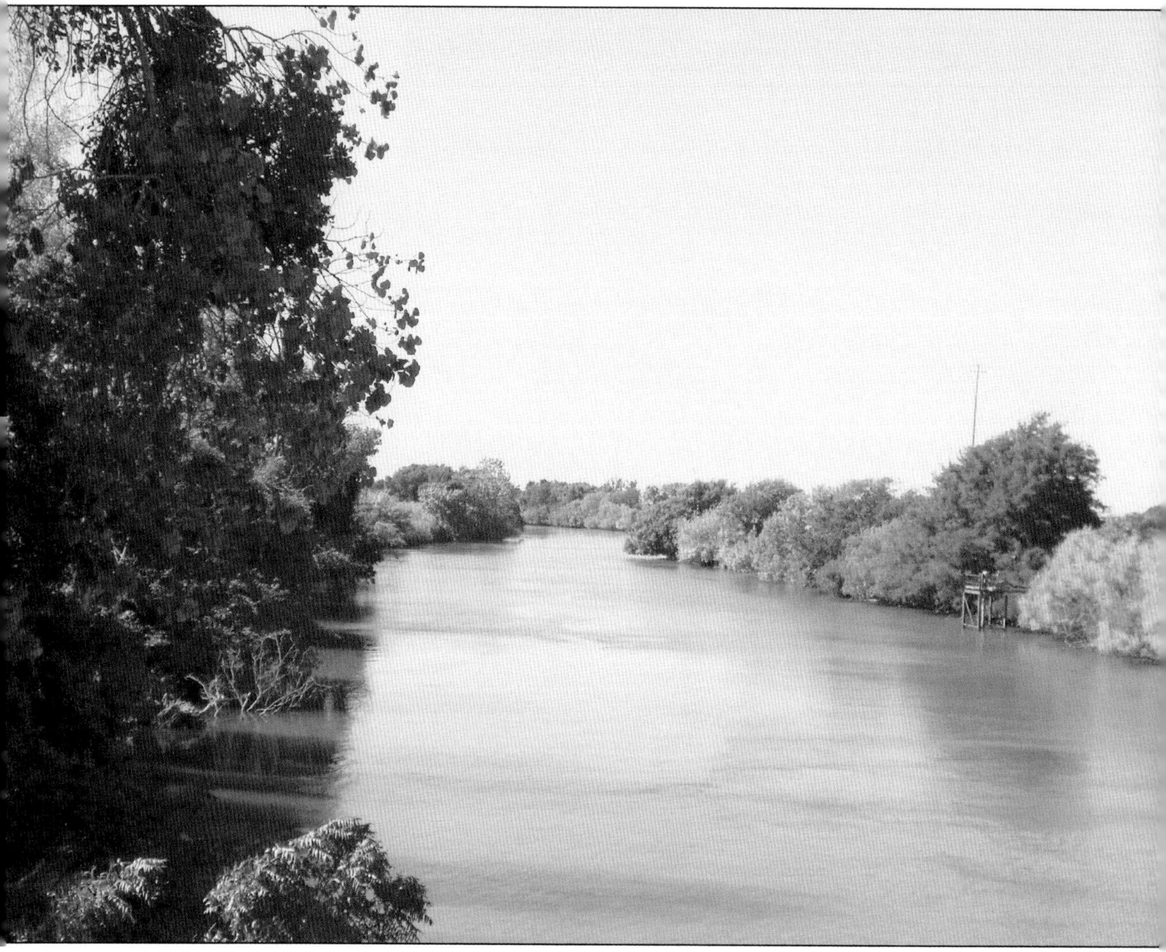

Sutter Slough looks extremely peaceful in this 2012 photograph taken from the bridge spanning the slough. (Photograph by Christina Pezzaglia.)

On the Cover: This image taken in 1935 shows L.W. McCall Contract Hauling and the Imperial Theatre, located on Market Street in Walnut Grove.

IMAGES
of America

TOWNS OF THE SACRAMENTO RIVER DELTA

Philip Pezzaglia

ARCADIA
PUBLISHING

ISBN 978-0-7385-9626-6

Published by Arcadia Publishing
Charleston, South Carolina

Printed in the United States of America

Library of Congress Control Number: 2012943373

For all general information, please contact Arcadia Publishing:
Telephone 843-853-2070
Fax 843-853-0044
E-mail sales@arcadiapublishing.com
For customer service and orders:
Toll-Free 1-888-313-2665

Visit us on the Internet at www.arcadiapublishing.com

Contents

Acknowledgments

The majority of the photographs in this book come from the archives at the Sacramento River Delta Historical Society, the Rio Vista Museum, and the Isleton Museum. Several additional photographs came from personal collections or other museums and historical societies and have been credited to those sources.

I would like to extend a heartfelt thank-you to the following organizations and individuals: the Sacramento River Delta Historical Society (SRDHS), Tom Herzog, Esther Koopman, and Bobbie Collier; the Isleton Museum, the Isleton Brannan-Andrus Island Historical Society (IBAHS), and Wendy MacDonald; the Rio Vista Museum (RVM); and the California State Library (CSL). Without the assistance of the aforementioned organizations and individuals and their willingness to allow me to view archives and learn from personal knowledge of the history of the delta, this book would not have been possible.

Most of all, I wish to thank my wife, Christina, and my daughters, Teresa and India, for being so very patient and supportive while I spent time researching and compiling this book. I greatly appreciate the time they spent accompanying me on several trips up and down the delta as well as the input and suggestions they made.

I also wish to thank my wife for taking several of the current photographs that appear in this book.

INTRODUCTION

The Sacramento River delta is one of the most beautiful places in California to live. And for those who do not reside in the area permanently, it has become an ideal place to vacation and enjoy boating, camping, and the many recreational facilities available as well as to explore the towns and communities that make the heart of the delta. The area is home to several quaint towns as well as former home to several towns that have disappeared and become just memories, now only seen in photographs displayed in local museums and in books written about the delta.

The communities that presently make up the Sacramento River delta are Rio Vista, Isleton, Ryde, Walnut Grove, Locke, Courtland, Hood, Clarksburg, and Freeport. Each has its own exciting tale of its founders and the origins of its name. With much determination and hard work, many generations have struggled to keep these delta towns alive. Unfortunately, there are a few communities that did not survive, namely Emmaton, Vorden, Paintersville, Webster, and Onsibo.

Many of the delta communities have similar origins; however, the passing of the 1861 Reclamation District Act by the California Legislature, which allowed for the drainage of delta lands and the construction of sturdier levees, probably had the greatest impact on the reclaiming of the delta and the founding of its towns. Each one of the delta communities holds a special place in the history of the area, and for that they should all be remembered, whether they continue to thrive or have been abandoned.

When Europeans first came to North America, it is estimated that California had a population of between 100,000 and 200,000 Indians. The Indians of California were rather passive, and perhaps because of this, they did not play an important role in California history. They were not hostile, except in a few isolated instances, usually letting the white man simply walk on undisturbed. Living in a favorable climate and hemmed in by high mountains to the east, the sea to the west, and the desert to the south, the Indians traveled little, engaging in no major wars and learning little except what came down from their past. As with most cultures that are not disturbed by outside influences, the lives of the Indians changed little from decade to decade, as they continued to live their lives governed by their heritage and beliefs.

The Spanish were the first Europeans to explore the western coast of America. Monterey Bay and Drakes Bay were explored, but San Francisco Bay was overlooked at first. When Gaspar de Portola and his men reached the area on November 1, 1769, they saw part of the great bay of San Francisco but were unimpressed, referring to it as an estuary.

In March 1772, Gov. Pedro Fages, accompanied by Father Crespi and others, tried to establish a mission in San Francisco Bay and saw the Sacramento River, calling it the "River of San Francisco." They traveled the waters as far as Antioch and then returned south, stopping long enough to survey the lands that led inward to the valley. These men are considered to be the first white men to view the river. Anza, in 1774, discovered that there were in fact two rivers, later called the Sacramento River and the San Joaquin River. Ayola, a Spanish lieutenant from Mexico, was the first seaman to explore San Francisco Bay thoroughly. He was very much impressed by the "estuary," as it had been called.

The first European vessels to explore the Sacramento River entered "the northern river of San Francisco" on October 23, 1811. This expedition, headed by Father Abella and Father Fortini and under the command of Jose Antonio Sanchez, braved the upstream current in a small boat. The group took a short voyage on the Sacramento before turning into the San Joaquin and heading back to the presidio of San Francisco.

Interest in the great river region lagged for a number of years, but on May 13, 1817, the first major exploration of the Sacramento River, from its mouth northward, began. Padres Duran and Abella, with 20 other men under the command of Lt. Louis Antonio Argullo, sailed in two launches up the river. At one point during their voyage, the party took refuge from a terrific wind behind the Montezuma Hills, near the present site of Rio Vista. They continued north until May 20, 1817, when they turned back. The group recorded its point of farthest exploration by carving a cross into an oak tree, the location of which is disagreed upon by researchers. Some believe it would be near the present-day town of Freeport. Other reports state that Padre Duran's diary describes that the Sutter Buttes were visible to the north and that the current swept them 14 leagues in the first day of their return journey. This would suggest that they had traveled farther north, to a point near the junction of the Sacramento and the Feather Rivers. In 1821, Lieutenant Argullo led a second expedition into the Sacramento Valley, this time on land. The group followed the Sacramento River north as far as the present-day site of the city of Redding, recording a number of Native American villages along the river.

The next exploration party to travel the Sacramento River was led by members of the Imperial Russian Navy. In 1824, Capt. Otto von Kotzebue sailed upstream from Fort Ross with two boats and 20 Aleut hunters. Some believe that Kotzebue's party may have reached as far as the mouth of the American River, while others claim that he only went as far as Freeport. It is noteworthy that a botanist with the Kotzebue expedition was the first to describe and name the California poppy (*Eschscholzia californica*).

The Spanish explorer Gabriel Moraga is credited with naming what would become the Feather River "El Rio de los Sacramentos." At the time, what would become the Sacramento River was still known as Rio de San Francisco. Over time, it became known as Rio del Santissimo Sacramento, or "River of the Most Blessed Sacrament," and eventually the Sacramento River.

In 1837, Great Britain sent Capt. Sir Edward Belchar and HMS *Sulphur* to chart the Sacramento River. Captain Belchar sent two boats upstream 150 miles. The information gathered on this voyage produced the first accurate charts of the lower Sacramento River.

The first American to explore the Sacramento River was Jedediah Smith, who followed it north as far as the Red Bluff vicinity in April 1828. Smith was under the impression that the Sacramento River was the legendary river Buenaventura, which was believed to flow west from the Rocky Mountains all the way to the Pacific Ocean.

On August 1, 1839, John Augustus Sutter chartered two schooners, the *Nicholas* and the *Isabella*, and set sail from San Francisco for the Sacramento Valley. At this point, there are multiple versions of the story. According to the July 1859 edition of *Hutchings' California Magazine*, Sutter chartered just the schooner *Isabella*, while Roger R. Olmsted's *Scow Schooners of San Francisco Bay* states that Sutter chartered two schooners, the *Nicholas* and the *Isabel*. Other accounts claim that either Jedediah Smith or John Fremont chartered the two ships.

Because of the numerous outlets of the Sacramento River, it took eight days to discover the main channel. When the explorers were approximately 10 miles below the current site of the city of Sacramento, 200 or more armed and rather hostile Indians intercepted them. However, the voyagers managed to win them over and were allowed to continue on their journey, accompanied by two of the Indians.

John Sutter founded Sacramento, originally called New Helevetia, on August 15, 1839. It included Sutter's settlement as well as the settlements of John Bidwell, Peter Lassen, John Sinclair, William Knight, William Chard, Theodore Cordua, and others, who all helped to promote regular traffic on the Sacramento River. In 1841, Sutter purchased Fort Ross for $30,000. The purchase included a schooner, which he renamed the *Sacramento*—not to be confused with the side-wheeler of the same name.

The first steamboat on the Sacramento, in 1847, was the *Sitka*, which is considered the first California river steamboat. William Leidesdorff, the former owner of most of the Folsom property, purchased it from the Russia America Company and had it reassembled on Yerba Buena Island. According to one source, the *Sitka* was a small 40-ton, 37-foot-long side-wheeler, which was so underpowered by its steam engine that it could barely make the journey. However, according to an article published in the July 1859 *Hutchings' California Magazine*, the *Sitka* was a stern-wheel vessel about 60 feet long and 17 feet wide. Its maiden voyage, under the command of Captain Leidesdorff, began on November 29, 1847, leaving from Yerba Buena for Sutter's Fort. The journey took six days, longer than it took a man making the journey on foot. On its return trip, it made such bad time that a team of oxen that left Sacramento at the same time arrived in Benicia before it. This vessel later had its engines removed and was converted into a sailing vessel, renamed the *Rainbow*. It sank in San Francisco Bay in late 1848.

When John Marshall discovered gold at Sutter's Mill on January 24, 1848, in Coloma, he had no way of knowing the impact that gold fever would have on California and the rest of the world. More than 100,000 gold-seekers descended on the goldfields of California in 1949, the majority of them traveling up the Sacramento River from San Francisco.

As river travel became more popular, better accommodations were needed. Sam Brannan brought the oceangoing vessel *Joven Guipuscoana* up the river, while Samuel J. Hensley and P.B. Reading brought in another oceangoing ship, the *Eliodora*. Both ships reached the Sacramento area during the early months of 1849, showing that the Sacramento River was open to navigation by large vessels. The first ship bearing cargo from the East Coast, the *Whiton* arrived in Sacramento via the Sacramento River on May 2, 1849.

The main problem with using sailing vessels on the river was that it took them a week or more to travel from San Francisco to Sacramento. The best solution to this problem was to enlist steamboats. After the poor performance of the *Sitka*, it was decided that there was a need to build steamships of greater size and power in order to bring both passengers and supplies to the various towns, mining camps, and landings on the waterways.

The next steamer to travel the Sacramento River was the side-wheeler *Sacramento*, which had been sent in pieces aboard a ship from New York to Sacramento, where it was assembled and named. It then met up with a line of schooners from San Francisco. Capt. John Van Pelt was the commander of the vessel.

The next ship to take up the San Francisco–Sacramento run was a small 36-ton steamship named the *Mint*, which was built in 1849. In October of that year, a large 400-ton propeller ship named *McKim* also became a part of the Sacramento–San Francisco run. The *McKim* had sailed from New Orleans through the Straits of Magellan to San Francisco in early 1849.

The first of the new, more powerful steamships to make its way up the river from San Francisco was the *Senator*, which arrived in Sacramento on November 5, 1849. It had come to San Francisco by way of Cape Horn on October 27. From that time on, it made three round-trips per week, carrying up to 300 passengers and 300 tons of freight per voyage. Its fares were $25 per passenger upriver and $30 per passenger downriver, and it charged $2 for each meal, $10 for staterooms, and $40 to $50 per ton for freight. During its first year on that run, its net profits exceeded $60,000 per month.

As more and more travelers headed upriver, a need for more steamships was evident. With his profits, one shipowner contracted to have more ships constructed, and before long, there was competition between shipowners, forcing fares and cargo rates down to one-third of what they had been. Time constraints became an issue, and there were competitions to see which vessel could become the fastest on the river. With this quest for speed came many boiler explosions, collisions, and ships running aground in shallow areas.

By 1853, there were six first-class steamships providing high-quality river travel from San Francisco to Sacramento. The California Steam Navigation Company soon came to dominate shipping on the mighty Sacramento. The company owned the ships *Confidence*, *Colusa*, *New World*, *Helen Hensley*, *Antelope*, *Governor Dana*, and *Sam Soule*. Soon after the company's incorporation in 1854, it gained control of several piers and wharfs on the river. With its ships and control of the landings, the company built up a virtual monopoly on the river and sent most of the other companies and private ships out of business.

The newly settled communities along the river began to grow—first with wharfs, hotels, general stores, schools, meeting halls, and later with post offices, banks, ferries, bridges, better roads and highways, canneries, train stations, and movie theaters. Eventually, churches were organized, lodges and fraternal organizations were established, and local government and fire departments were created. With the influx of settlers to the area and the variety of work created, many settlements developed into small communities of varying ethnicities, including Chinese, Japanese, Hindu, and Filipino.

It has been more than 160 years since the first communities were established within the confines of the delta. Knowing that, one ponders whether or not those early pioneers ever imagined what the delta would be like today.

One

Rio Vista

The original town of Rio Vista was established in 1858 by Col. Nathan H. Davis approximately one mile below the mouth of Cache Slough. Three years earlier, Davis had purchased 17,752 acres of John Bidwell's Los Ulpinos Mexican land grant for $400.

Because so many settlers had come to California in the Gold Rush, Davis intended to subdivide part of the land. He called this settlement Los Brazos del Rio because it was situated near where the river branched off into three waterways, eventually known as the Sacramento River, Steamboat Slough, and Cache Slough.

Located halfway between San Francisco and Sacramento, the settlement saw a rush of miners, machinery, and supplies come to the goldfields by ship. Once a wharf was constructed, steamships could make daily stops at the small but rapidly growing settlement.

Later, Davis realized that a local post office was the one thing the small settlement lacked, so he petitioned for one. It was approved with the provision that the name of the settlement be changed. Vista del Rio was agreed upon by residents as the new name, but was only used for a very short time.

In 1858, shortly after her husband, Charles Kirkpatrick, became postmaster, Mrs. Kirkpatrick presented the settlers with the idea of once again changing the name of the town—this time to Rio Vista, or "River View"—and the settlers agreed.

Unfortunately, the original site of Rio Vista was destroyed by storms and high floodwaters on January 9, 1862. No lives were lost, but the town's approximately 150 residents were forced to relocate to the town's present location.

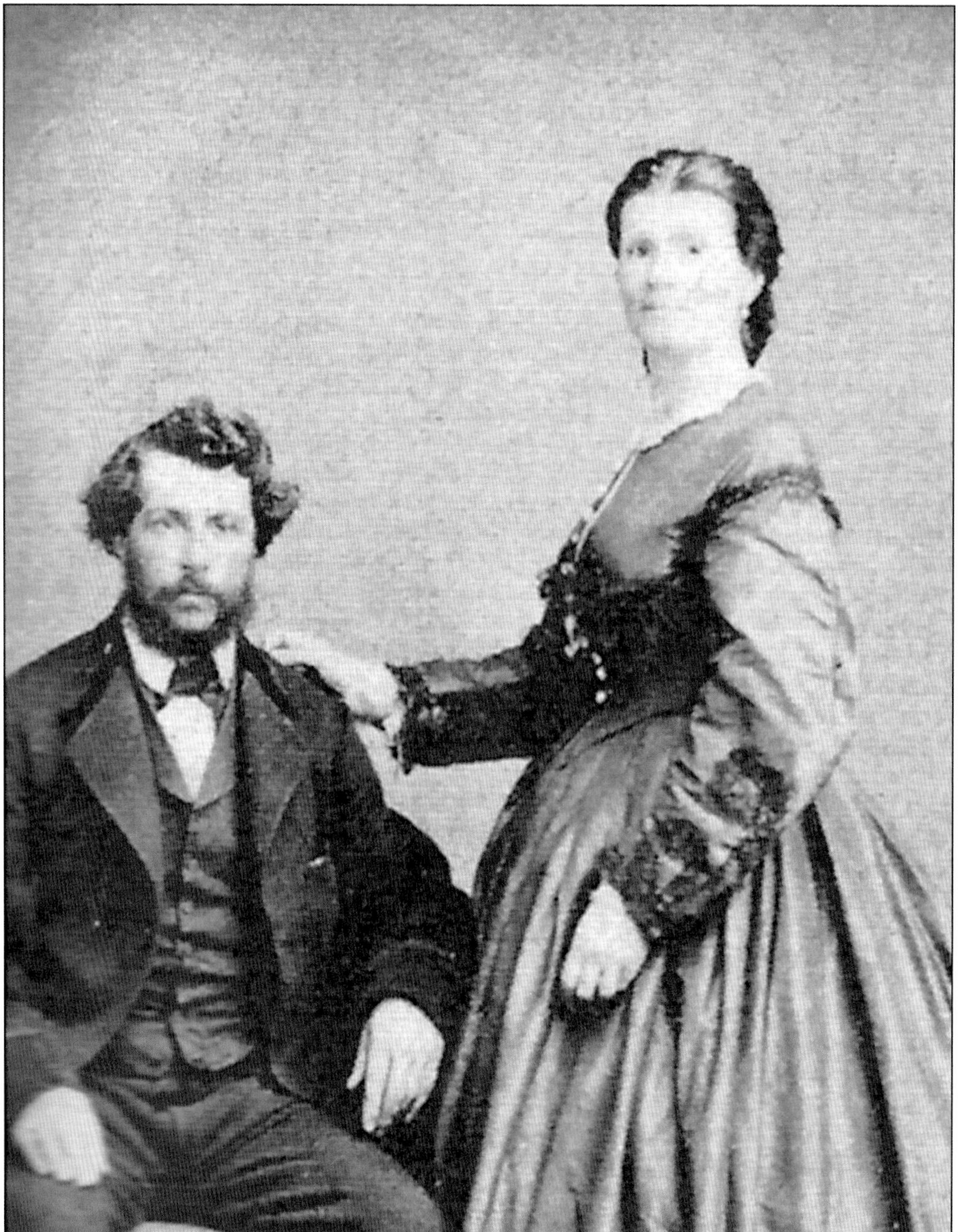

Robert C. Carter Jr. was born in the Redding area of London, England, on February 3, 1834, and immigrated to the United States with his parents in 1841. The family initially lived in San Francisco, eventually moving inland and settling in Brazos del Rio in 1859. With his father, Carter opened a salmon cannery, which is considered to be the first one operated on the West Coast. After the 1862 flood, the family was one of the first to relocate to the new Rio Vista settlement. Carter reestablished his salmon cannery and then established a tin shop. He also organized the first local hook and ladder company, on October 21, 1871, and originated and carried out the plan for the first water company, the Rio Vista Water Works, in 1875. (RVM.)

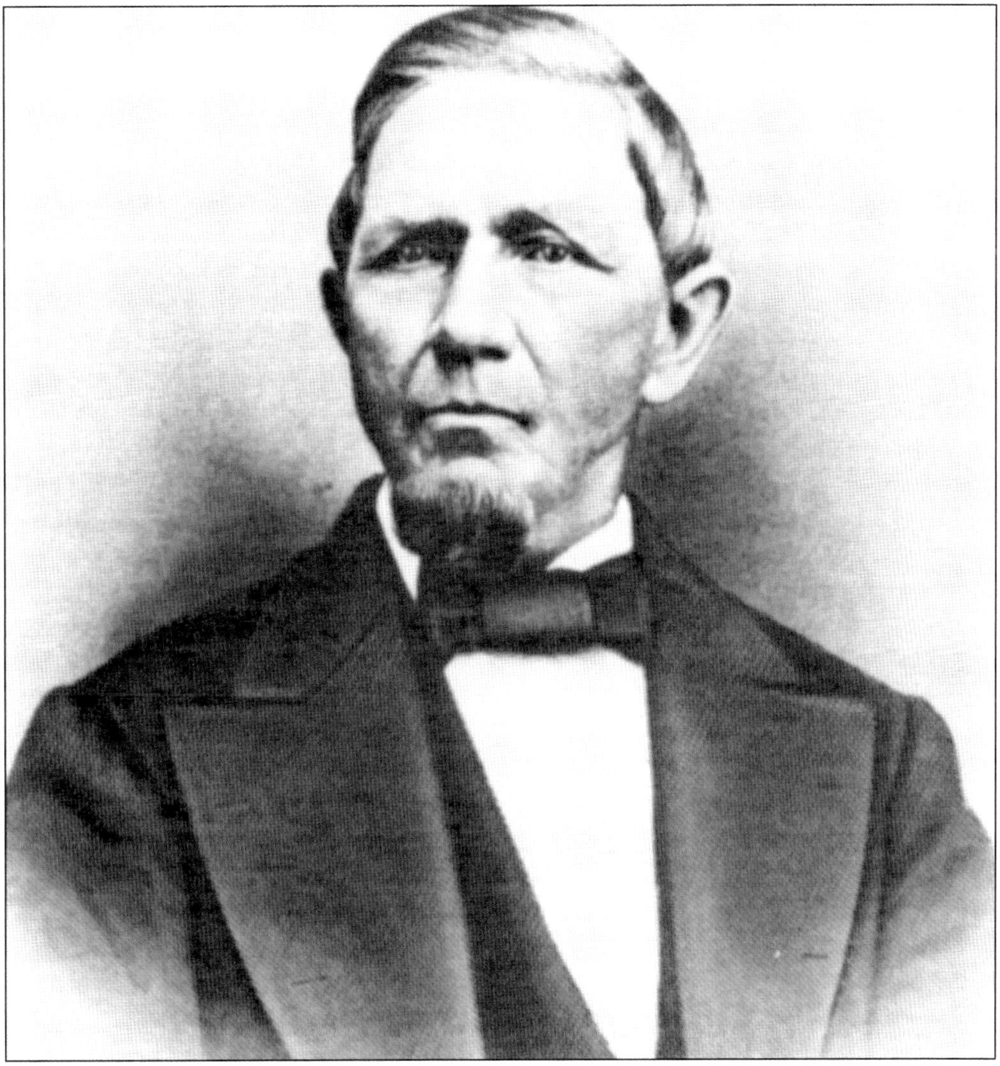

Joseph Bruning (1822–1902) was born in Vichtee, in the Grand Duchy of Oldenburg, Germany, and arrived in San Francisco in 1850. After his arrival, he immediately went to work in the mines on the Yuba River. He took the money he made, moved back to San Francisco, and worked in the hotel business until 1858. Due to ill health and doctor's orders, Bruning and his wife, Gertrude, decided to leave San Francisco in 1858 and move to the country. He bought land in the Los Ulpinos land grant, which extended west from the Sacramento River and south into the Montezuma Hills. He then built a house and took up farming on a rather large scale. After watching the establishment and destruction of the original Rio Vista settlement, he donated his land to establish a new settlement, and helped improve the town. For this, he will be forever remembered as Rio Vista's first benefactor. (RVM.)

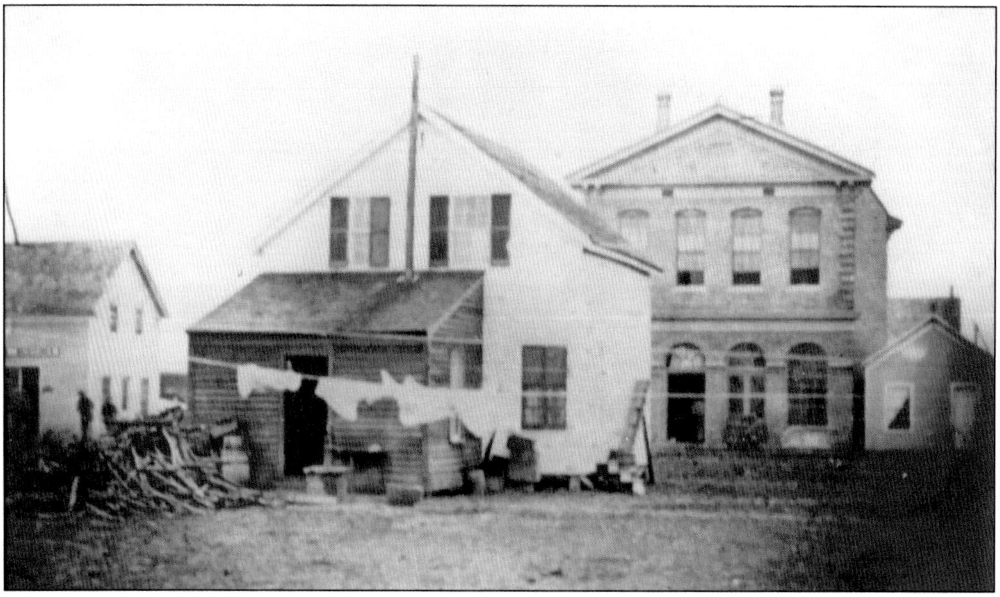

These two photographs, taken in 1874, are some of the earliest available of Rio Vista. The brick, two-story Bruning Building, on the west corner of Main and Second Streets, is seen above. The main floor was occupied by the firm of Pine and Palmer, and the upstairs was used as a hall by several secret orders. The hall was destroyed in the fire of July 20, 1892, which decimated a large portion of Main Street. The image below shows a typical day in 1870s Rio Vista, with a steamship docked at the public wharf. On the right side of the street heading towards the river are Luowis Fallman's blacksmith shop, Fallman's house, the home of James Simpson, the Bruning Building, Simpson's saloon, and some other small stores. (Both, RVM.)

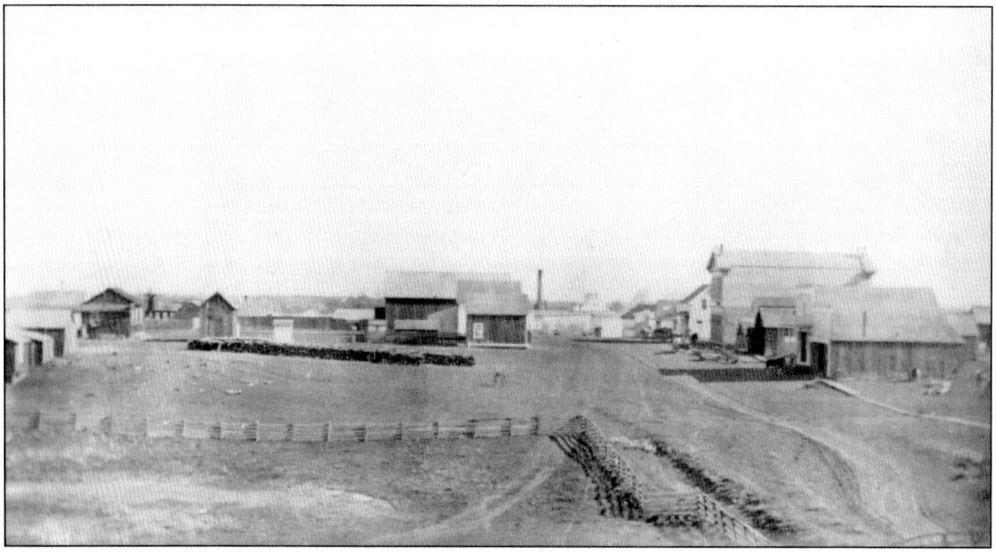

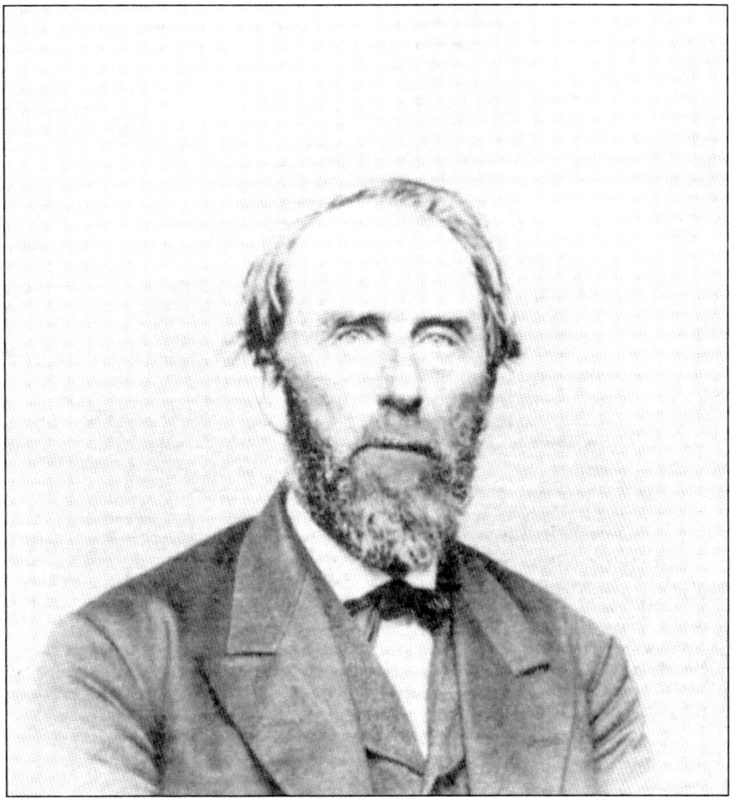

John M. Sidwell was one of the early pioneers who resided in the first Rio Vista and relocated to its second site. In March 1862, he and three other men met with Joseph Bruning to ask him for a plot of land on which to rebuild the Rio Vista settlement, which he agreed to donate. Sidwell eventually constructed and operated the Hotel Sidwell, the second hotel in Rio Vista. (RVM.)

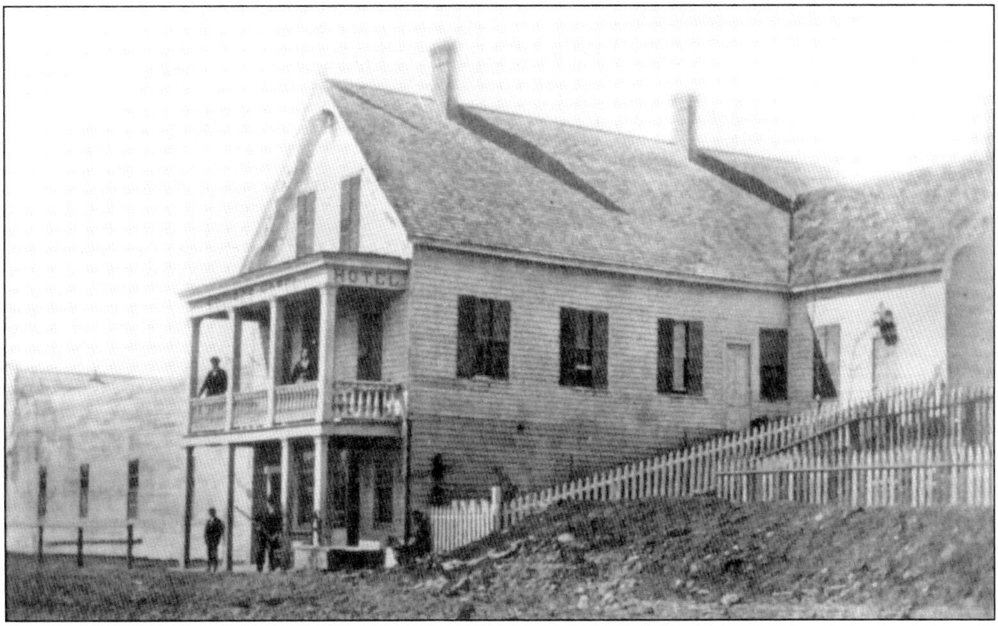

William Squires owned and operated the first hotel in Rio Vista, in 1862. He had previously owned and operated a hotel in the original Rio Vista before relocating after the flood. The hotel, seen here, was on South Front Street. In the 1880s and 1890s, the hotel was known as the Russ House as well as the Central Hotel. (RVM.)

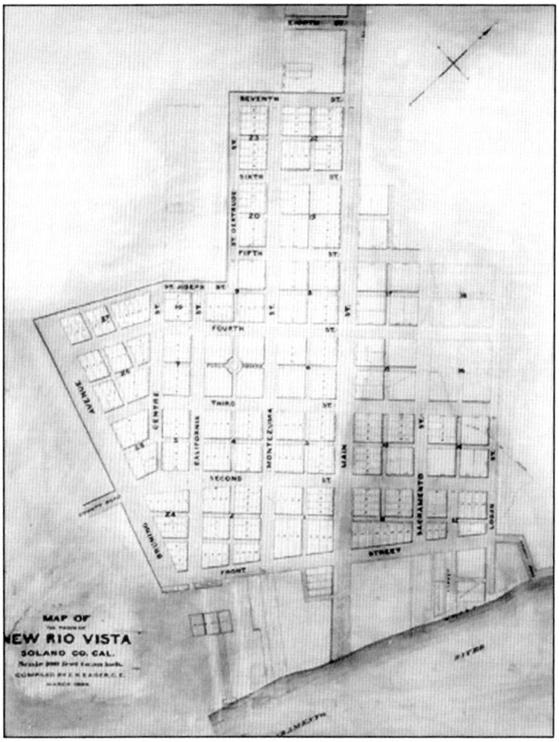

This March 1886 map of "New Rio Vista," drawn by E.N. Eager, civil engineer, was the third map drawn of Rio Vista. In the time since the last map was drawn in 1878, few changes had occurred in town, with the exception of Wharf Street being renamed Logan Street and Bruning Street being added to the town. (RVM.)

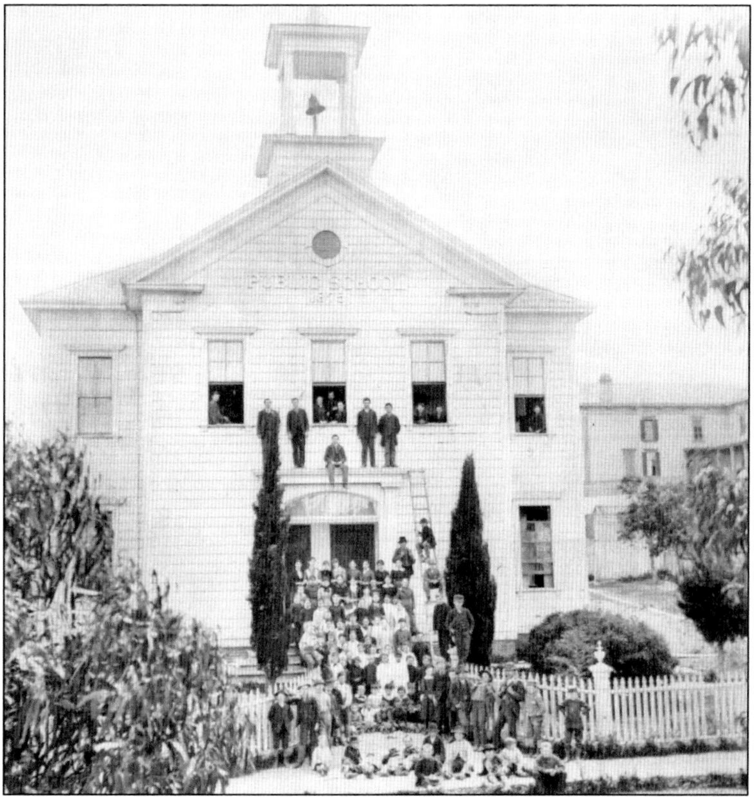

Students pose in front of the Rio Vista public school on May 7, 1884. The first public schoolhouse was built in the summer of 1862, and when the enrollment outgrew the building in 1875, this new schoolhouse was constructed on the same site, on Montezuma Street. It was destroyed by fire in 1917. (RVM.)

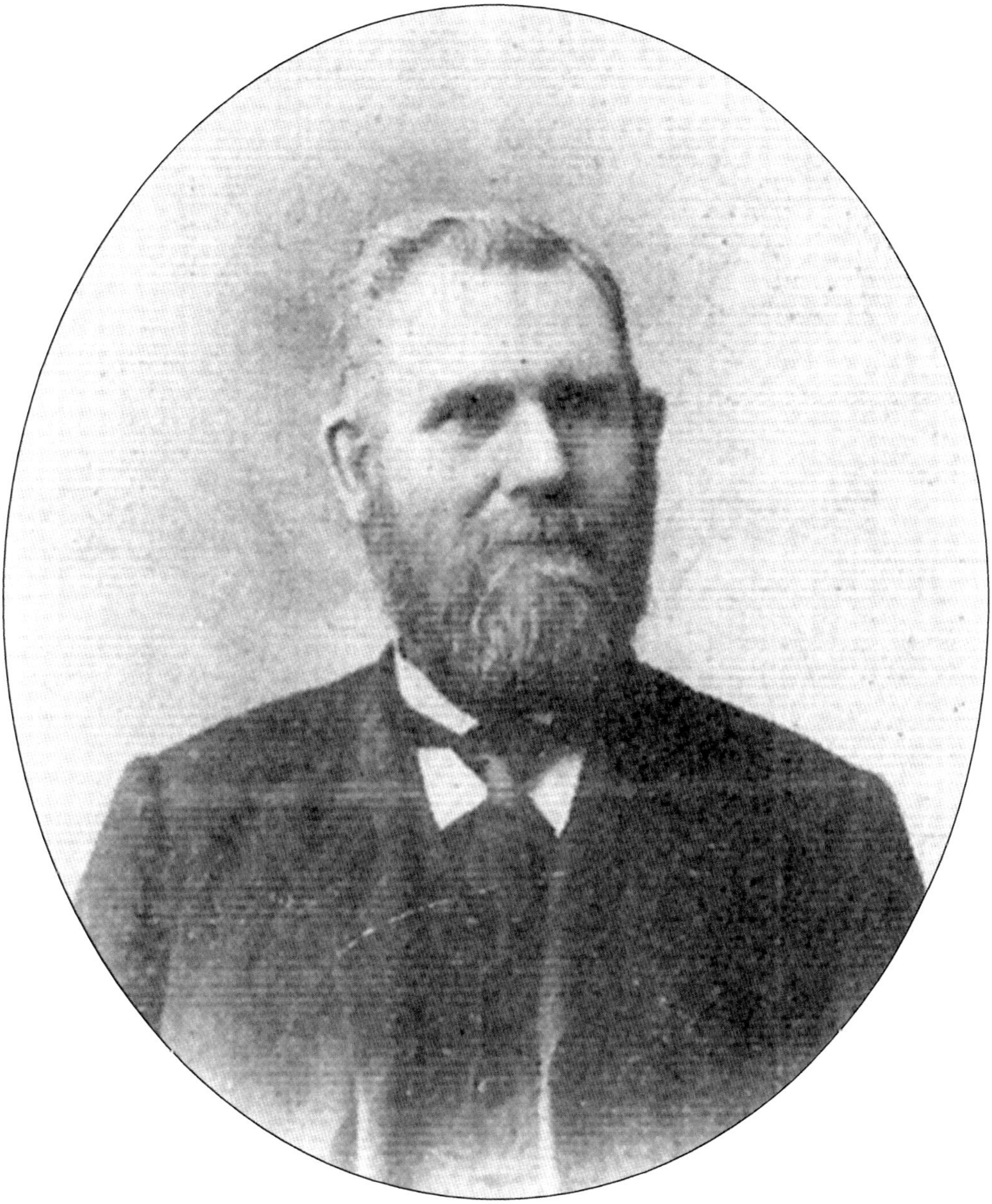

Lyman Luther Palmer began to document Rio Vista's history the moment he arrived in the settlement, on July 20, 1873. Though he only lived in the town until 1879, he was a teacher and the principal of the public school as well as the superintendent of the Sunday schools at First Congregational Church and at the Methodist church. He was also an active member of Rio Vista Lodge No. 208, Free and Accepted Masons, and established the first local newspaper, the *Weekly Gleaner*, which was published from September 6, 1877, to February 22, 1879. In 1914, he published *Historical Sketch of Rio Vista, Cal. and Reminiscent Sketches Forty Years Ago*, the most valuable written time capsule of early local history. (RVM.)

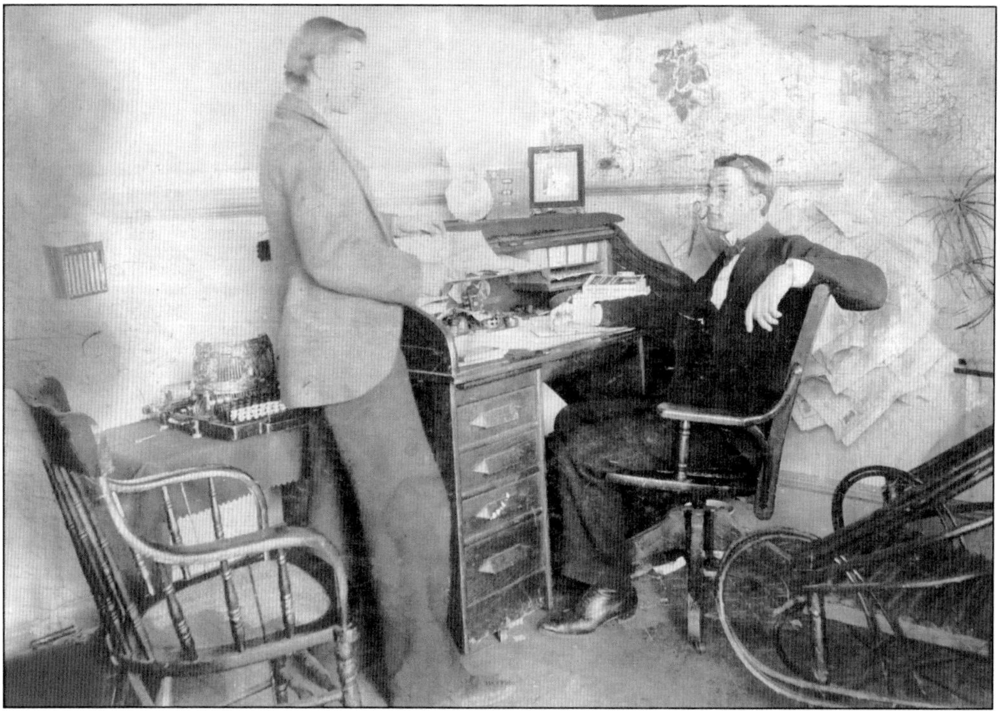

The *Sacramento River News* was established by David G. Holt in 1890. It is the oldest business still in operation in Rio Vista and has served the communities of the delta for more than 120 years. The newspaper became the *River News* in 1895, and later, the *River News-Herald*. The newspaper's second owner, William L. Dunn (left), is seen here with his brother Archie. Dunn owned the paper from 1895 to 1898. (RVM.)

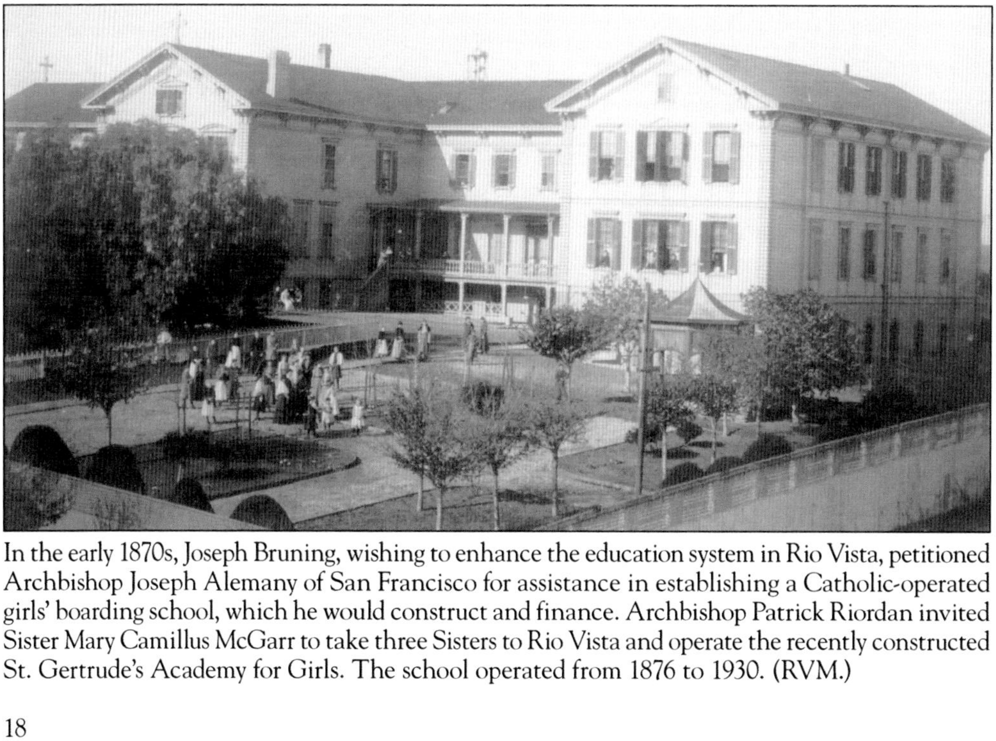

In the early 1870s, Joseph Bruning, wishing to enhance the education system in Rio Vista, petitioned Archbishop Joseph Alemany of San Francisco for assistance in establishing a Catholic-operated girls' boarding school, which he would construct and finance. Archbishop Patrick Riordan invited Sister Mary Camillus McGarr to take three Sisters to Rio Vista and operate the recently constructed St. Gertrude's Academy for Girls. The school operated from 1876 to 1930. (RVM.)

Martin Christensen, a native of Graese, Denmark, came to Rio Vista in 1875. In December 1893, at the time of Rio Vista's incorporation, he was elected president of the board of trustees, a position commonly referred to as mayor. Pictured are Christensen and his four sons: from left to right, (seated) Fred, Alvin, and Martin; (standing) Martin Jr. and John. Martin Jr. and John both went on to serve as mayors. (RVM.)

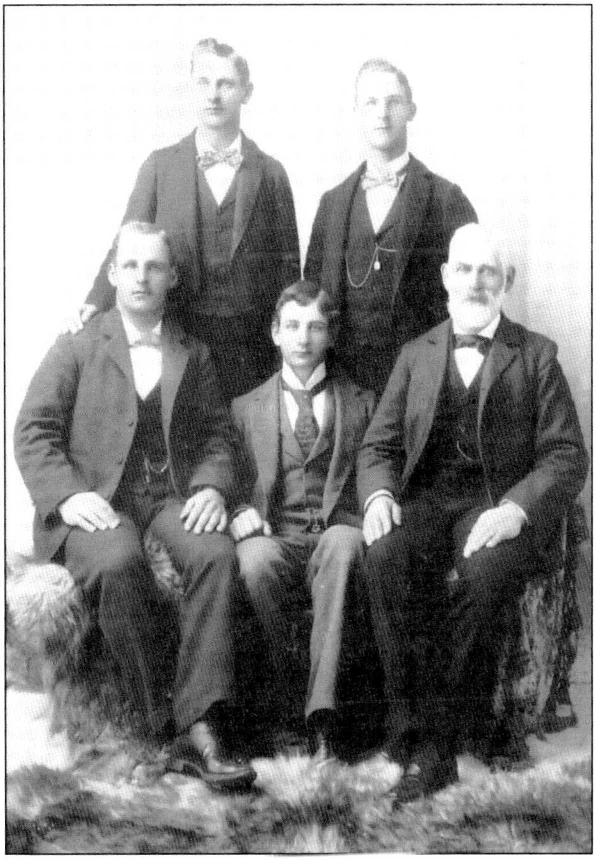

Matthew Stewart purchased Thomas Kiernan's undertaking establishment (pictured) on Main Street in mid-December 1891. The building was ruined in the devastating fire of July 20, 1892, which destroyed the majority of Rio Vista's downtown. After the fire, Stewart erected this new 28-foot-by-42-foot undertaking parlor on the lot adjacent to his home on Montezuma Street. This photograph dates from the 1890s. (RVM.)

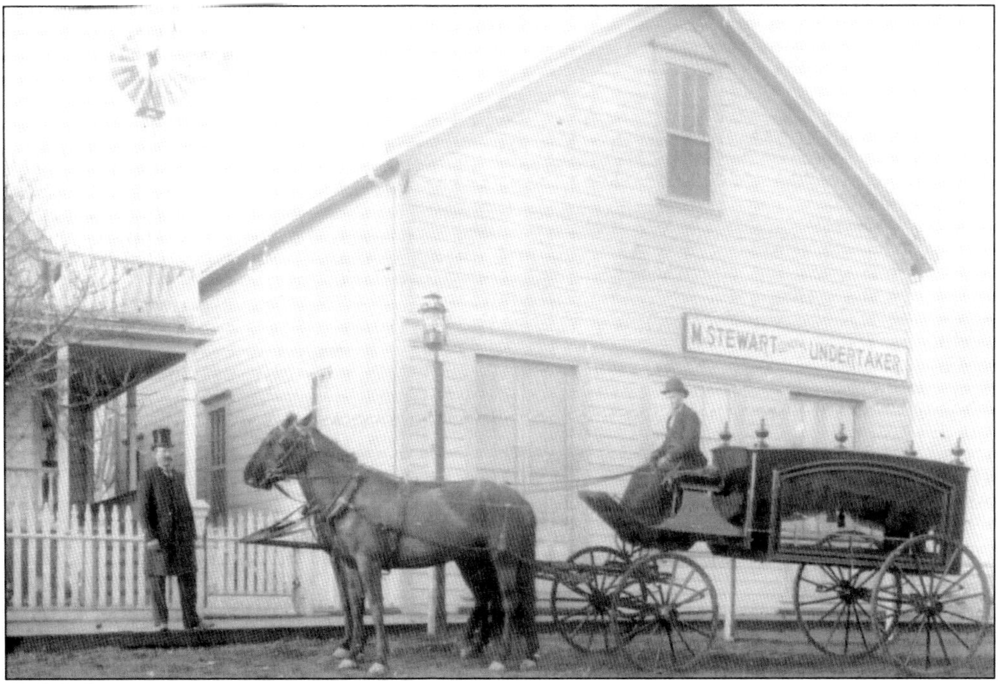

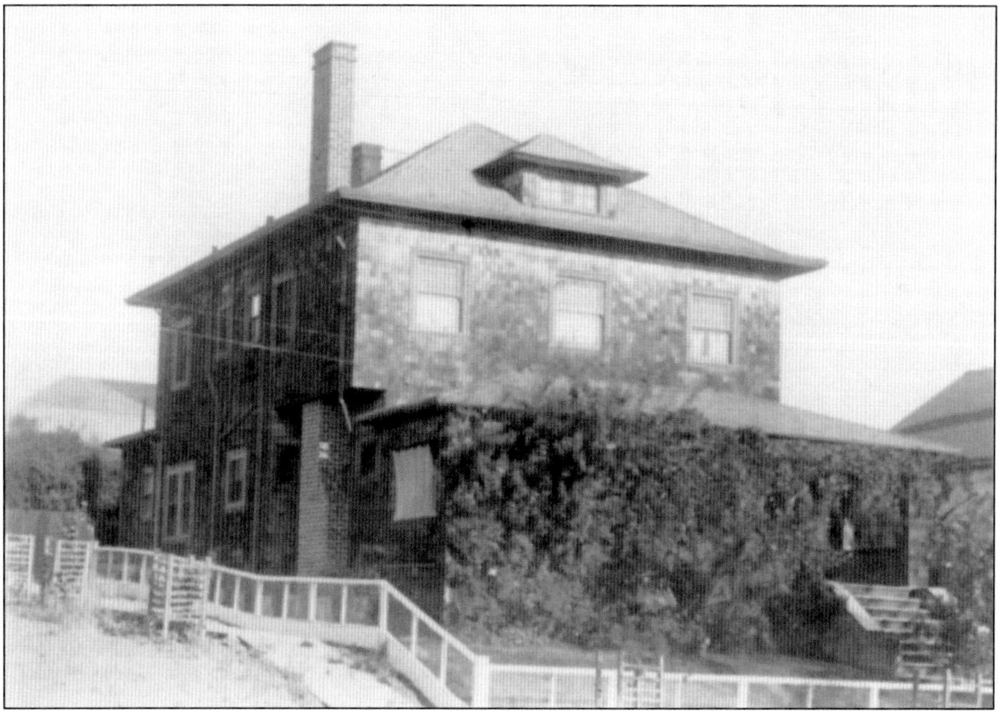

Sen. Thomas McCormack purchased the land on which to build this fine home in 1898. Local contractor Fred Johnson was hired to construct the house, which he completed in 1902. The historic residence is one of several on Second Street that were built around 1900. (RVM.)

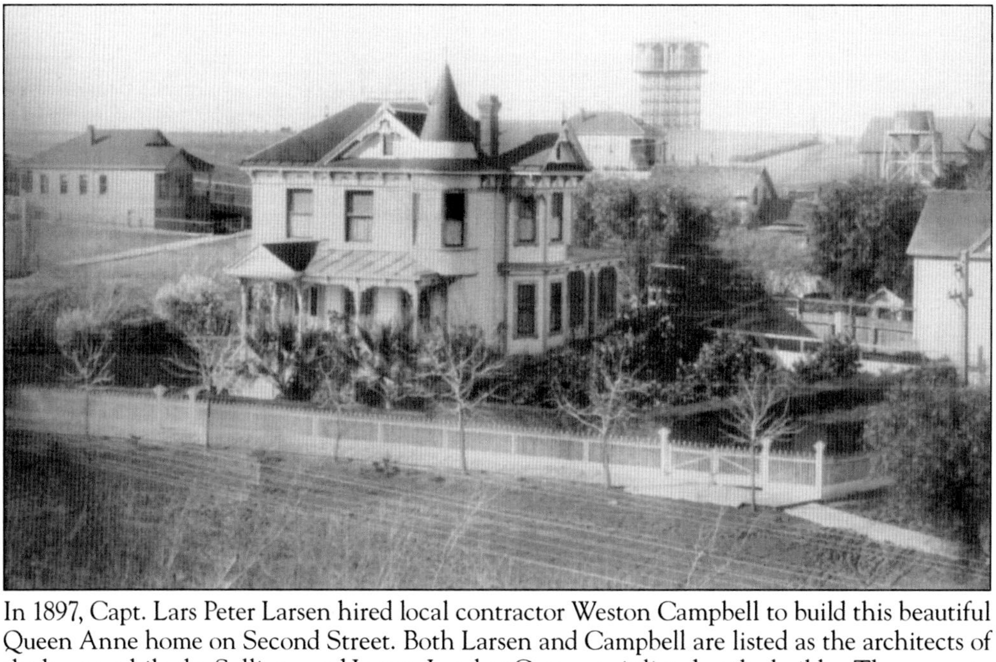

In 1897, Capt. Lars Peter Larsen hired local contractor Weston Campbell to build this beautiful Queen Anne home on Second Street. Both Larsen and Campbell are listed as the architects of the house, while the Sullivan and Larsen Lumber Company is listed as the builder. The property covered one quarter of the block, including the stately home and a lovely adjoining yard with a barn, a carriage house, and an outhouse. (RVM.)

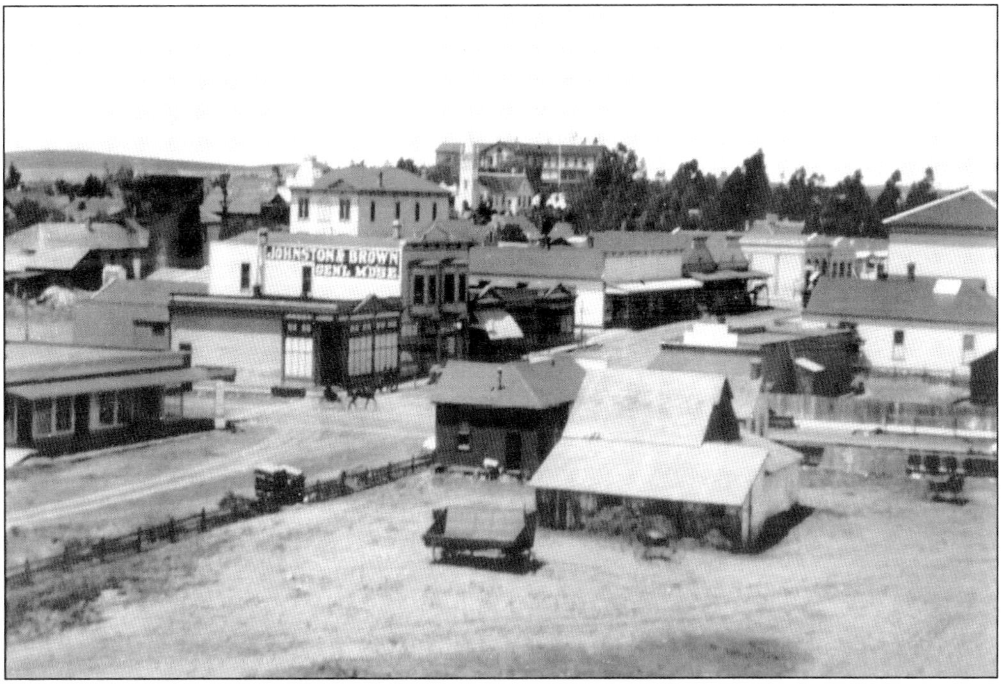

This 1899 photograph shows how the downtown was reconstructed after the fire of 1892. On the far left side is Chase's general store. To the right along Main Street are the Cobweb Saloon and Johnston & Brown General Merchandise. The Knights of Pythias Hall, St. Joseph's Catholic Church, and St. Gertrude's Academy for Girls are in the background. (RVM.)

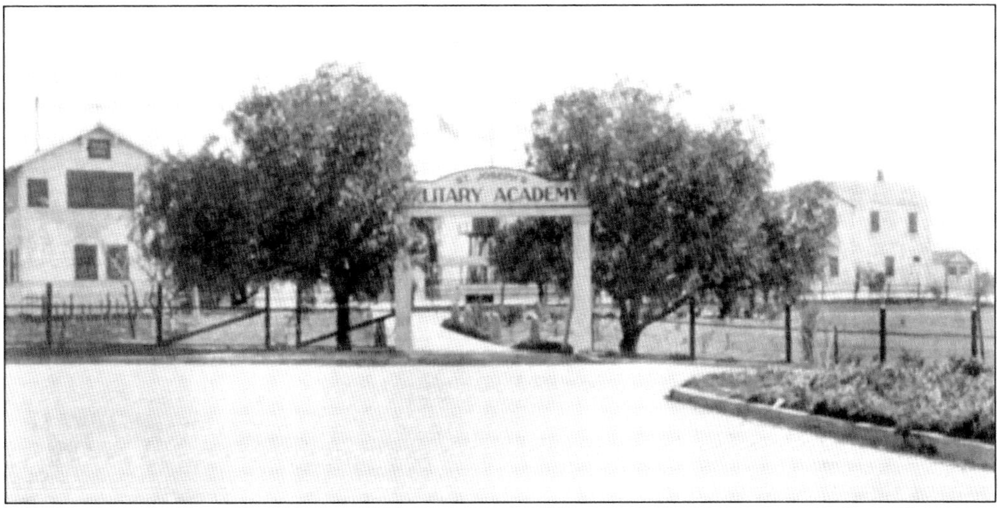

On August 3, 1903, St. Joseph's Military Academy for Boys opened its doors at the foot of Bruning Street. The school was operated in conjunction with St. Gertrude's Academy, and many of the classes were held at the girls' academy; however, the boys' academy had a military curriculum that was overseen by an Army captain who was retained as the school commandant. (RVM.)

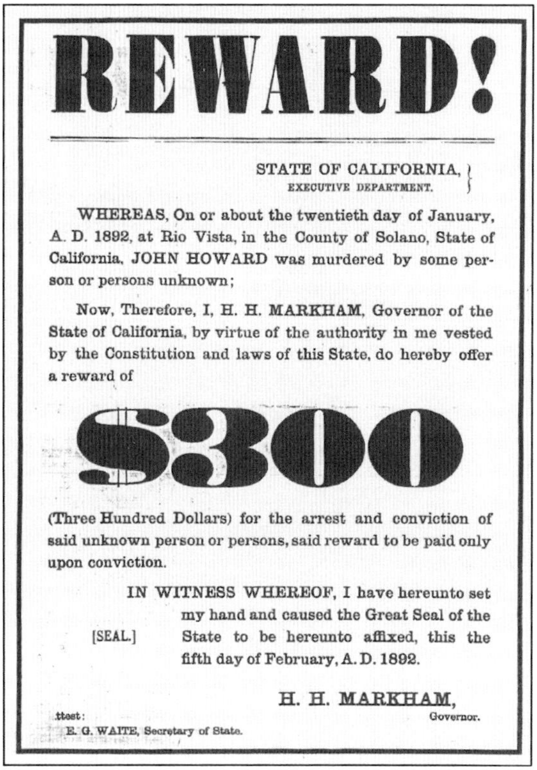

REWARD!

STATE OF CALIFORNIA,
EXECUTIVE DEPARTMENT.

WHEREAS, On or about the twentieth day of January, A. D. 1892, at Rio Vista, in the County of Solano, State of California, JOHN HOWARD was murdered by some person or persons unknown;

Now, Therefore, I, H. H. MARKHAM, Governor of the State of California, by virtue of the authority in me vested by the Constitution and laws of this State, do hereby offer a reward of

$300

(Three Hundred Dollars) for the arrest and conviction of said unknown person or persons, said reward to be paid only upon conviction.

IN WITNESS WHEREOF, I have hereunto set my hand and caused the Great Seal of the State to be hereunto affixed, this the fifth day of February, A. D. 1892.

[SEAL.]

H. H. MARKHAM,
Governor.

ttest:
E. G. WAITE, Secretary of State.

In Rio Vista's history, Wanted posters have been issued only twice. The first was in 1892, the second in 1914. It took two years and one month to sentence the last of the three would-be burglars involved in the killing of night watchman John Howard in 1892. (RVM.)

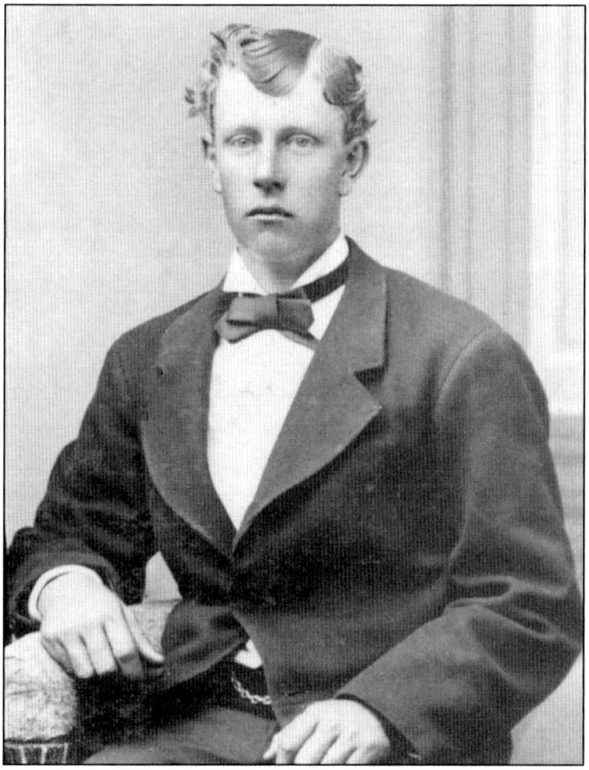

In the early-morning hours of January 20, 1892, Howard, the night watchman, was checking the wharfs when he unexpectedly surprised a man who was about to blow the California Transportation Company's safe open. The would-be robber turned on Howard and emptied the contents of a shotgun into his stomach. Howard quickly pulled his revolver and returned fire, but his injuries proved fatal and he died that morning. (RVM.)

This Wanted poster was issued for the man who murdered marshal Jarvis Powell Emigh. As Emigh made his normal rounds about town in the early hours of August 29, 1914, he entered the local post office while robbers were attempting to blow the safe. As Emigh reached into his pocket, William Clay, one of the robbers, shot him. It was later found that Emigh was not reaching for a gun, but for his chewing tobacco. (RVM.)

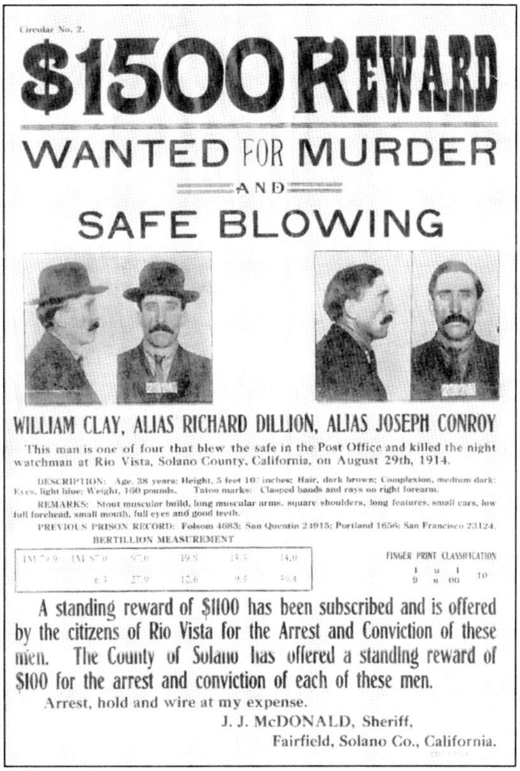

Circular No. 2.

$1500 REWARD

WANTED FOR MURDER

AND

SAFE BLOWING

WILLIAM CLAY, ALIAS RICHARD DILLION, ALIAS JOSEPH CONROY

This man is one of four that blew the safe in the Post Office and killed the night watchman at Rio Vista, Solano County, California, on August 29th, 1914.

DESCRIPTION: Age, 38 years; Height, 5 feet 10½ inches; Hair, dark brown; Complexion, medium dark; Eyes, light blue; Weight, 160 pounds. Tatoo marks: Clasped bands and rays on right forearm.

REMARKS: Stout muscular build, long muscular arms, square shoulders, long features, small ears, low full forehead, small mouth, full eyes and good teeth.

PREVIOUS PRISON RECORD: Folsom 4683; San Quentin 24915; Portland 1656; San Francisco 23124.

BERTILLION MEASUREMENT

1M 79.9	1M 87.0	97.0	19.8	15.5	14.0
	6.5	27.9	12.6	9.5	50.4

FINGER PRINT CLASSIFICATION

1 u 1 / 9 u 00 10

A standing reward of $1100 has been subscribed and is offered by the citizens of Rio Vista for the Arrest and Conviction of these men. The County of Solano has offered a standing reward of $100 for the arrest and conviction of each of these men.

Arrest, hold and wire at my expense.

J. J. McDONALD, Sheriff,
Fairfield, Solano Co., California.

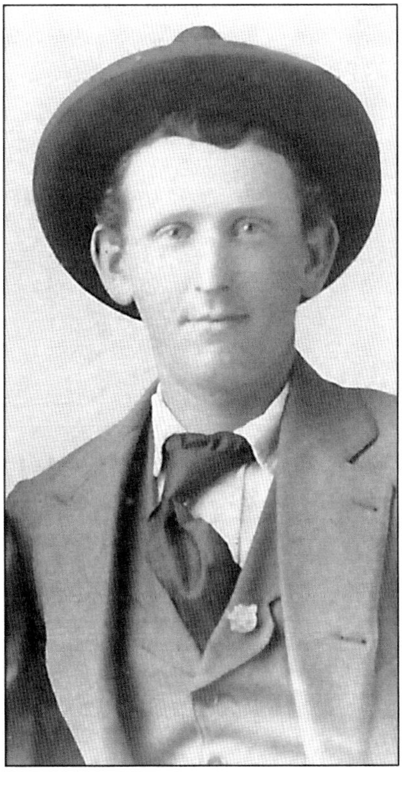

This photograph of Jarvis Powell Emigh was taken in 1898. Emigh was one of 10 children born to Jerome and Eudora (Allender) Emigh. He was named after his grandfather, Jarvis Emigh, and his uncle, Thomas Powell Emigh. The elder Emigh brothers had come to Rio Vista during the 1870s. Jarvis Powell was 36 when he was murdered, leaving behind his wife, Stella (McDowell). (RVM.)

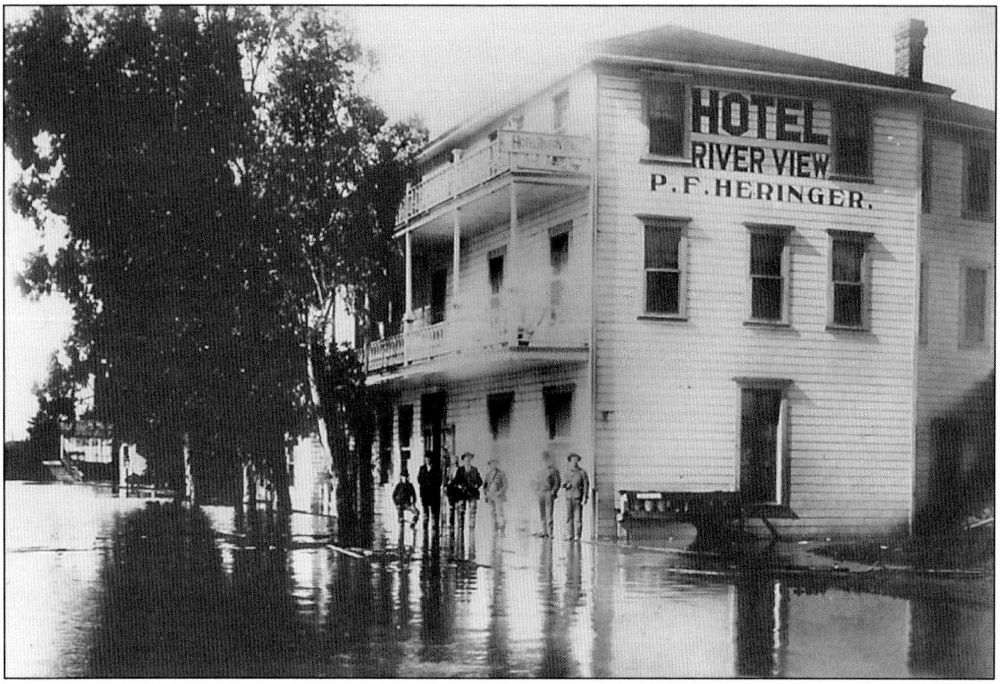

In 1907, the Sacramento River rose high enough to flood some of the stores in Rio Vista. The Hotel Riverview, on the North Front Street site of the former Squires Hotel, is seen here with water entering the main floor. Upriver, the town of Isleton also felt the wrath of these same floodwaters (page 35). (RVM.)

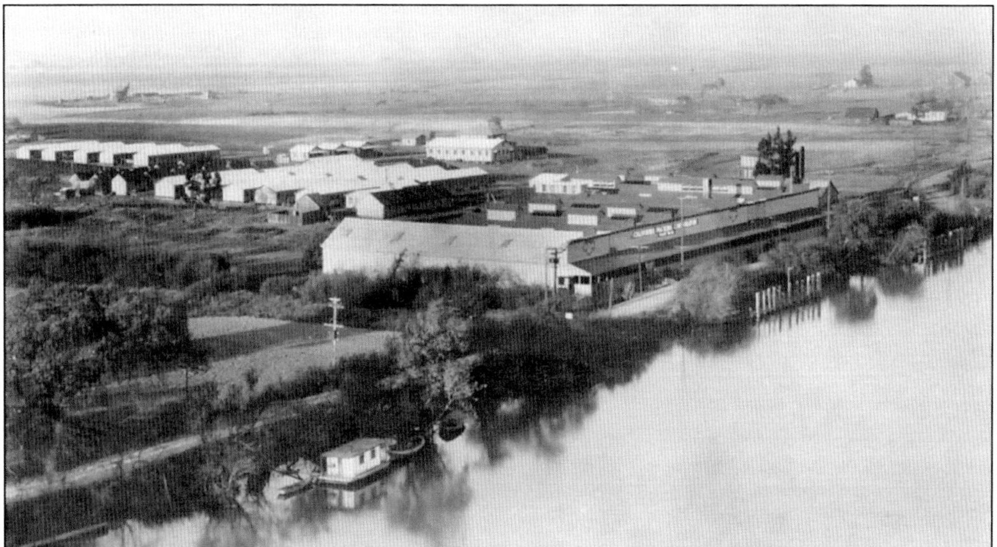

Many of the towns on the Sacramento River had packing plants. California Packing Corporation's Plant No. 22 was just north of the Rio Vista Bridge. In the 1930s, this Del Monte brand facility was considered one of the largest asparagus canneries in the world. The plant closed in 1945. In 1949, Blackwelder Manufacturing moved onto the property, which is now owned by the Dutra Group. (RVM.)

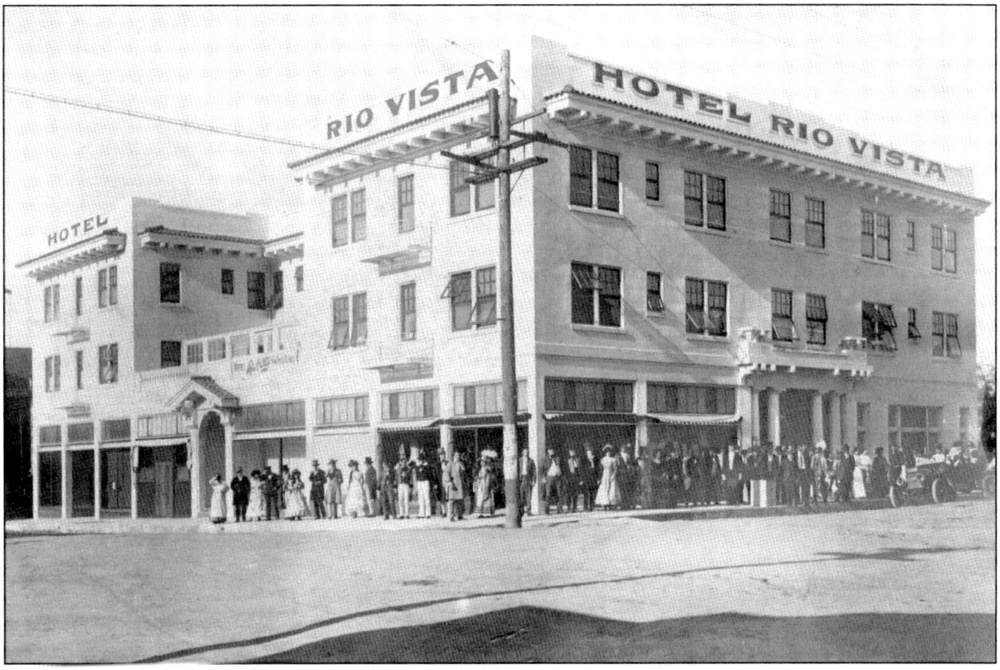

The cast and crew of the silent film *Cameo Kirby* take a moment to pose for a photograph in front of the Hotel Rio Vista on November 6, 1914. This was the first of many film crews to come to Rio Vista. From 1914 to 2012, more than 40 motion pictures had scenes filmed between Rio Vista and Freeport. (RVM.)

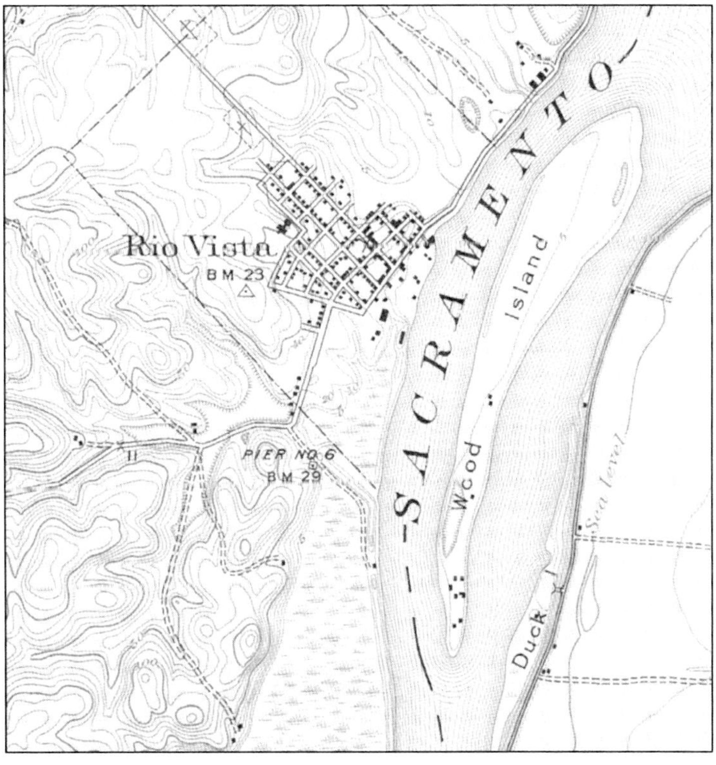

This enlarged section of a 1910 map shows Wood Island. The island was originally named Gillespie Island and was located within the Georgiana Township. It was eventually annexed to Rio Vista by an act of the California Legislature in 1875–1876. In the early 1870s, the name was changed Wood Island. The island was removed by suction dredging in 1927 to create a deepwater channel. (RVM.)

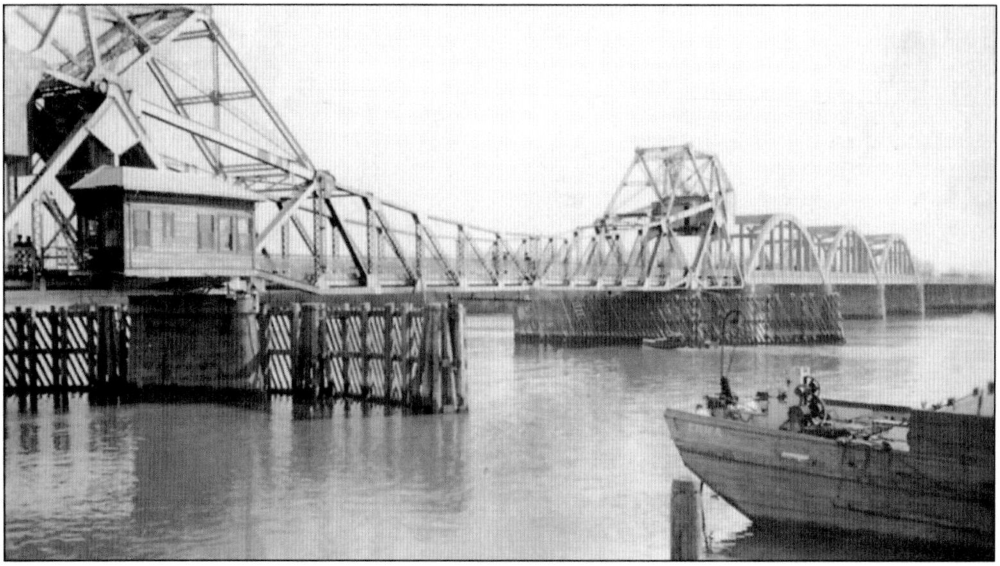

The original Rio Vista Bridge (above) was a Strauss bascule-type bridge that was operated by a system of counterweights, gears, and motors to rotate the "leaves" of the bridge up and down away from the centerline of the river, providing clear passage for river traffic. In 1943, construction began on the new Rio Vista Bridge (below), which was not completed and formally dedicated until April 1, 1960. The company Lord & Bishop constructed the substructure of the new two-lane bridge just 60 feet upstream of the existing Rio Vista Bridge. The east portion of the new bridge, completed in 1945, consisted of 1,300 feet of steel trusses, at a cost of $960,500. The striking Rio Vista Bridge was given the American Iron and Steel Institute's award for the "Most Beautiful Movable Steel Bridge" when it was completed in 1959. (Both, RVM.)

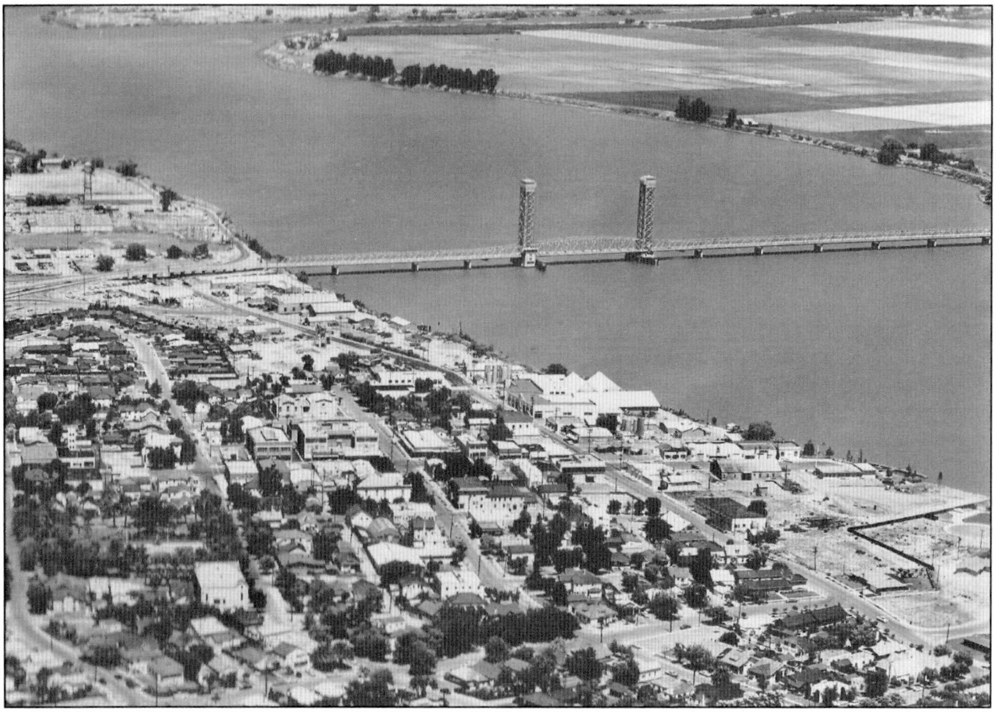

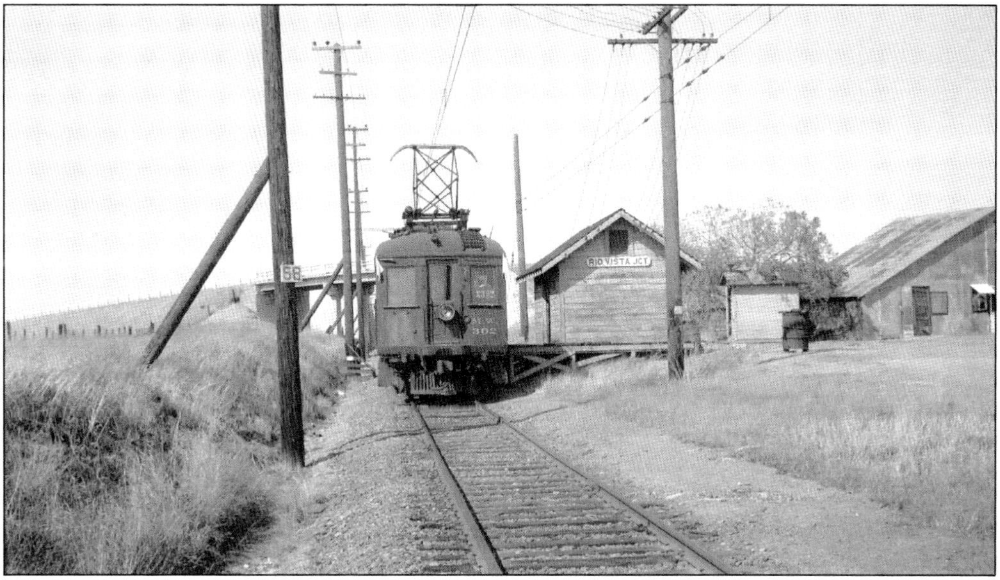

In 1913, the Oakland, Antioch and Eastern Railway established a junction outside of Rio Vista, as part of the 93-mile route from San Francisco to Sacramento. The name Rio Vista Junction was not adopted until 1922; former names include Curtis (1913) and Creed (1914). In 1919, the route was reorganized into the San Francisco–Sacramento Railroad, eventually becoming the Sacramento Northern Railway in 1928. Passenger service was discontinued on August 28, 1940. Freight service, however, continued for several decades. In 1985, the old junction became the Western Railway Museum. (John Harder collection.)

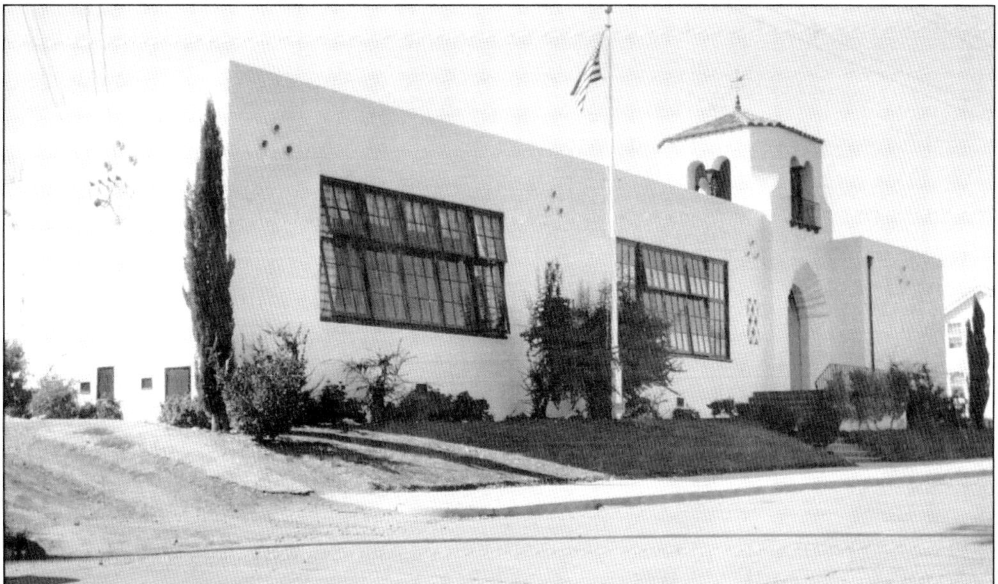

A decade after the Rio Vista public school was destroyed by fire, this school was built on the same site and named after the town's most generous benefactor, Joseph Bruning. The school opened in 1929 and continued to operate until 1967, when the district was reorganized. It has been used as the offices of the River Delta Unified School District since then. (RVM.)

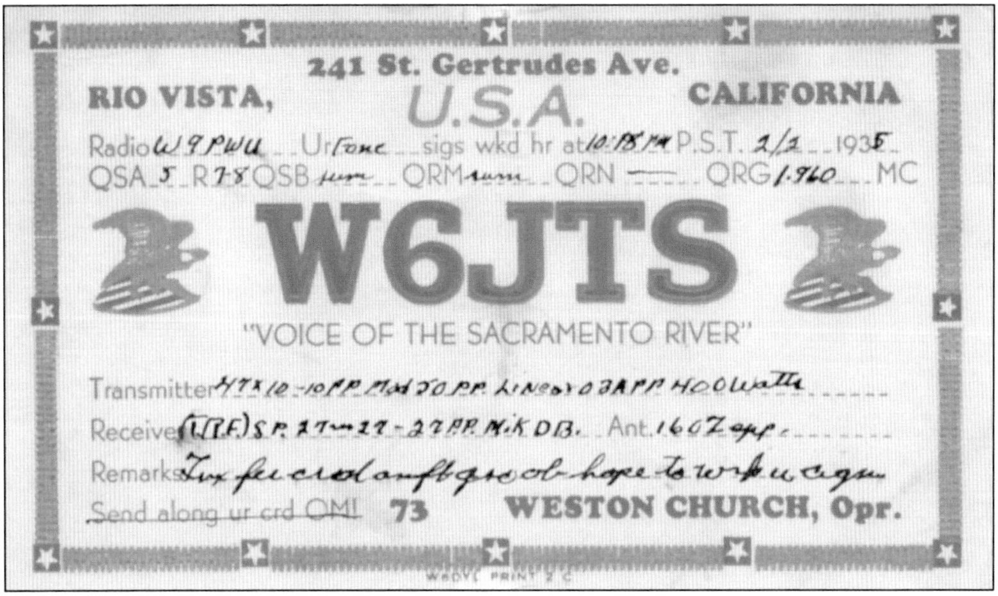

WJTS, the "Voice of the Sacramento River," was the first radio station established in the delta. It was owned by Weston Church and operated out of his home on St. Gertrude Avenue in the 1930s. In 1972, Rio Vista High School's KRVH became the second radio station in Rio Vista, with studios approximately a block and a half up the street from Church's home. (RVM.)

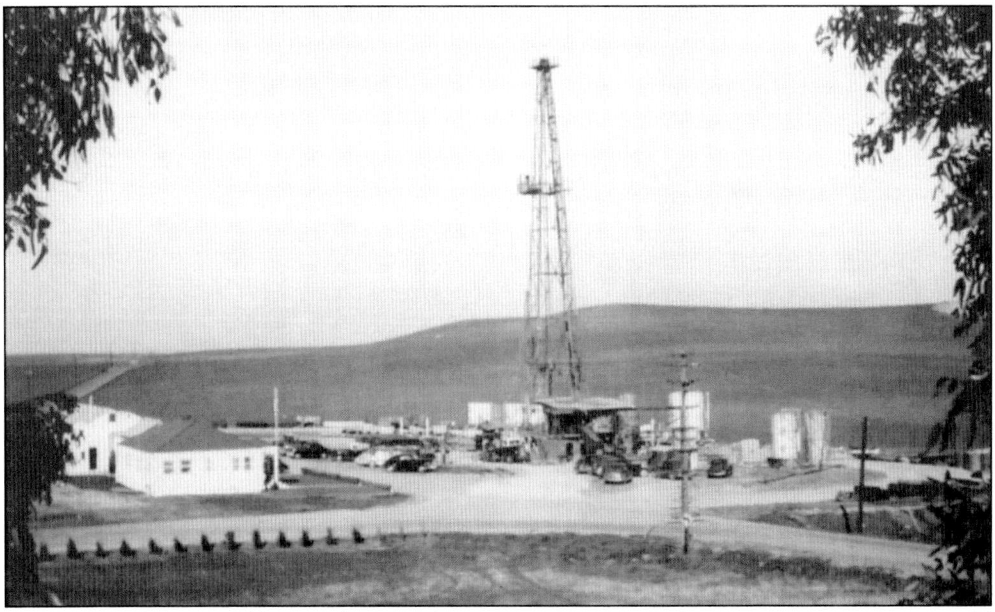

This was the first gas well on Arthur Emigh's property, just two miles west of town. No one could predict the impact it would have on the farmers and the town in the years to come. The Amerada Petroleum Corporation later bought Emigh No. 1, as it was properly named on June 18, 1936. The total depth was 4,485 feet, and it took 44 days to complete. (RVM.)

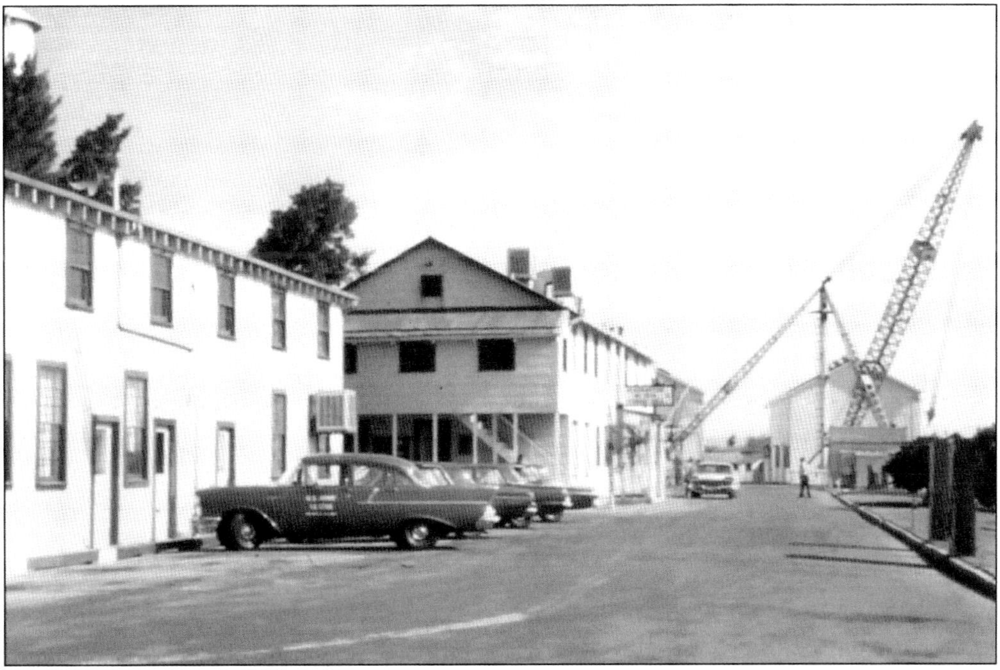

This former Army base is south of town on 28.1 acres and was originally established in 1911 under the name US Engineer Storehouse, Rio Vista. Over the next 80 years, the name changed nine times, and the base officially closed in 1991. This photograph was taken in the 1960s. (RVM.)

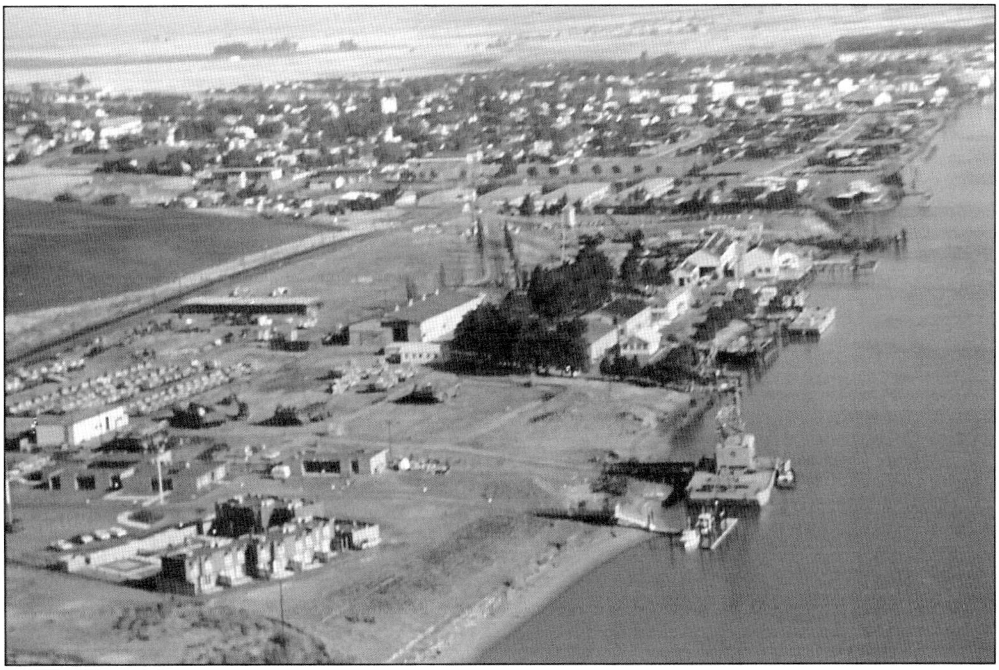

US Coast Guard Station Rio Vista, of the Eleventh Coast Guard District "Guardians of the California Delta," patrols 1,000 miles of waterways in the Sacramento–San Joaquin River delta. The base was first opened on a section of the Army base property. On June 3, 1967, a separate station just south of the original base was commissioned. (RVM.)

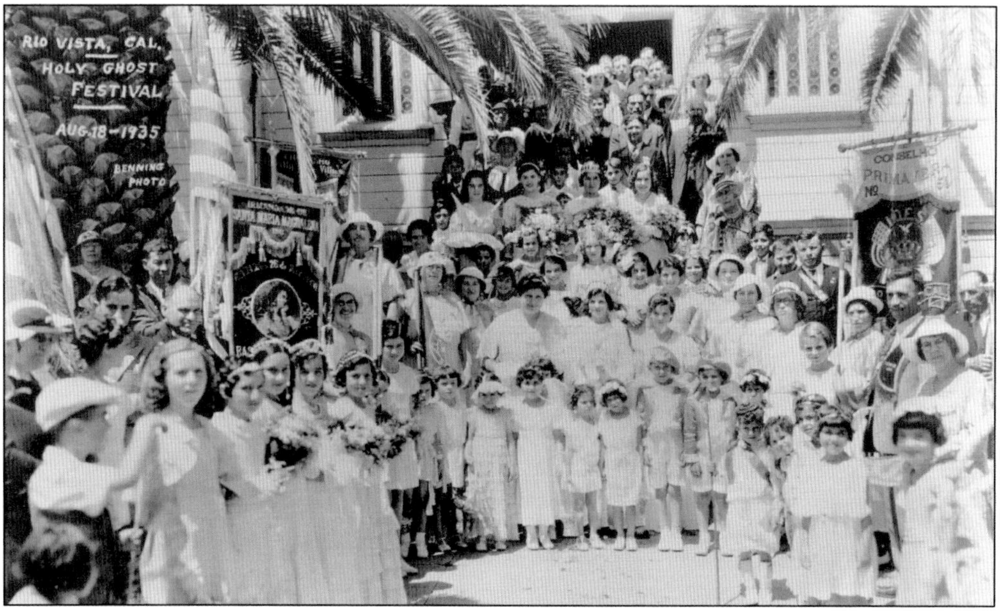

The first Holy Ghost Festival was held in Rio Vista in 1899, the year the Rio Vista–Isleton Club was organized, and has continued as an annual event ever since. This photograph, taken on August 18, 1935, shows the event's many participants standing in front of St. Joseph's Catholic Church on South Fourth Street. (RVM.)

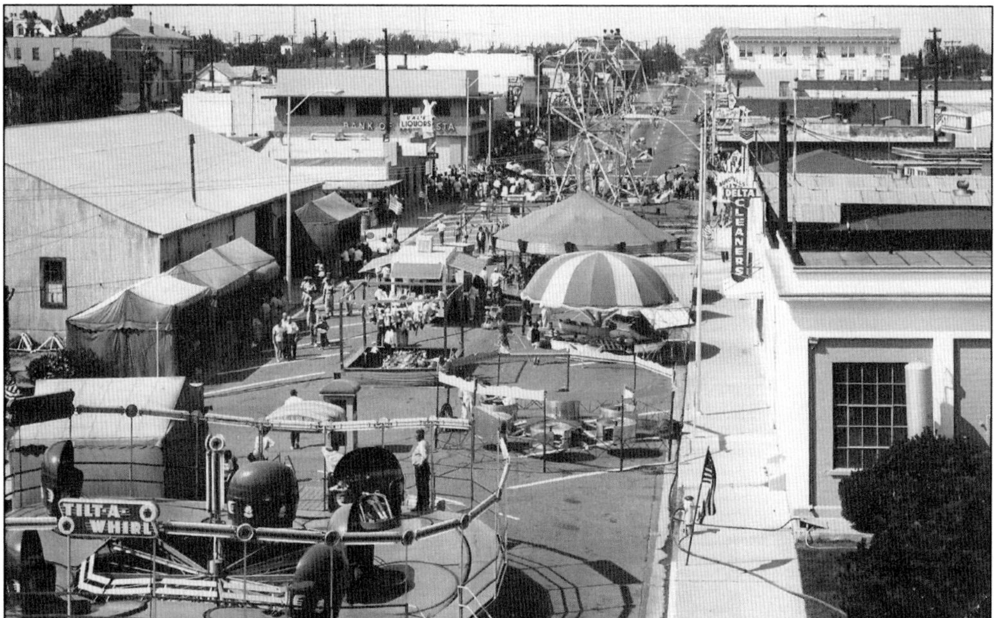

The community of Rio Vista is home to several long-standing festivals. The First Congregational Church has held its annual Harvest Festival every year since 1870, and the Rio Vista–Isleton Club has held a Holy Ghost Festival every year since the club was established in 1899. The annual Rio Vista Bass Derby and Festival was established in 1933, discontinued in 1939, and reestablished in 1949. (RVM.)

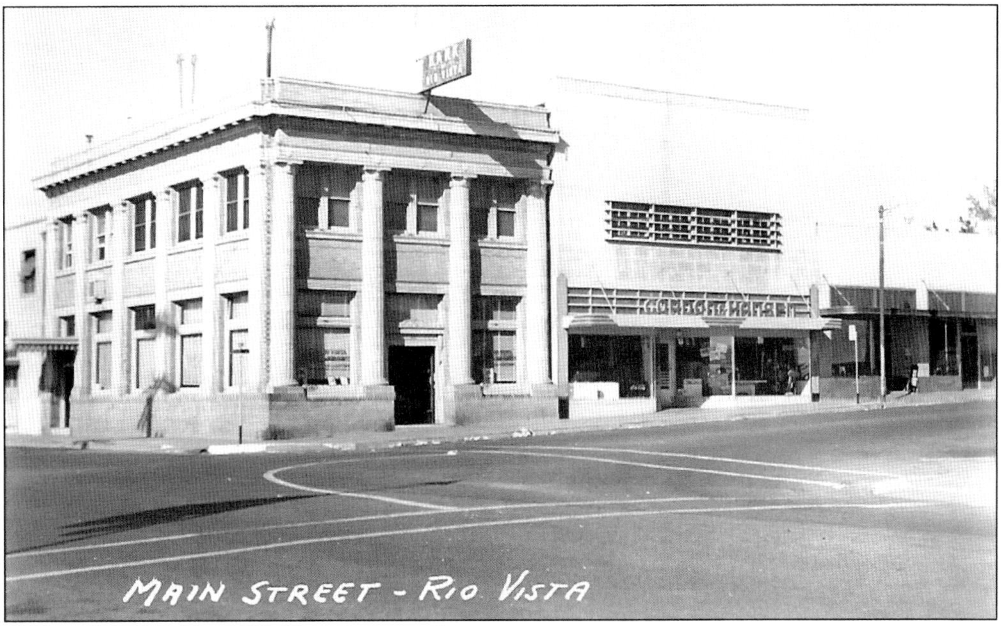

The Bank of Rio Vista is the third-oldest business in Rio Vista, opening in April 1904. Over the years, the bank has opened branches in Isleton, Walnut Grove, and Valley Springs. This building was initially built for a rival bank, the First National Bank of Rio Vista, in 1917. The structure's original, grandiose architecture is seen here prior to a remodeling in the late 1950s. (RVM.)

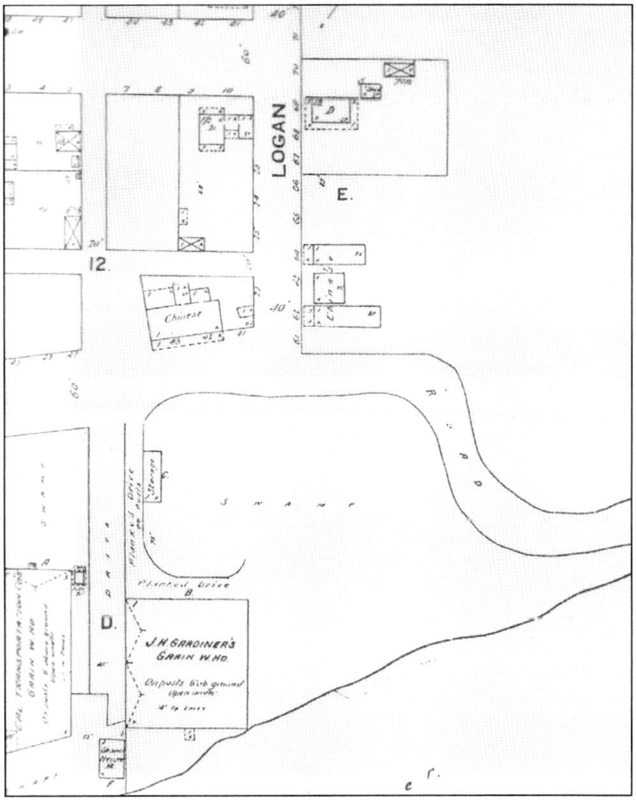

This enlarged section of an 1896 Sanborn Fire Map makes note of several Chinese-owned buildings. Rio Vista's Chinatown existed from 1870 to 1920 at the north end of Front Street, coming back as far as Sacramento Street. The majority of the Chinese in the Rio Vista community came from the Sze Yap region of China, specifically Taishan County. (RVM.)

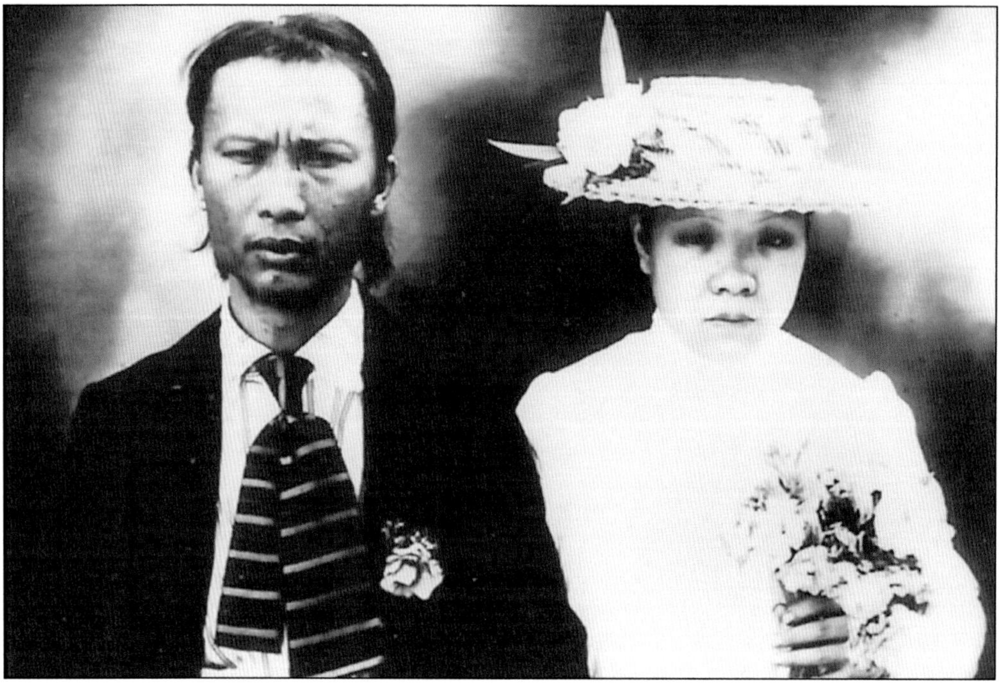

After finding little wealth in the gold mines, a great number of Chinese arrived in Solano County when work became available building the railroads from 1868 on. When the railroads were completed, many found work in the orchards or built levees. The township of Rio Vista saw the arrival of its first Chinese citizen in the 1870s. This unidentified local couple is seen here on their wedding day. (RVM.)

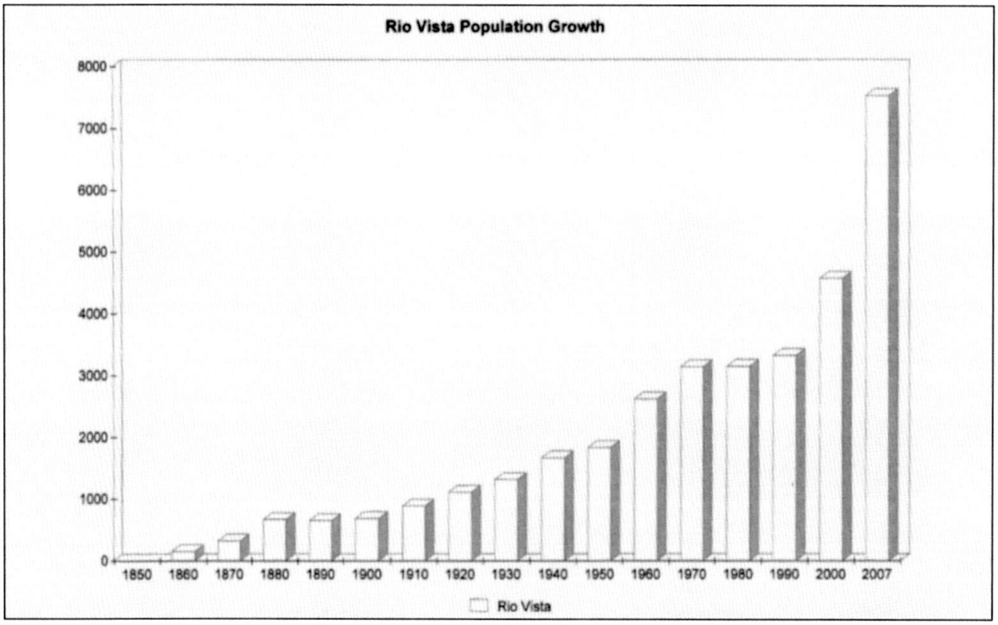

This graph, compiled by the author, shows the growth of Rio Vista from 1860 to the present. At the time of the flood of 1862, the original settlement of Rio Vista had a population of approximately 150. In the 2010 census, the population of Rio Vista was 7,360. (Author's collection.)

Two

Isleton

Five miles upriver from Rio Vista on Andrus Island is the town of Isleton, established by Josiah Pool in 1874. Pool was born in 1829 and came to California in 1852 after spending several years in the military, serving under Gen. Zachary Taylor in the Mexican War in 1846 and 1847. Pool came to Andrus Island in 1851 some reports say 1857 and settled on 164 acres, which would later be known as the Pool Ranch.

In 1869, he purchased property and moved to Rio Vista, just north of Newtown Landing on what would be referred to as the River View Creamery Ranch. In 1874, Pool, still having a fondness for Andrus Island, traded his 800-acre property in Rio Vista with a gentleman who owned property on Andrus Island. That year, he had a townsite platted and recorded and, with his friend John Brocas, named it Isleton, meaning "town on an island."

Almost immediately after taking possession of the property, Pool began to build himself a town. Even though he met with some opposition from other inhabitants of the island, he never felt discouraged, only optimistic. The first thing any community in the delta needed was a wharf, and Pool constructed one in 1875. His wharf was large enough to accommodate steamers, and before long, Isleton was receiving four steamers a day and two in the winter months. He petitioned to get a local post office and then became the postmaster, an uncommissioned position. Before long, a hotel sprang up, along with livery stables and many fine homes.

By 1878, the community boasted a hotel, two stores, a livery stable, a post office, a factory, a wharf, and several houses. After the devastating floods of 1878 and 1881, which left Pool in financial hardship, he moved out of the town he established and relocated to Tucson, Arizona, where he lived until he passed away in 1902 at the age of 73.

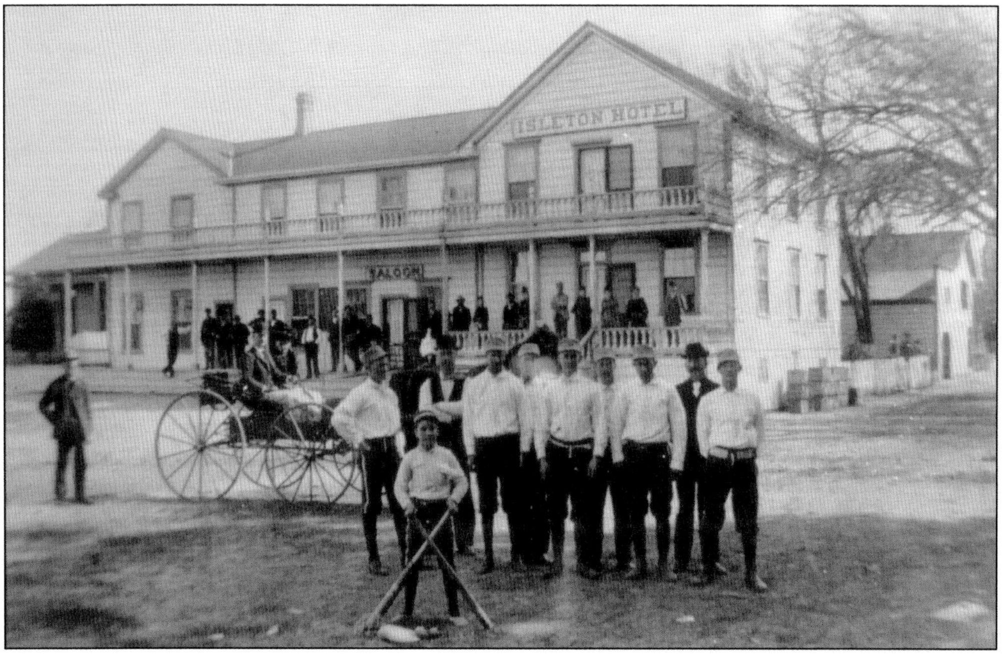

This is one of the earliest known photographs of Isleton. Taken in 1880, it shows the Isleton baseball team posing in front of the Isleton Hotel. Baseball was a very popular sport in this era, and many of the delta communities had local teams, which traveled either by steamship or horse and buggy to meet their opponents. The hotel was built in 1876 at the corner of D and Main Streets. (SRDHS.)

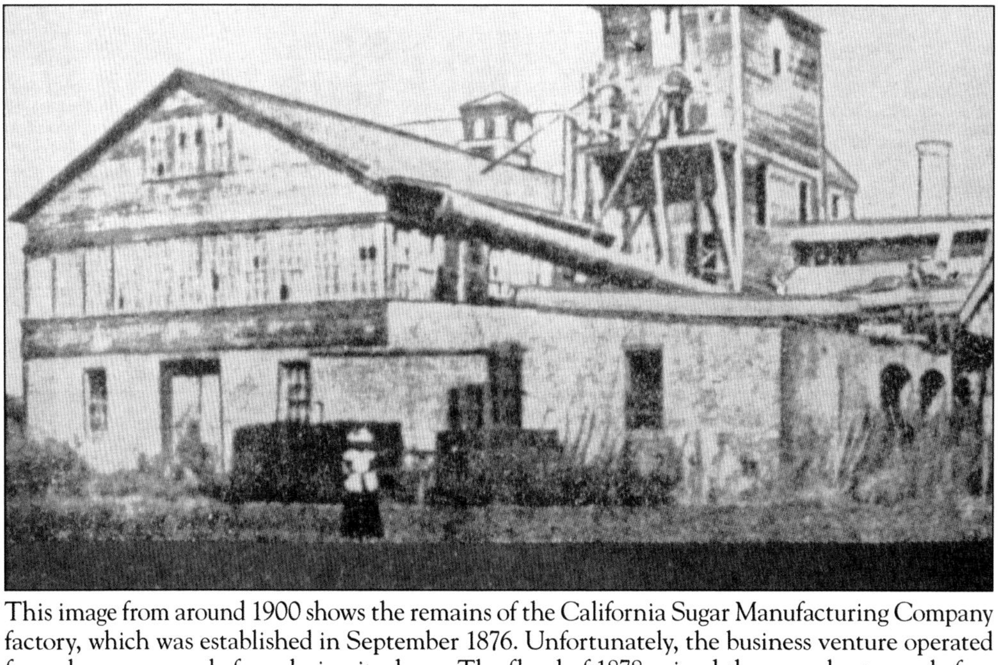

This image from around 1900 shows the remains of the California Sugar Manufacturing Company factory, which was established in September 1876. Unfortunately, the business venture operated for only one season before closing its doors. The flood of 1878 ruined the sugar beet crop before the second season, forcing the plant to close. Years later, a section of this mill was incorporated into the Sun Garden Cannery. (IBAHS.)

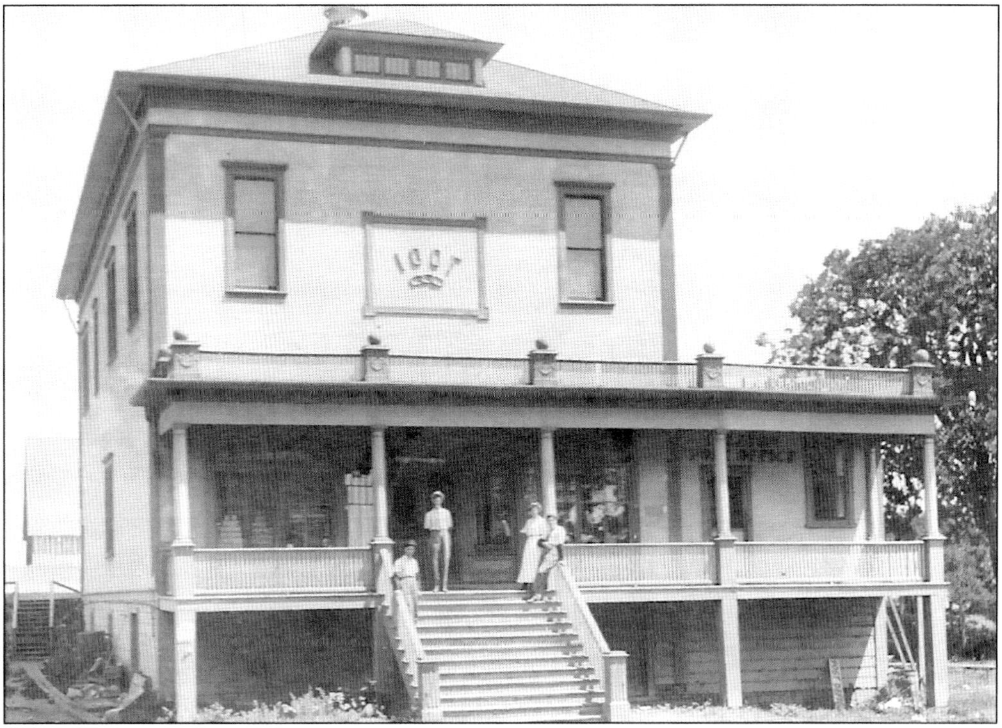

The Gardiner Company building is probably the most recognized structure in Isleton. In the early spring of 1875, the general store was one of the first businesses to open, under the partnership of J. Fitch Wilcox and Philip Hogate Gardiner. Shortly after, the partnership dissolved. However, the Gardiner family name has been synonymous with both Isleton and the building since the 1870s. (IBAHS.)

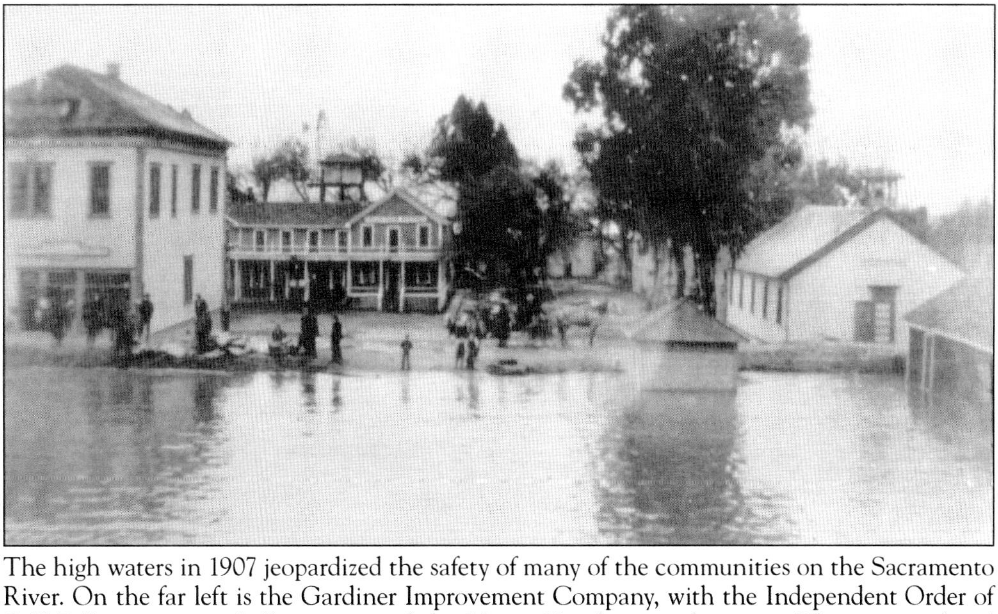

The high waters in 1907 jeopardized the safety of many of the communities on the Sacramento River. On the far left is the Gardiner Improvement Company, with the Independent Order of Odd Fellows meeting hall upstairs and the Isleton Hotel across the street. The town endured floods in 1878, 1881, 1890, 1907, and 1972. (SRDHS.)

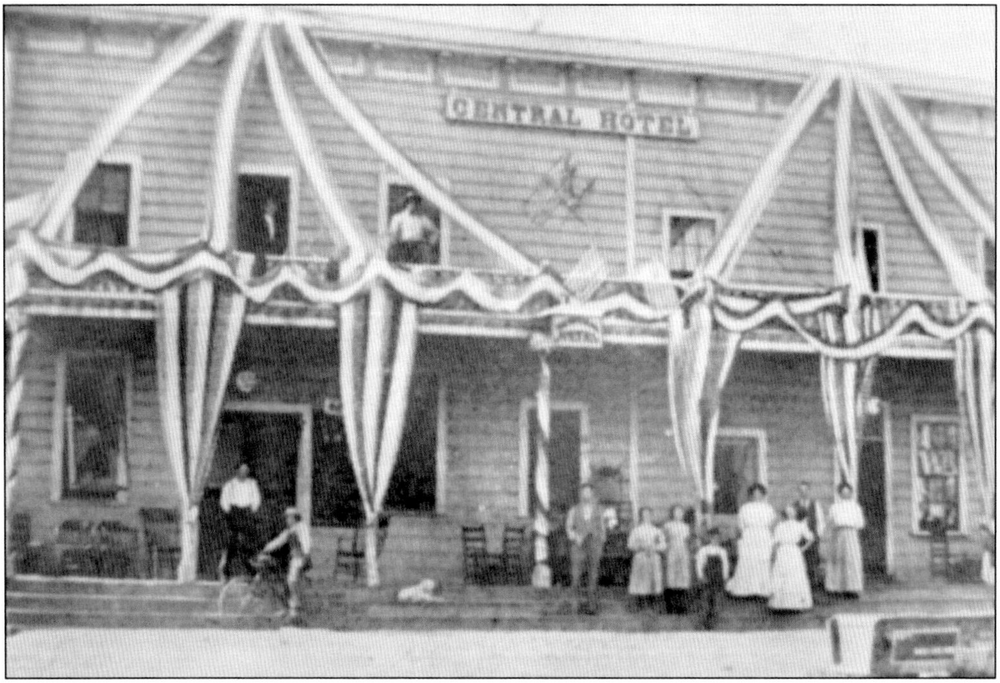

The Central Hotel was just one of a handful of fine hotels on the Sacramento River allowing weary travelers a place to stay and have a warm meal. The lodging was built in 1904 on property on what would become Second Street—the current site of Isleton Joe's. The hotel suffered the same fate as many fine buildings in the delta, succumbing to fire on June 30, 1930. (SRDHS.)

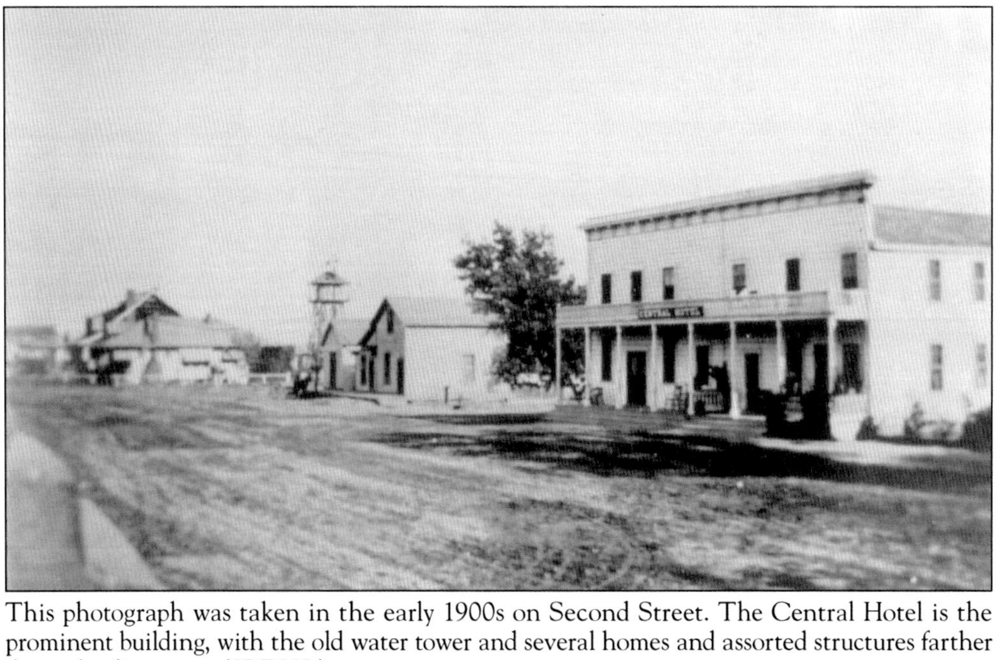

This photograph was taken in the early 1900s on Second Street. The Central Hotel is the prominent building, with the old water tower and several homes and assorted structures farther down the dirt street. (SRDHS.)

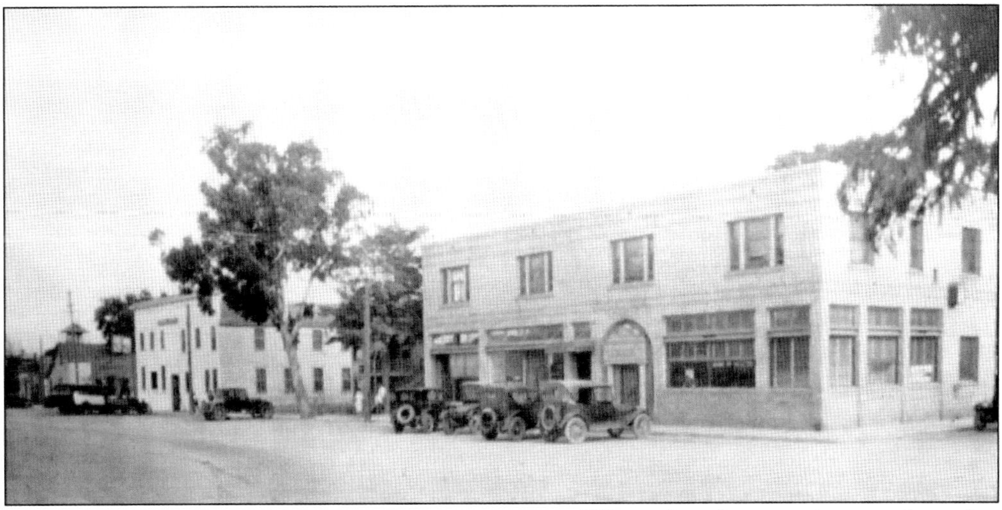

As the towns grew, local banks came into existence. When this photograph was taken, this building was occupied by the Bank of Isleton. Later, Bank of America used the same building. To the left is the Central Hotel, and just past that is Dunn's Dodge dealership. Both the dealership and the Central Hotel were destroyed by fire on June 30, 1930. (SRDHS.)

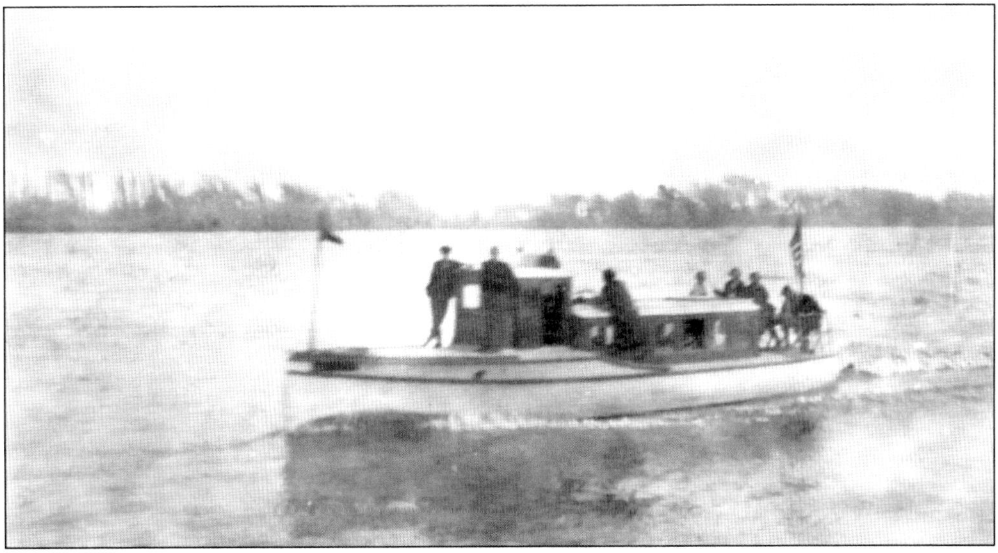

Before bridges were constructed, only a handful of ferries were in operation, and students were ferried to and from school aboard "school boats" such as this one. Isleton students attended the Georgiana School, which was approximately halfway between Isleton and Walnut Grove and was part of the Georgiana School District, established in 1866. Isleton established its own school district in 1878. (SRDHS.)

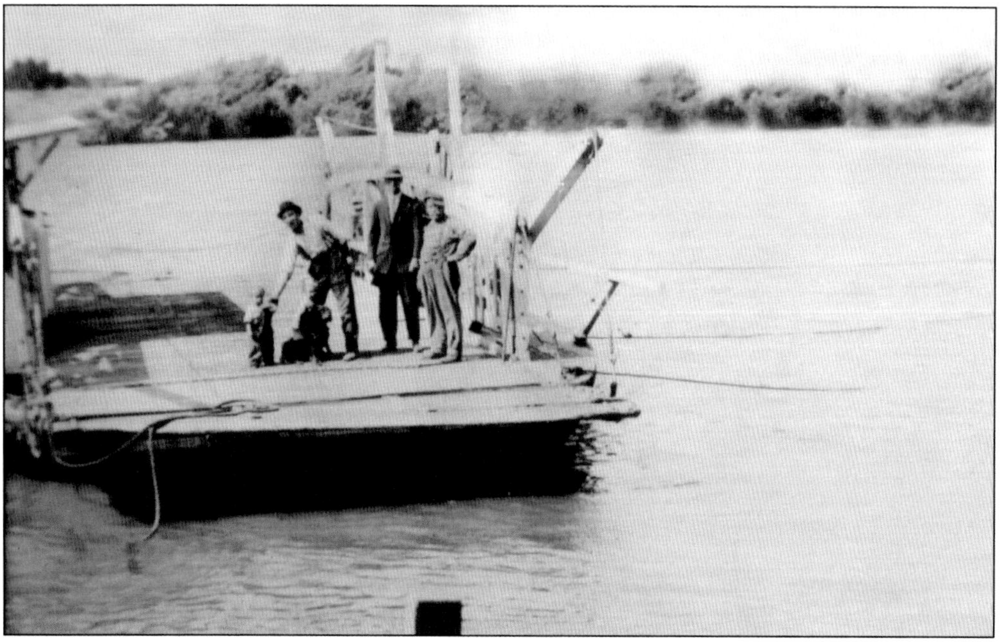

The Isleton ferry crossed from Isleton to Grand Island and was in operation until 1923, when the Isleton Bridge opened. The ferry was propelled by a hand-crank operated by George Fisher and Sam Dorsey. Seen here, from left to right, are Sam Dorsey Jr., Sam Dorsey, Dennis Dorsey, and Herb Crew. (SRDHS.)

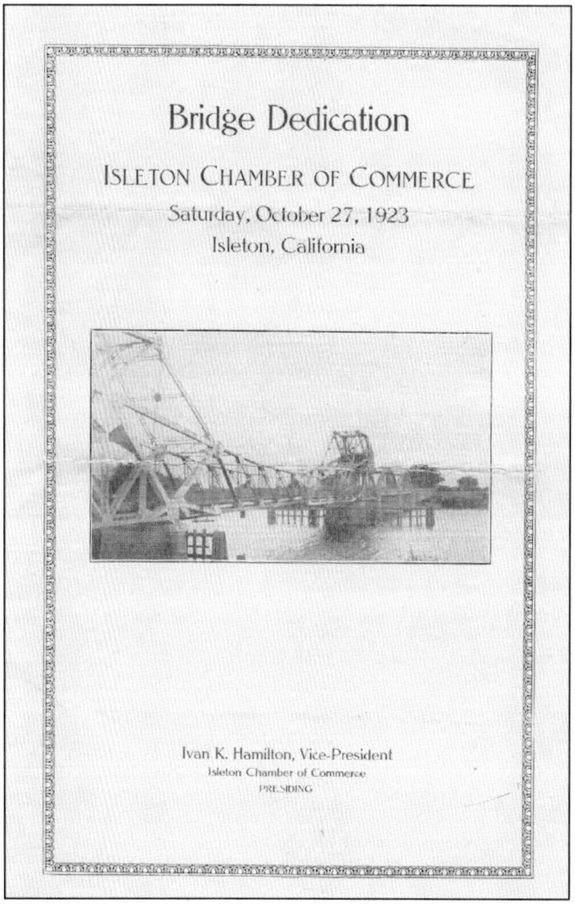

Bridge Dedication

ISLETON CHAMBER OF COMMERCE

Saturday, October 27, 1923

Isleton, California

Ivan K. Hamilton, Vice-President

Isleton Chamber of Commerce

PRESIDING

The Isleton Bridge is a cantilever bridge and was constructed between 1920 and 1923 by the Strauss Bascule Bridge Company of Chicago. This photograph was taken during the dedication of the bridge on October 27, 1923. This was the fourth of four bridges on the Sacramento River delta designed by Strauss, the others being the original 1916 Walnut Grove Bridge, the 1918 Original Rio Vista Bridge, and the 1923 Paintersville Bridge. (SRDHS.)

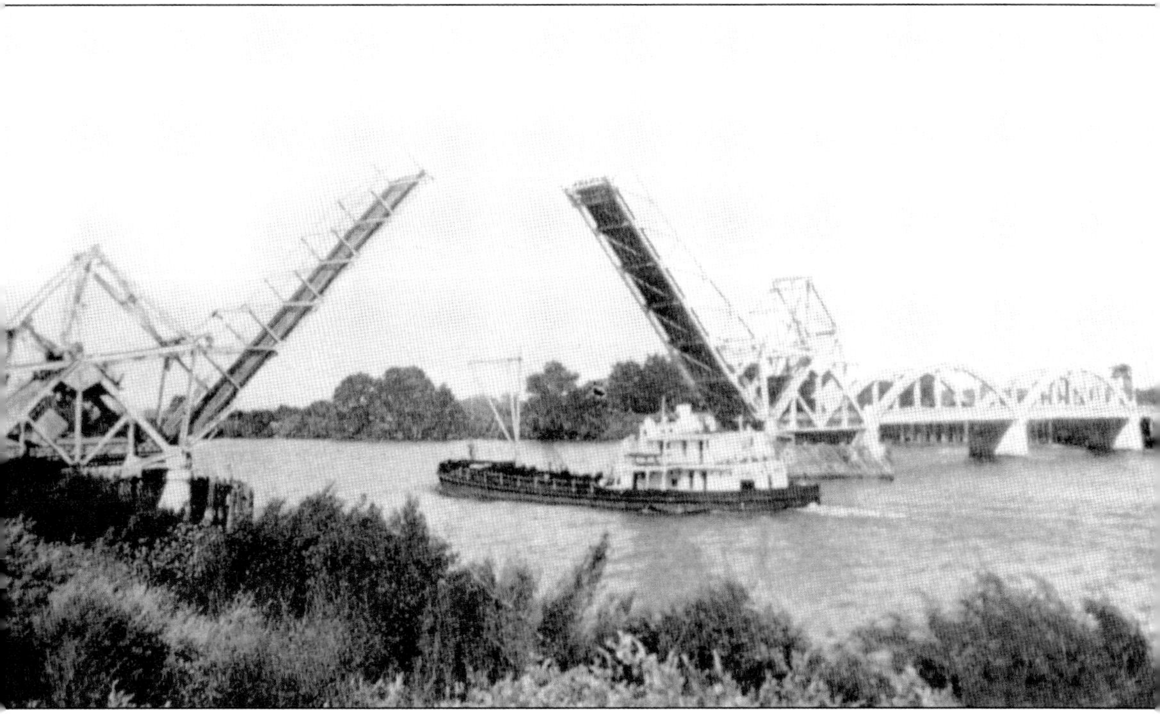

This rather picturesque image shows the bridge at Isleton in the open position as a barge makes its way along the Sacramento River. The delta communities of Rio Vista, Isleton, Walnut Grove, Paintersville, and Freeport all have bridges spanning the Sacramento River. At one time, the river was used for transportation and fishing. Today, both still occur; however, recreational boating, sailing, and water-skiing are more common activities. (SRDHS.)

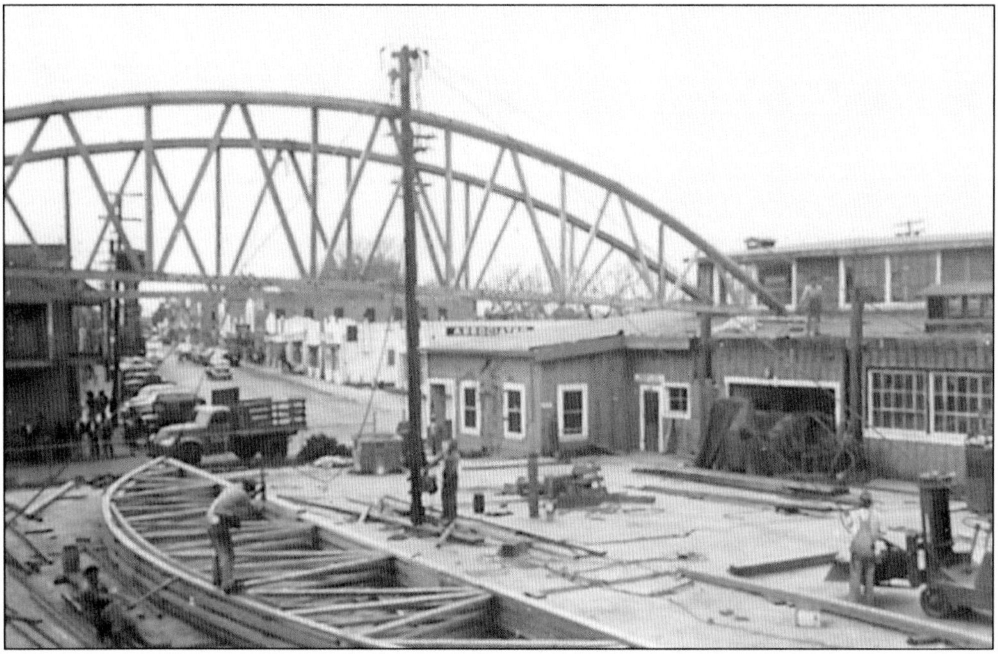

This rare image was taken as additional construction work was underway at the National Packing Company, with Isleton's Chinatown in the background. There were canneries in many of the delta settlements, including Rio Vista, Isleton, Ryde, Locke, and Hood. (SRDHS.)

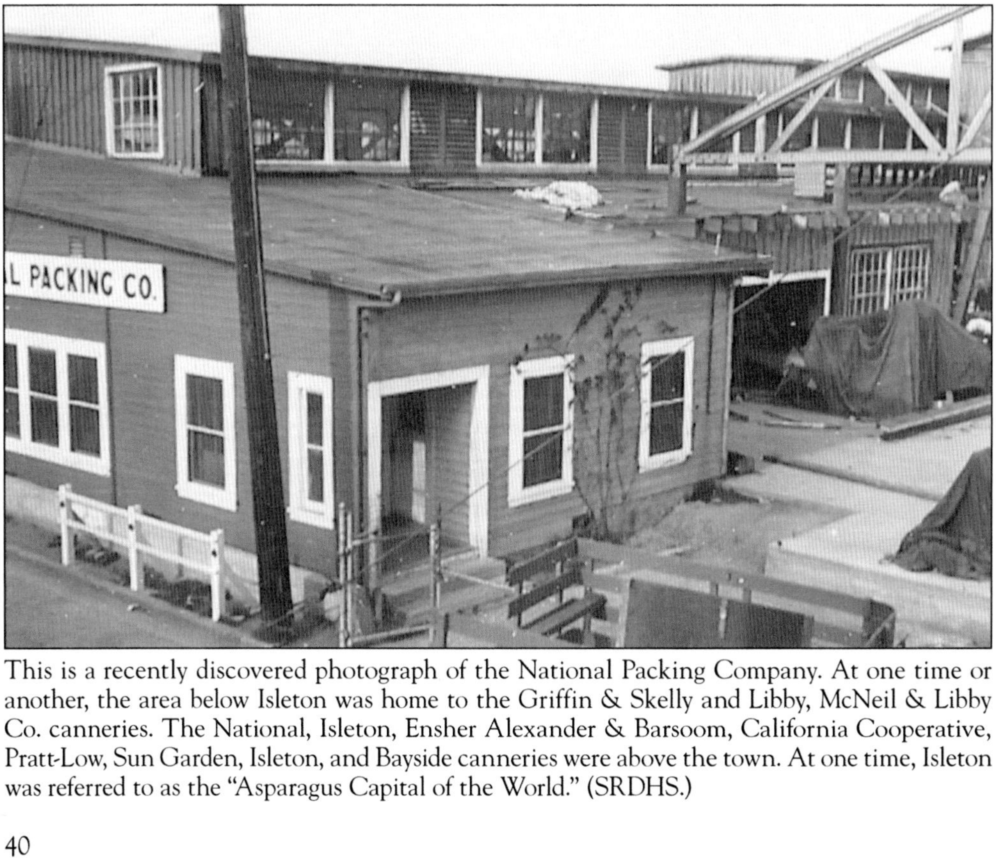

This is a recently discovered photograph of the National Packing Company. At one time or another, the area below Isleton was home to the Griffin & Skelly and Libby, McNeil & Libby Co. canneries. The National, Isleton, Ensher Alexander & Barsoom, California Cooperative, Pratt-Low, Sun Garden, Isleton, and Bayside canneries were above the town. At one time, Isleton was referred to as the "Asparagus Capital of the World." (SRDHS.)

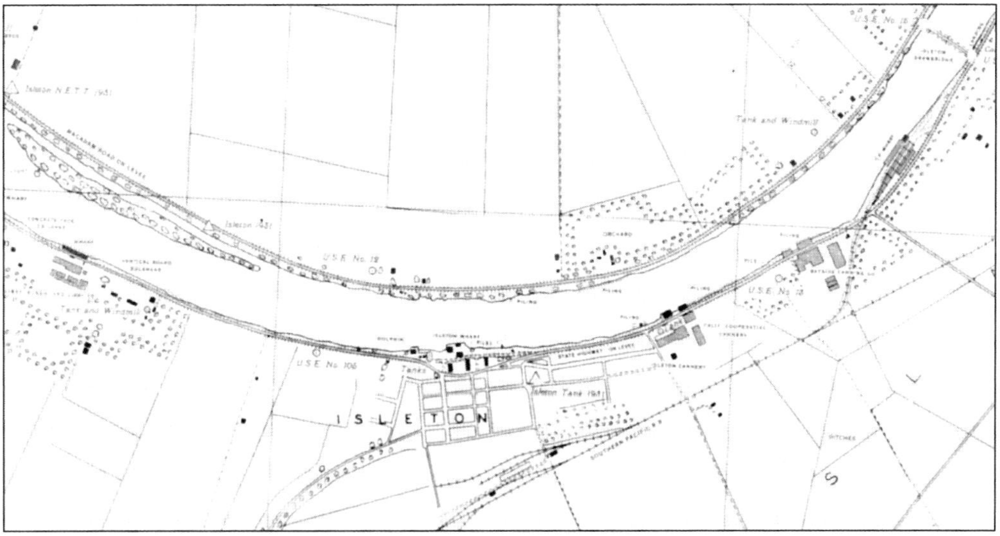

This enlarged section of a 1931 photolithographic print, from a compilation of aerial photographs, shows Isleton, the Libby, McNeil & Libby Co. cannery below town, and the canneries of Isleton, California Cooperative, and Bayside above town. Maps like this help put into perspective the communities and the distances between the many area canneries. (RVM.)

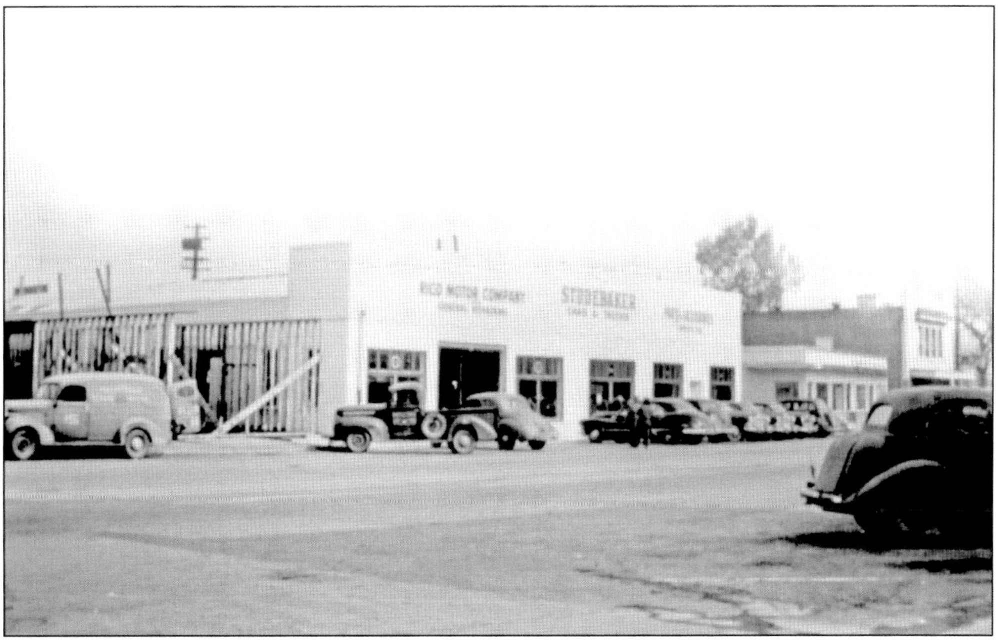

The north side of Second Street (Highway 160) is seen here in 1949. Beginning in the left corner of the image and continuing right are the framework for the construction of the Del Rio Hotel, Rico Motor Company, Balsmeier Plumbing, and the Isleton Playhouse. All but the theater building are still standing today, but Balsmeier Plumbing is the only one of the four businesses still in operation. (SRDHS.)

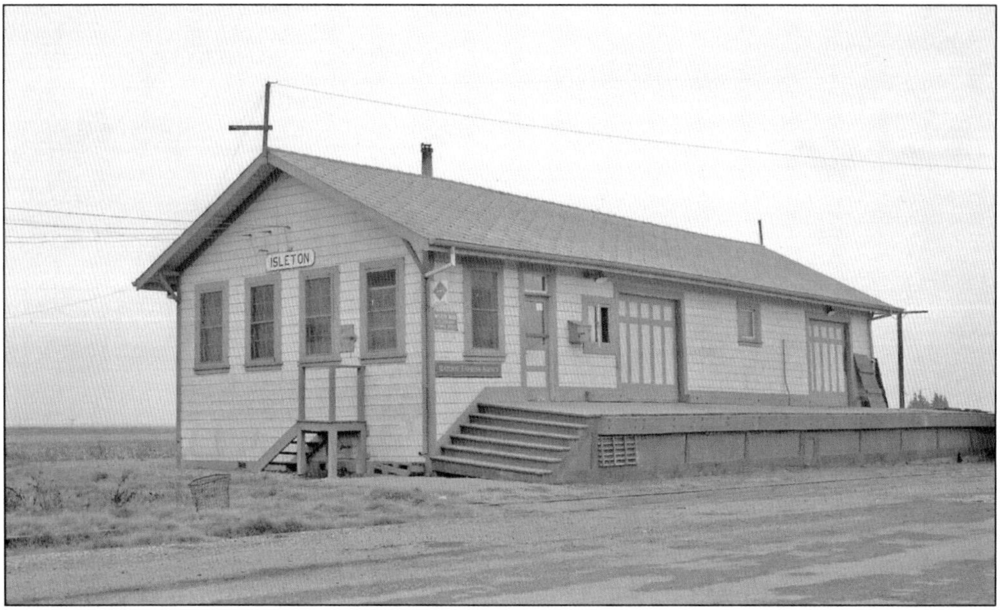

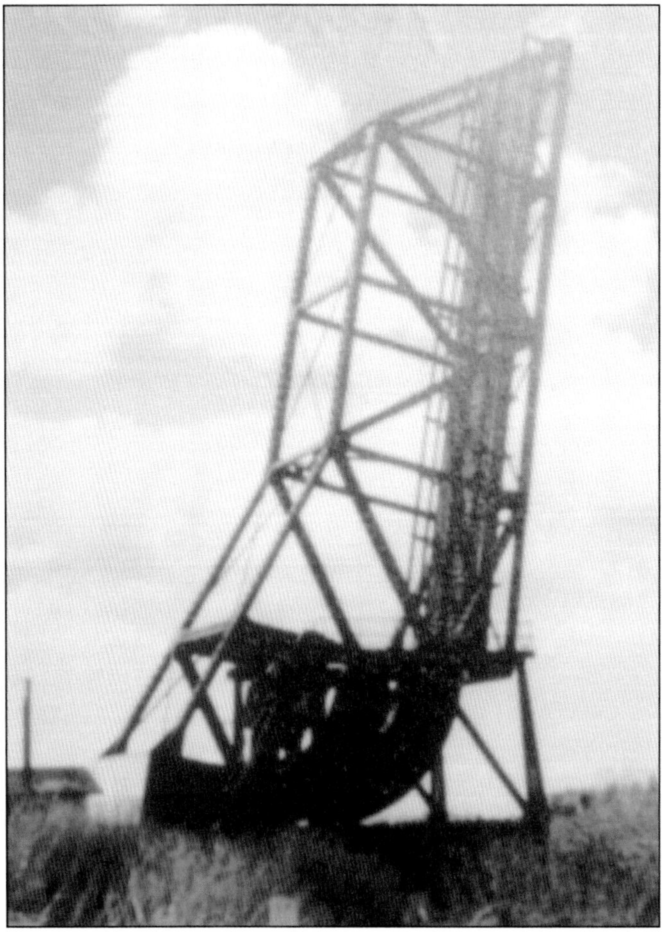

The Southern Pacific station at Isleton was the last one built on the route. In 1929, tracks were laid from Walnut Grove to Isleton, crossing the Georgiana Slough approximately 1.5 miles north of Isleton. The station officially opened in November 1929. Originally, the railroad was to continue to Antioch, but that never became a reality, making the Isleton station the final destination on the route. The Isleton branch operated until June 21, 1972, when a levee broke and a disastrous flood engulfed Isleton. No train ever came as far as Isleton after that flood, but the town did remain on the Southern Pacific Railroad timetable until 1977. In June 1975, the Southern Pacific filed with the Interstate Commerce Commission (ICC) to abandon the track from Hood to Isleton, which took effect in 1977. (Above, John Harder collection; left, SRDHS.)

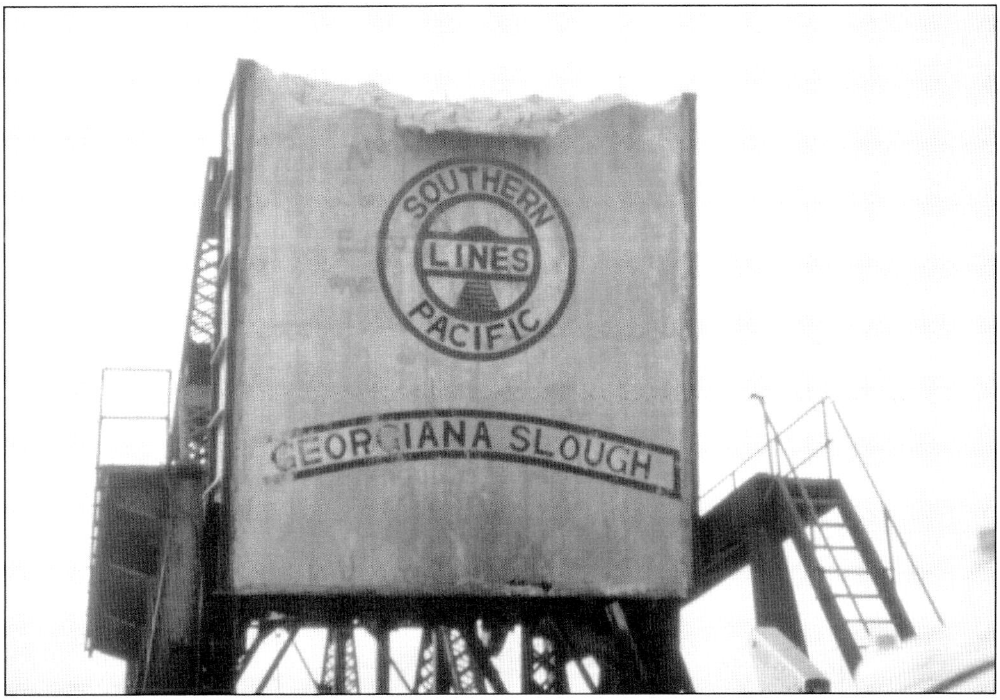

In order for the Southern Pacific Railroad to lay tracks from Walnut Grove to Isleton in 1929, a bridge crossing the Georgiana Slough was required to connect Tyler Island to Andrus Island. This bridge was normally left open to allow for boat traffic and only lowered when required for rail traffic. The historic bridge was dismantled in 1982. (SRDHS.)

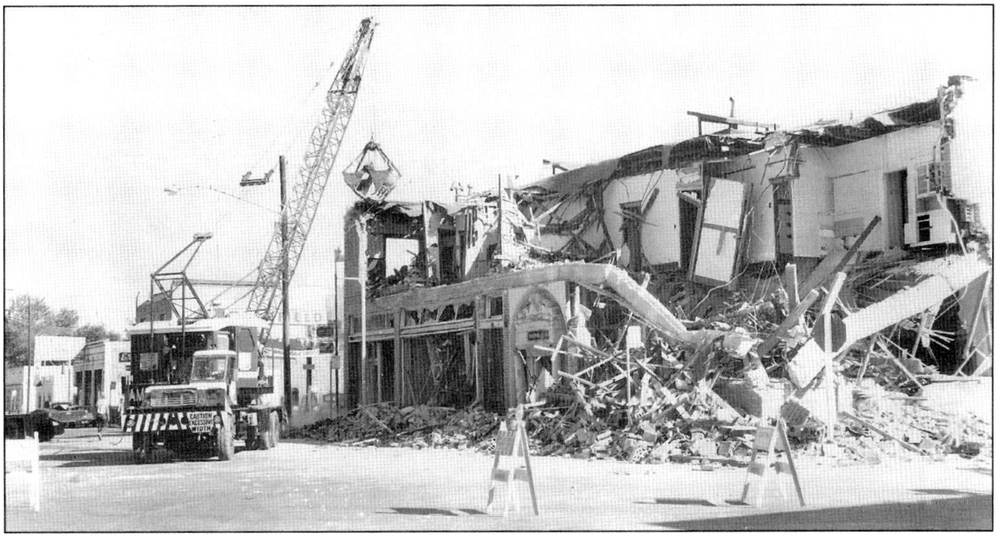

Crews tear down the former Bank of America building on the corner of Second and A Streets. H.R. Dunn & Sons Dodge dealership is in the background. Dunn's automotive originally sold Dodges and Plymouths, then just Dodges, and finally Dodges, Chryslers, and Plymouths. At one time, the business also had a location on Front Street in Rio Vista. Compare this to the image on page 37. (SRDHS.)

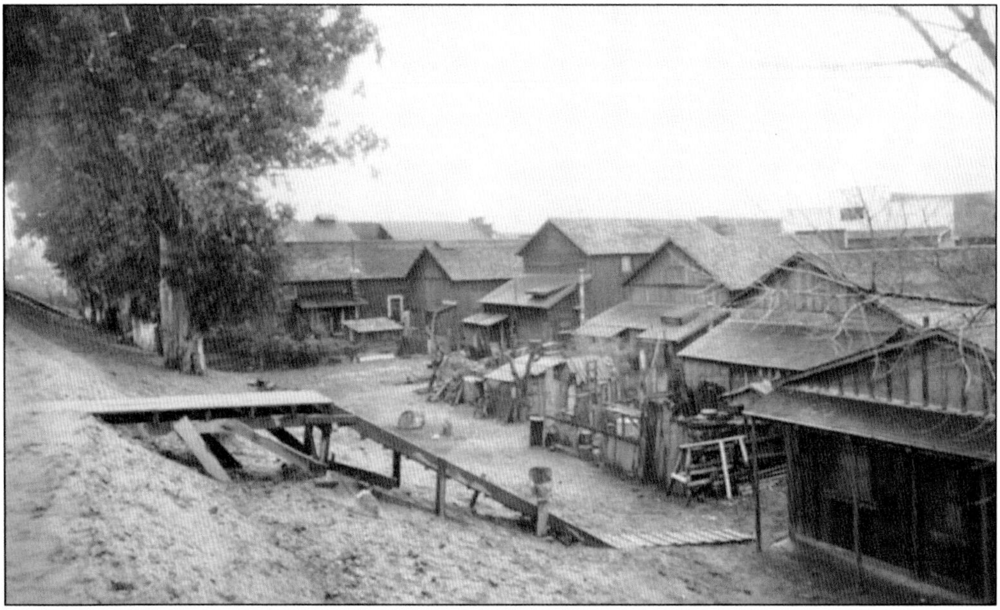

This photograph shows the original Chinese community, or Chinatown, established in the late 1800s near Jackson Slough, the site of the present city hall, and Wilson Park. This original Chinatown was destroyed by fire on November 30, 1915, after which the Chinese population relocated to property offered by John Gardiner just a short distance upriver, in what is now Isleton's Main Street Chinatown. (SRDHS.)

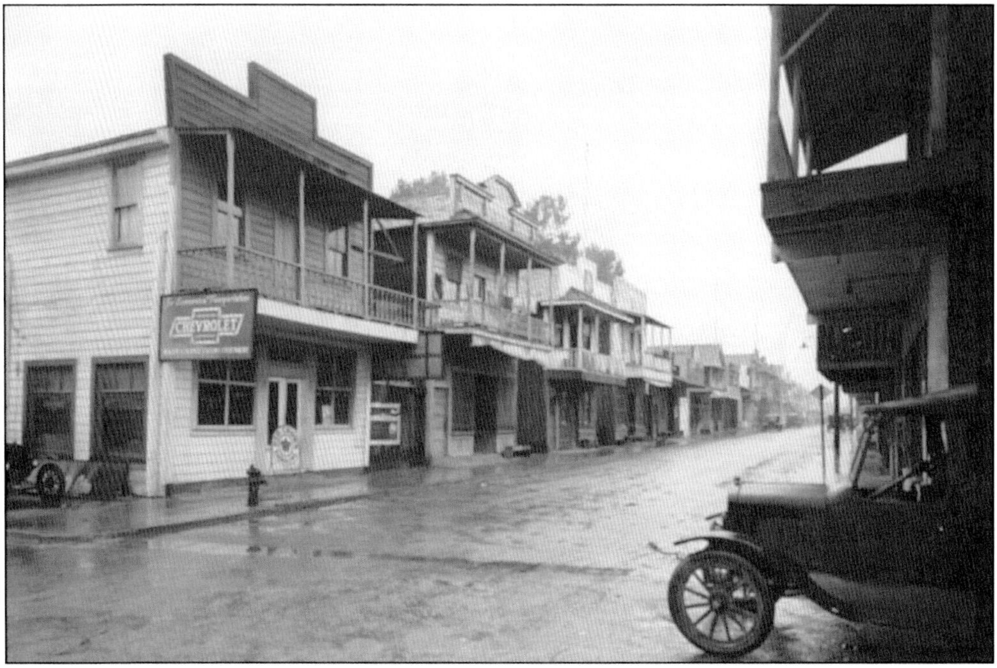

This photograph and the ones on the next two pages was taken in 1926, after Chinatown was reestablished following the 1916 fire, but before the Memorial Day 1926 fire, which destroyed Isleton's Chinese section for a second time. Unfortunately, when the fire broke out, the members of the Isleton Volunteer Fire Department were all attending a Memorial Day picnic. (CSL.)

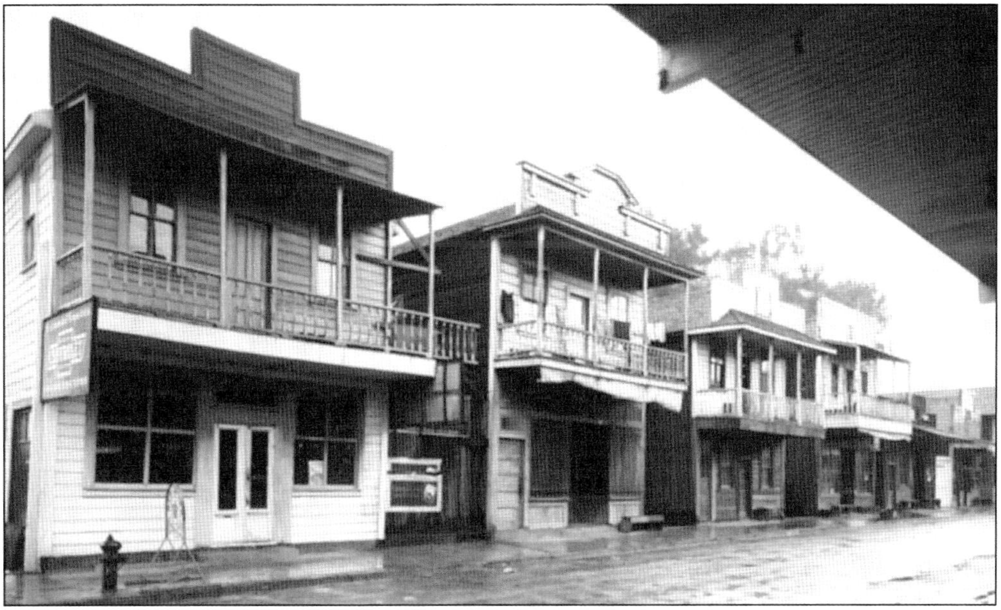

On Memorial Day 1926, a Chinese woman was heating milk on a kerosene cook stove. When the milk boiled over, she attempted to save it and accidentally set her hand towel on fire. In minutes, her home was engulfed in flames, and within 30 minutes, the majority of Chinatown was on fire. More than $750,000 worth of damage occurred. (CSL.)

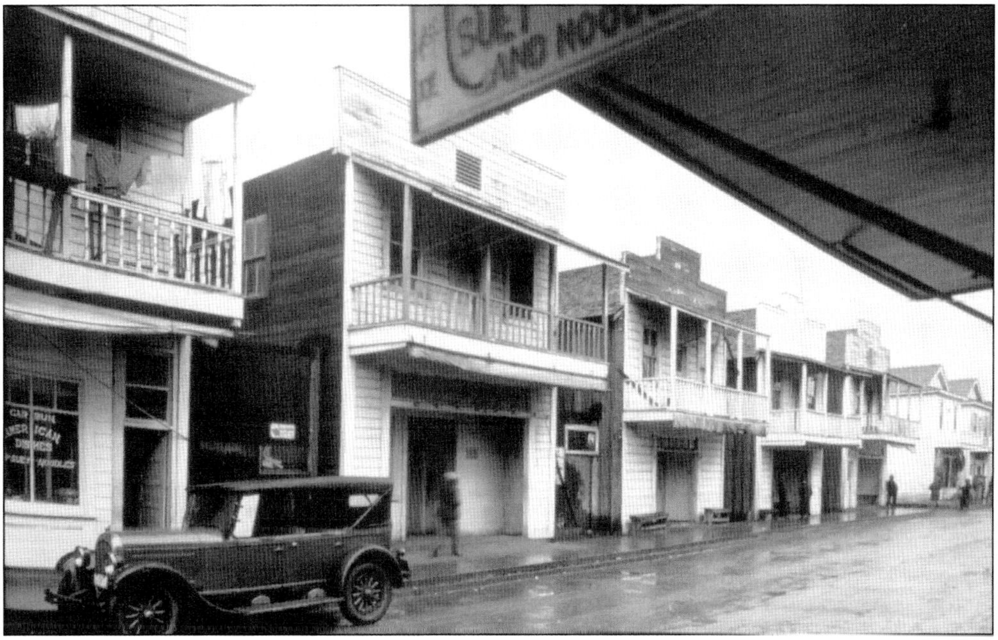

Luckily, no lives were lost, and only seven individuals were treated for burns. Schools, public buildings, and private residences were pressed into service to accommodate the recently homeless. A total of 110 Chinese and Japanese stores and homes were destroyed, leaving 1,500 people homeless. Among the more notable buildings destroyed were the Chinese Masonic Hall, the Josh House, the Young Men's Christian Association, the Quong Wo Sing, the Wah Hing Company, and the Chan Kee Hashimoto Company. (CSL.)

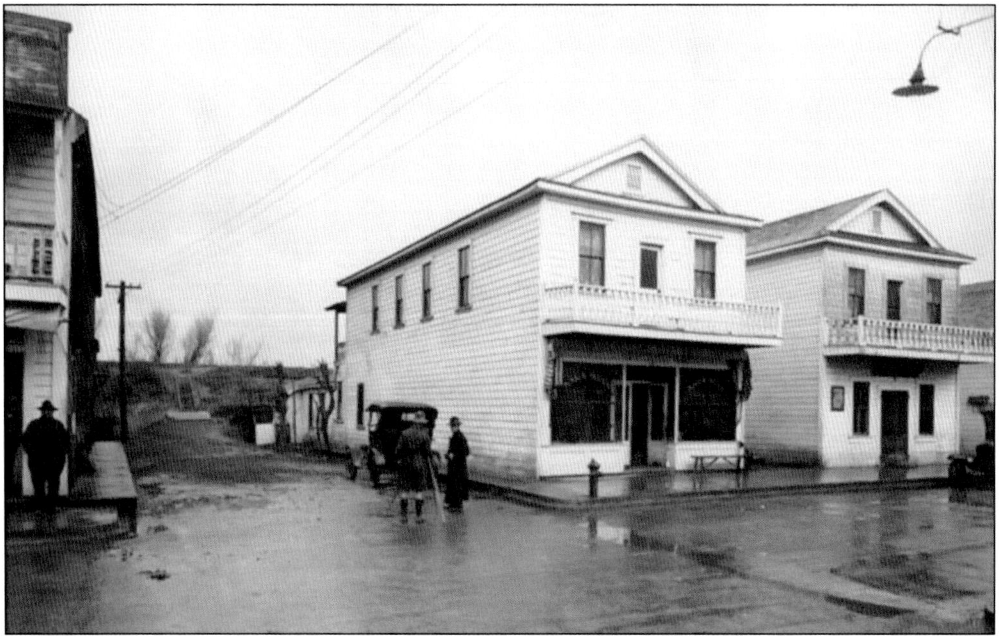

The intersection of F and Main Streets, seen here, was the division line between the Chinese and Japanese sections of Isleton. The buildings on the left were Chinese, and the ones on the right were Japanese. All of these structures were destroyed in the 1926 fire. (CSL.)

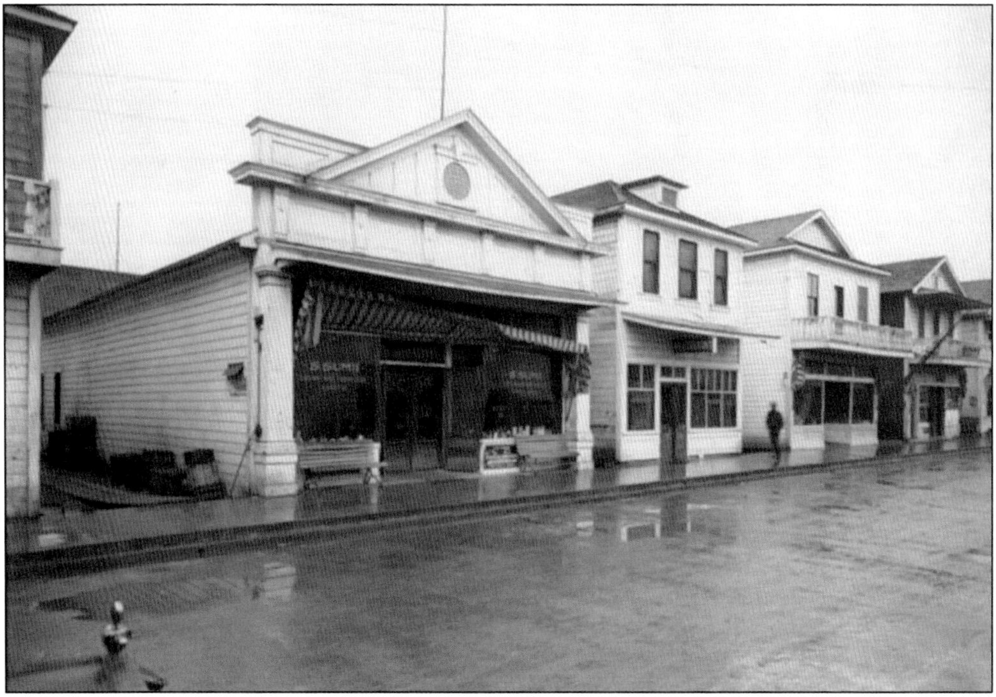

The devastating fire reminded many Chinese and Japanese residents of November 1915, when 35 buildings in Isleton were destroyed by fire. Of those 35, more than 20 were in the Chinese section, including a movie theater, a Chinese laundry, three gambling houses, a notions store, Oriental School, and several general merchandise stores. (CSL.)

The Bing Kong Tong building, at 29 Main Street, was constructed after the devastating 1926 fire. The association held its grand opening in 1933. This was where the local Chinese would go to settle differences within their community. There were similar associations in both Walnut Grove and Locke. When the first Chinese school was no longer big enough, this building was used for Chinese language and cultural studies. (SRDHS.)

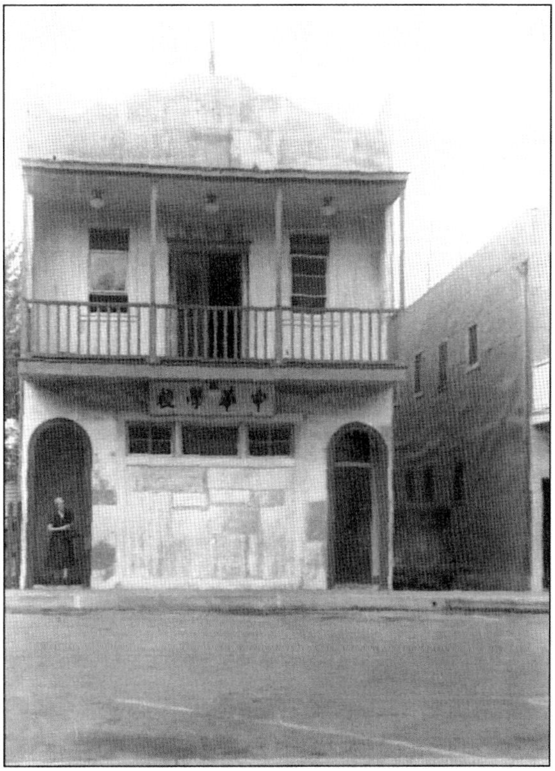

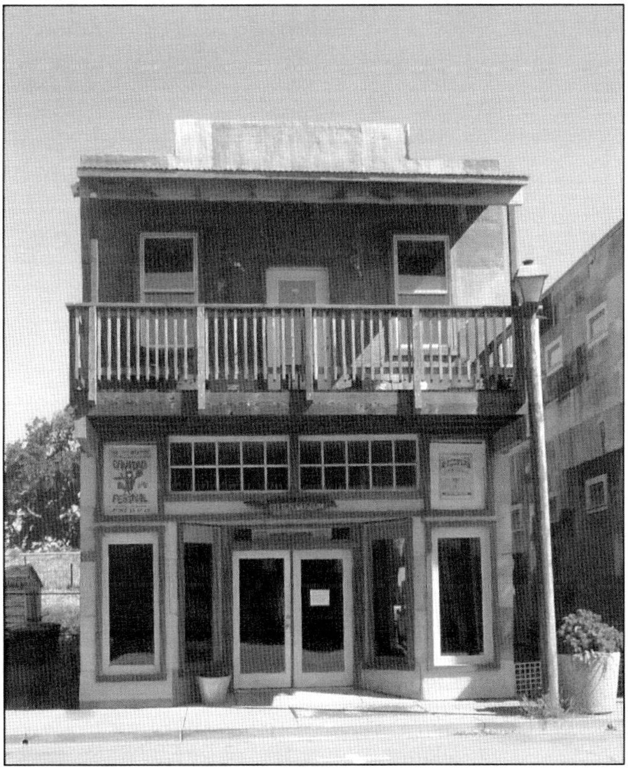

The Isleton Museum is located at 33 Main Street in what was once a gambling hall named Sun-Ah-Jo, or "New Asia." On display are items specific to the multicultural history of the town of Isleton. Rio Vista, Isleton, and Locke are the only three delta communities with local museums. (Author's collection.)

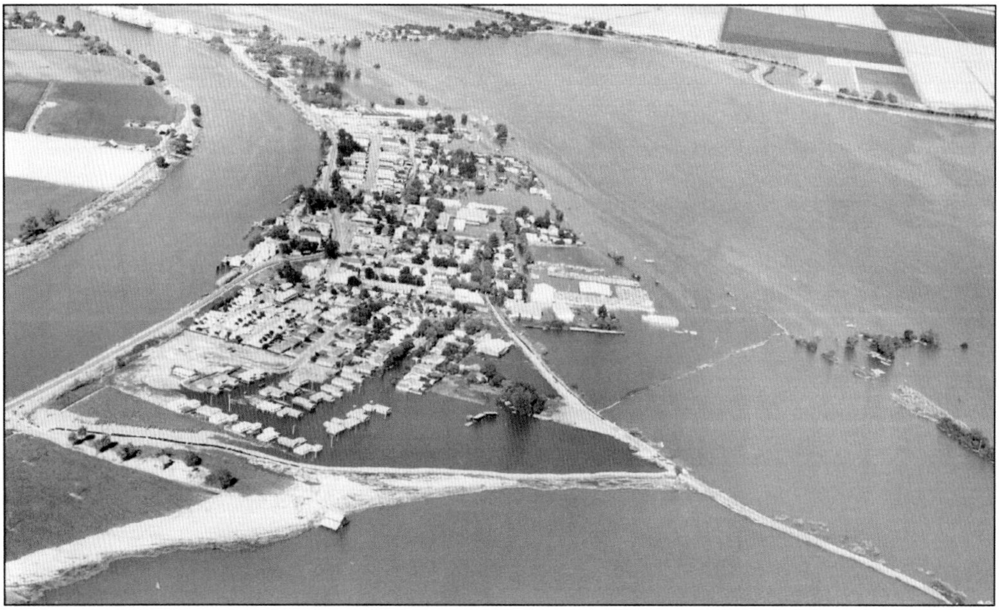

On June 21, 1972, the first levee break occurred on the San Joaquin River six miles south of Isleton, dumping 58 billion gallons of water over 12,000 acres onto Andrus and Brannan Islands. The following day, approximately half of Isleton was under floodwaters. For several months, pumps worked around the clock to siphon the islands dry. It took nearly six months to repair the levee and pump out the water. (RVM.)

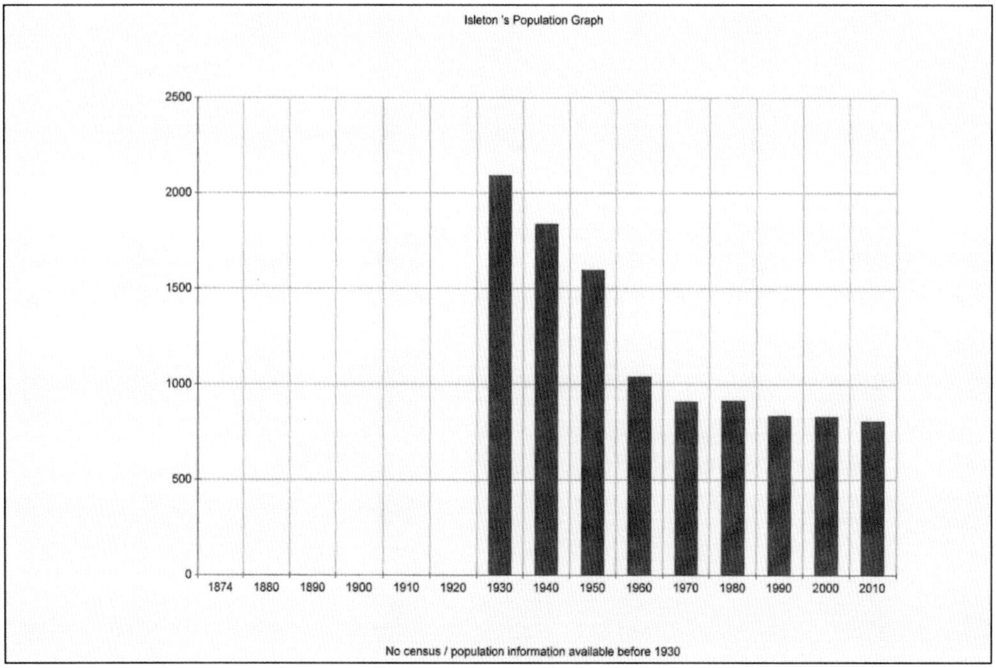

It is quite apparent from this graph that the population of Isleton has decreased consistently since 1930. No census information is available from before 1930, and because of the seasonal arrival and departure of cannery workers and their families, it is hard to accurately pinpoint the number of local year-round residents. (Author's collection.)

Three

Ryde

The small, unincorporated community of Ryde is on Grand Island, a few miles above the Isleton Bridge, and is designated in Reclamation District No. 3. Originally, the island was part of what was known in the early 1850s as Sutter Township. However, in August 1854, the court of sessions ordered that a new township be organized and named Georgiana. Its boundaries were formalized in October 1856.

By the early 1870s, several small proprietors and a few large proprietors owned the 17,000 acres that made up Grand Island. Gen. Thomas Hansford Williams, the former California attorney general under Gov. John B. Weller, and his law partner, David Bixler, owned approximately 2,000 of those acres.

In 1870, Williams purchased an additional 9,000 acres from George Roberts, with the two men acting as business associates in some of the holdings. Williams reclaimed much of the property and farmed it. His crops were fruitful until the floods of 1878, 1879, and 1881, which caused some losses.

Williams passed away in 1885, and his estate was put into the hands of administrators. Williams was from the Isle of Wight, just off the southern coast of England. There was a beautiful town on the island's coast named Ryde, which resembled the area where he had erected a hotel. He always said that because of the geographic similarities, the community should be named after its European counterpart.

In 1891, W.A. Kesner purchased 40 acres from the Williams estate and moved his family there. The Kesners operated a hotel and saloon there for a number of years. In 1893, Kesner petitioned and received a post office, becoming postmaster and founding Ryde. Reportedly, Thomas Williams's son actually suggested the name of his father's birthplace.

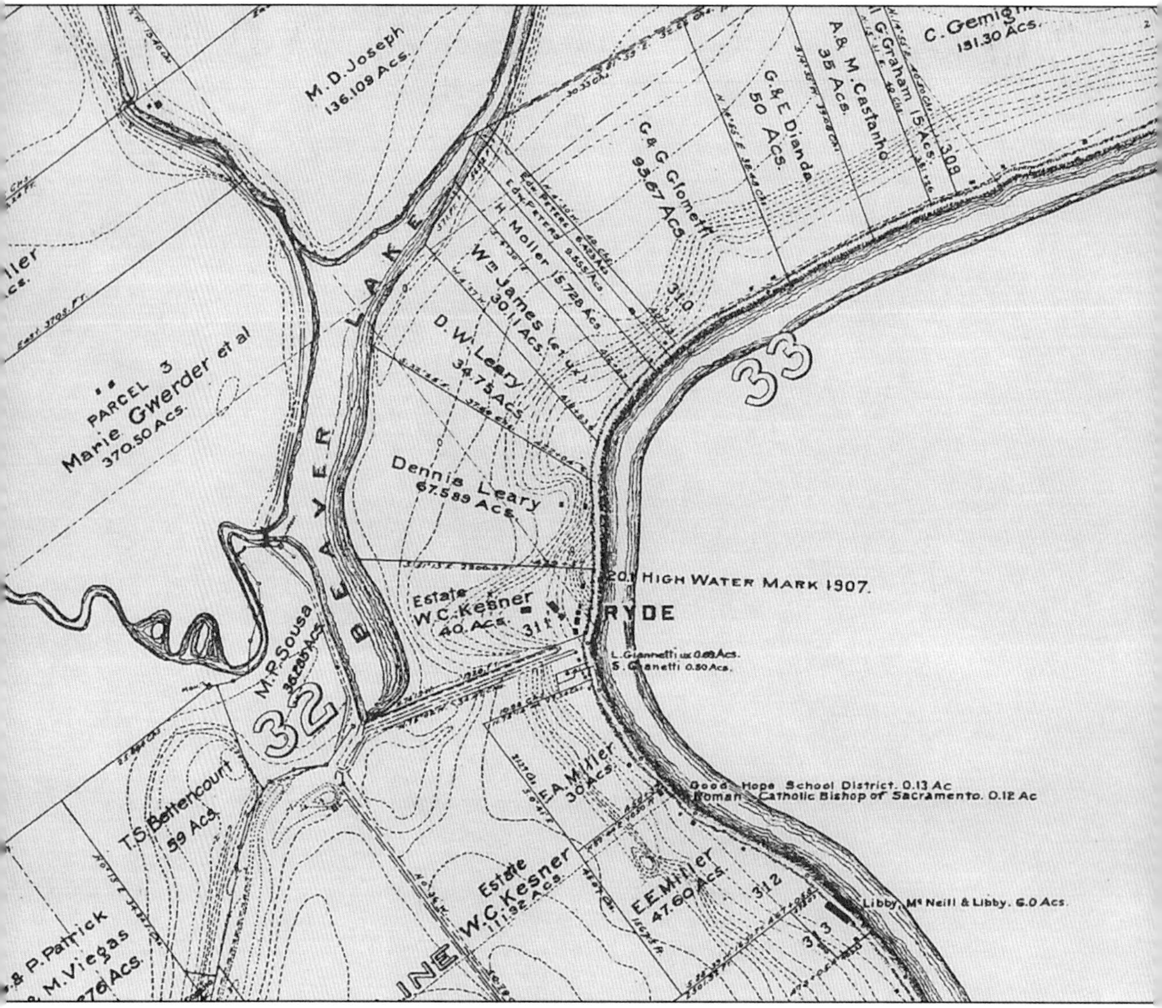

This enlarged section of a 1913 map of Grand Island map shows Ryde and the surrounding landowners' properties. Descendants of the Gwerder, Bettencourt, Souza, Leary, and James families, among others, are still residing in the delta. Note Beaver Lake, near which Beaver Union School was constructed. Notice the notation for the high water that occurred in the floods of 1907. (RVM.)

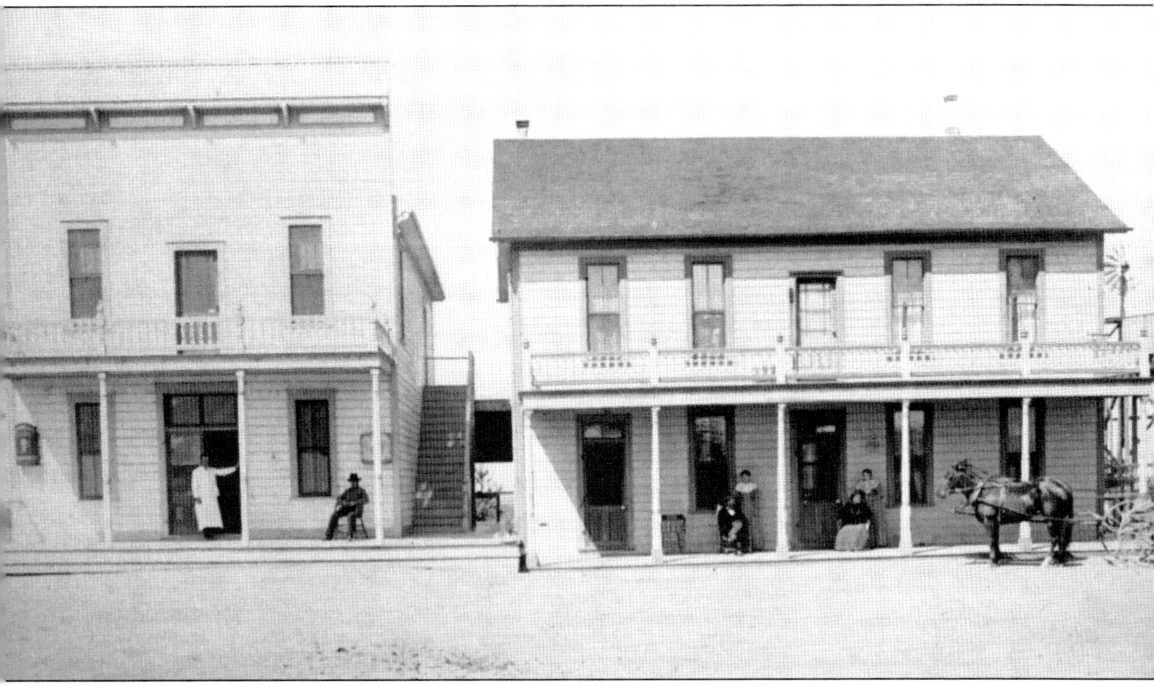

This image was taken between 1886 and 1918 and shows the original Ryde Hotel on the left and an unidentified building on the right. Images of the new hotel, built after the 1918 fire, only show one structure where these two buildings once stood. (SRDHS.)

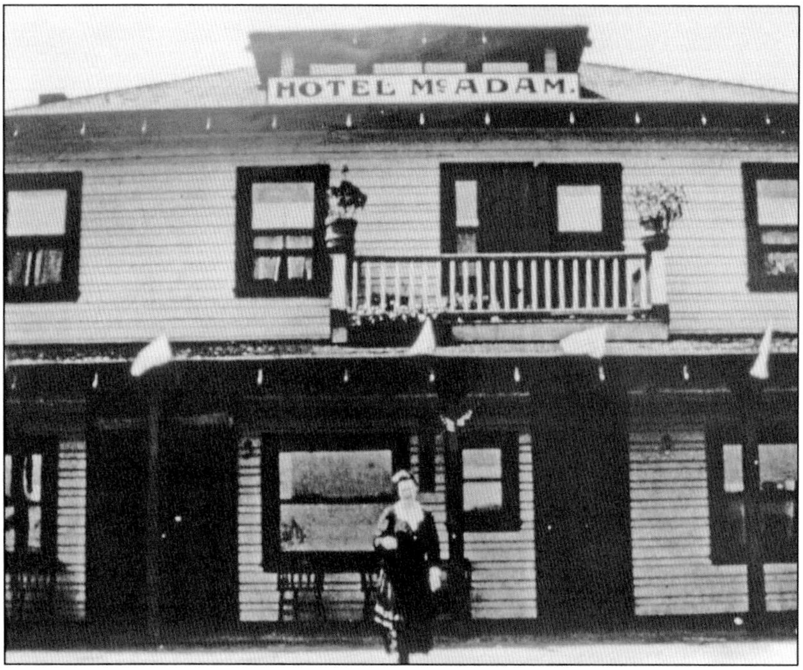

The second Hotel Ryde, also known as Hotel McAdam, was built on the site of the original hotel soon after it burned in 1918. (SRDHS.)

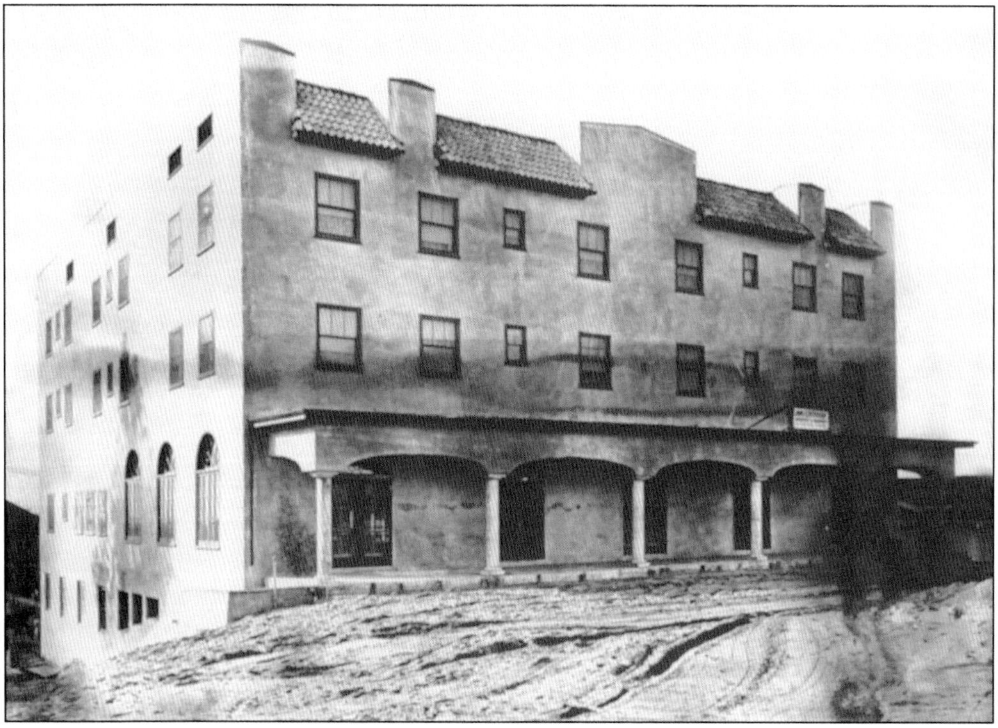

By the mid-1920s, the Ryde Hotel was getting more business than it could accommodate, so property owner Severina Gianetti hired Sacramento architect Jens C. Peterson to design a Mission-style stucco building. Sacramento contractor J.A. Saunders was hired to build it, and construction began on June 1926. The new three-story, 50-room Ryde Hotel formally opened for business in March 1927. This is a rare image of the construction as it neared completion. (CSL.)

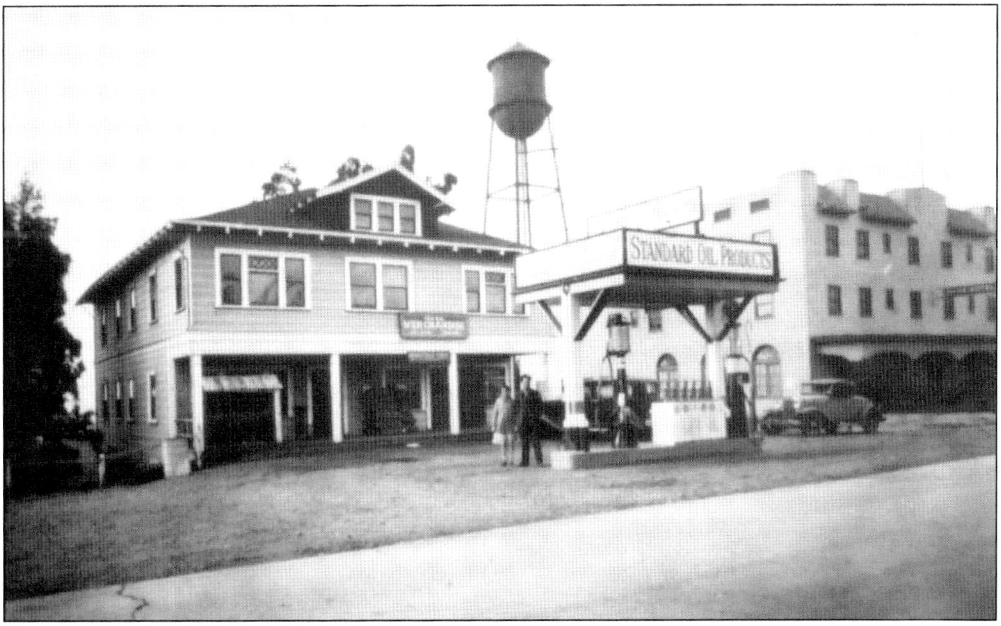

After the new Hotel Ryde went into operation, the old hotel functioned as a grocery store, eventually closing its doors and being torn down in the 1930s. In the 1930s, it was said that Hollywood stars such as Al Jolson, Clark Gable, and Jean Harlow all stayed at the hotel. Herbert Hoover also reportedly announced his candidacy for the presidency at the Ryde Hotel. (SRDHS.)

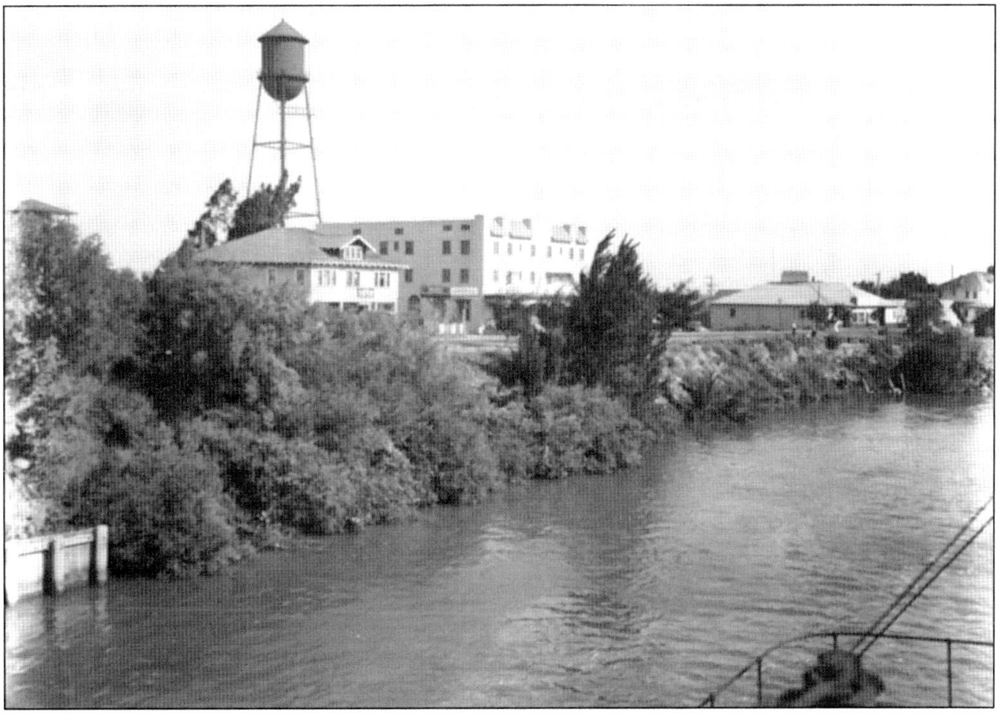

Through the decades, the stories regarding the speakeasy, Hollywood stars, and the goings-on in the Prohibition era would become legendary throughout the delta. This photograph of Ryde captures the community in its heyday. (CSL.)

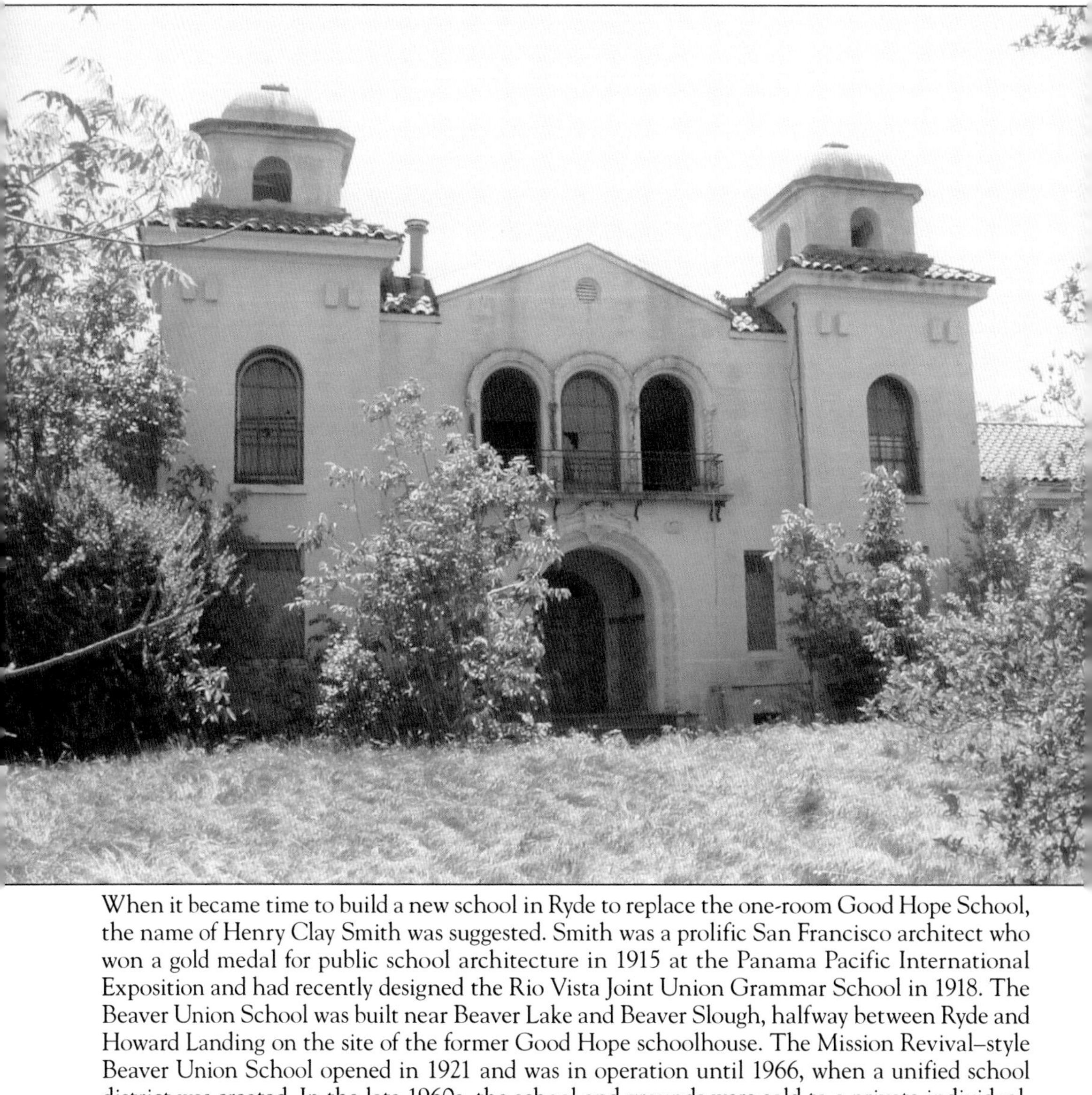

When it became time to build a new school in Ryde to replace the one-room Good Hope School, the name of Henry Clay Smith was suggested. Smith was a prolific San Francisco architect who won a gold medal for public school architecture in 1915 at the Panama Pacific International Exposition and had recently designed the Rio Vista Joint Union Grammar School in 1918. The Beaver Union School was built near Beaver Lake and Beaver Slough, halfway between Ryde and Howard Landing on the site of the former Good Hope schoolhouse. The Mission Revival–style Beaver Union School opened in 1921 and was in operation until 1966, when a unified school district was created. In the late 1960s, the school and grounds were sold to a private individual. (Author's collection.)

Four

Walnut Grove

In 1849, New York native John Wesley Sharp headed west to California with his wife, son, and daughter. After arriving in California in late 1849, the Sharps spent their first winter in the settlement of Coloma, near Dry Creek. As the seasons changed and spring came upon them, the Sharps followed the Sacramento River down to a point where they found a large thicket of walnut and oak trees near where the Georgiana Slough branched off the Sacramento River.

The Sharp family spent their first night in the delta on the site, and Sharp felt it would be ideal to purchase the land and construct a home there, as it was at the point where Tyler and Georgiana Sloughs made a junction with the old river channel of the Sacramento River. These sloughs offered direct access to the Mokelumne and San Joaquin Rivers. In 1850, Sharp acquired 160 acres of rich farmland at the aforementioned site from the state by invoking the recently passed Federal Swamp and Overflow Act, which provided for the title of wetlands to be transferred from the federal government to the states.

He erected a fine home, and, being a blacksmith by trade, opened a blacksmith shop that served the surrounding farmers. Before long, Sharp found himself establishing a town. When it came to naming the town, he remembered how he was so taken by the grove of walnut trees there that he chose to name the settlement after the trees he had camped under on that first night the year before. One of Sharp's first actions was to build a wharf, making the town accessible by water, its lifeline to San Francisco and Sacramento. Additional settlers gradually arrived, businesses were established, and the town continued to grow. Sharp donated the land for the first school as well as the site for the California Transportation Company to place the first steamboat landing.

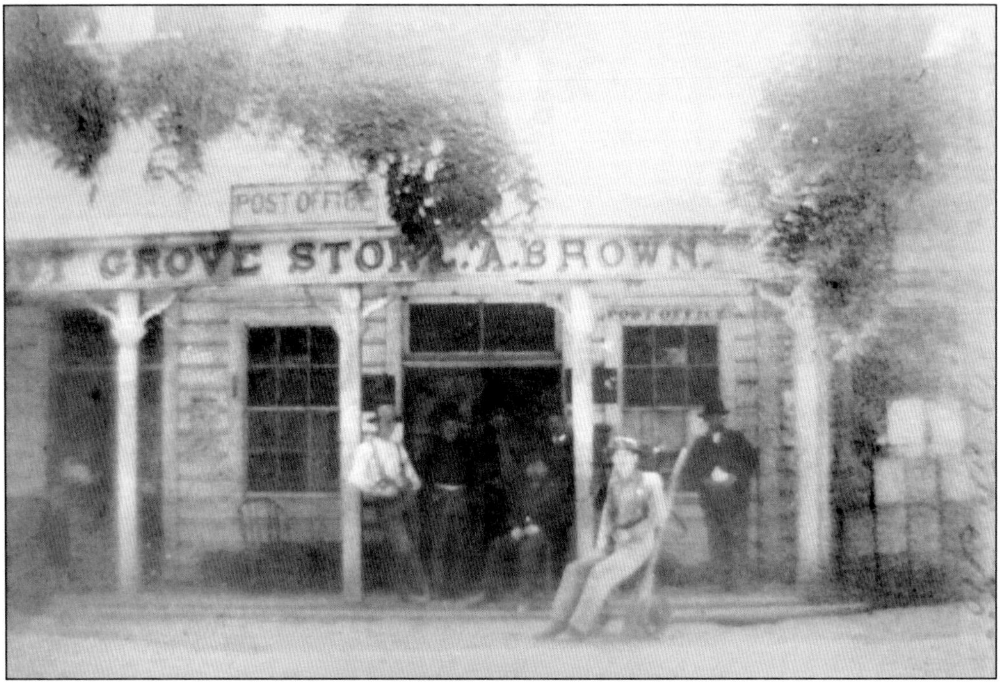

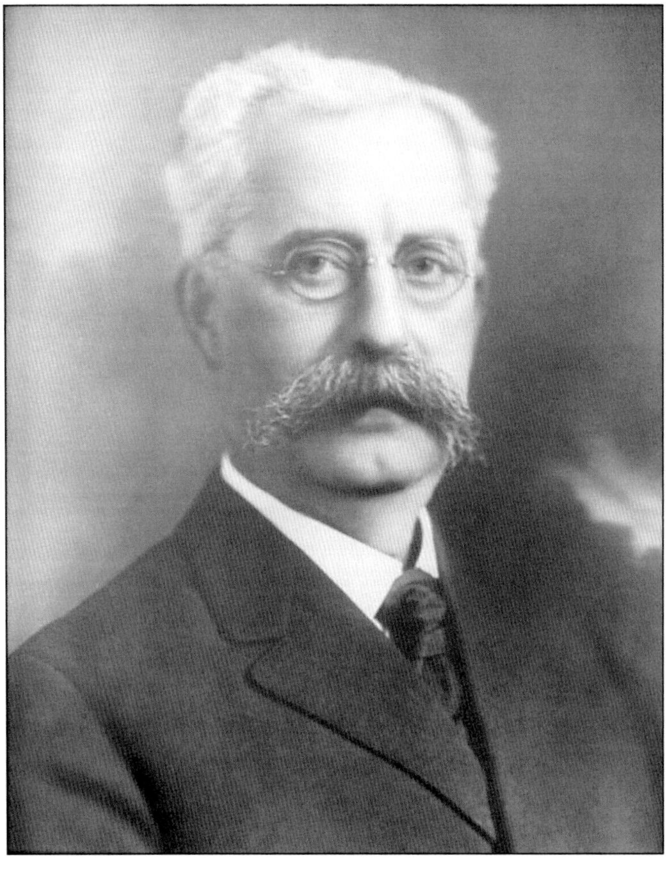

Alex Brown opened this general merchandise store pictured in 1881 on the levee road. After the building was destroyed in the big fire of 1915, Brown erected a new building down the street from the former site. Today, a bistro is on this property. (SRDHS.)

Alex Brown moved to Walnut Grove in 1879 with his widowed mother, Agnes, and his five siblings. Prior to his arrival, he had been employed as an apprentice in a grocery store in Lawrence, Massachusetts, and had found work doing odd jobs in San Francisco. (SRDHS.)

John S. Brown, eldest son of Alex Brown, managed the express office in his father's general store, which was affiliated with the Sutter Bank of San Francisco. Initially, John provided primitive banking services, but as the town grew, he saw the need for a bank and established the Bank of Alex Brown in 1913. John served as president of the bank until his death in 1952. (SRDHS.)

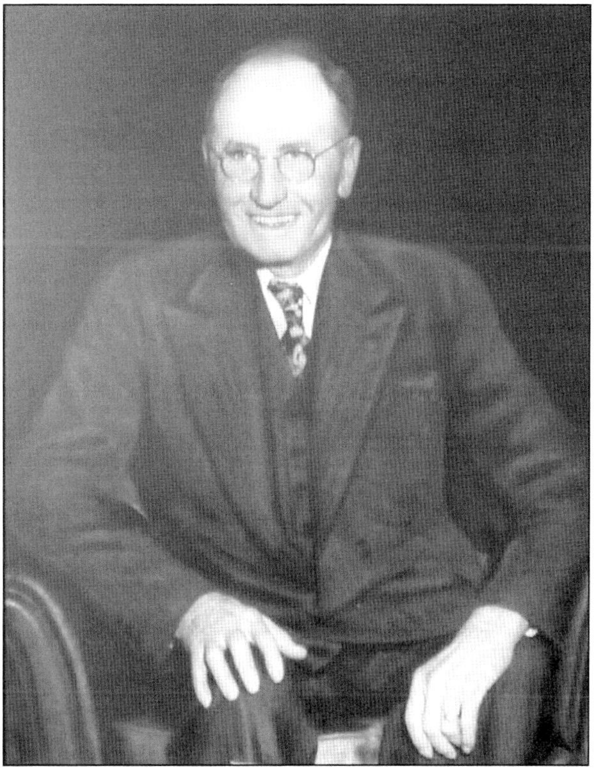

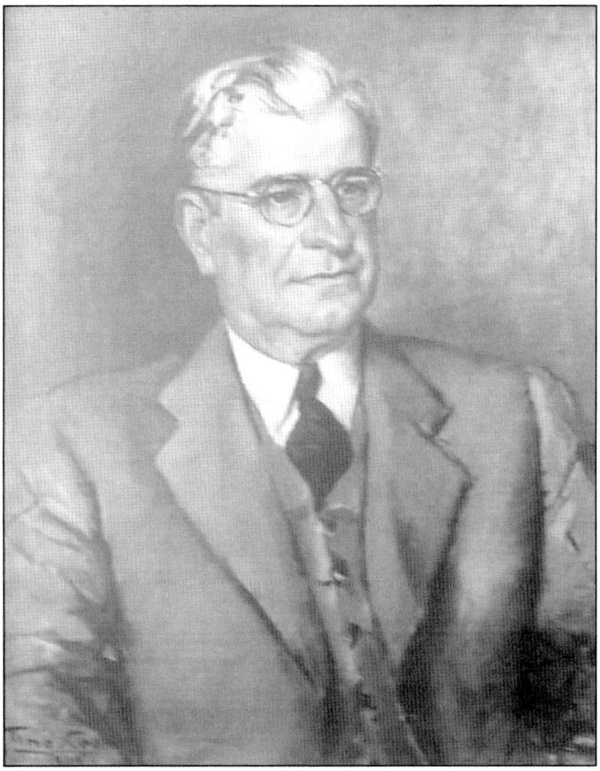

Arthur Alexander Brown was the second child of Alex and Kate Brown. He married Amy Dye and they had two children, Kathryn and Myron. Amy was the daughter of Sperry Dye and Elizabeth Sharp, who were both from early local pioneer families. When his brother John passed away, Arthur assumed the position of president of the Bank of Alex Brown until his own death in 1959. (SRDHS.)

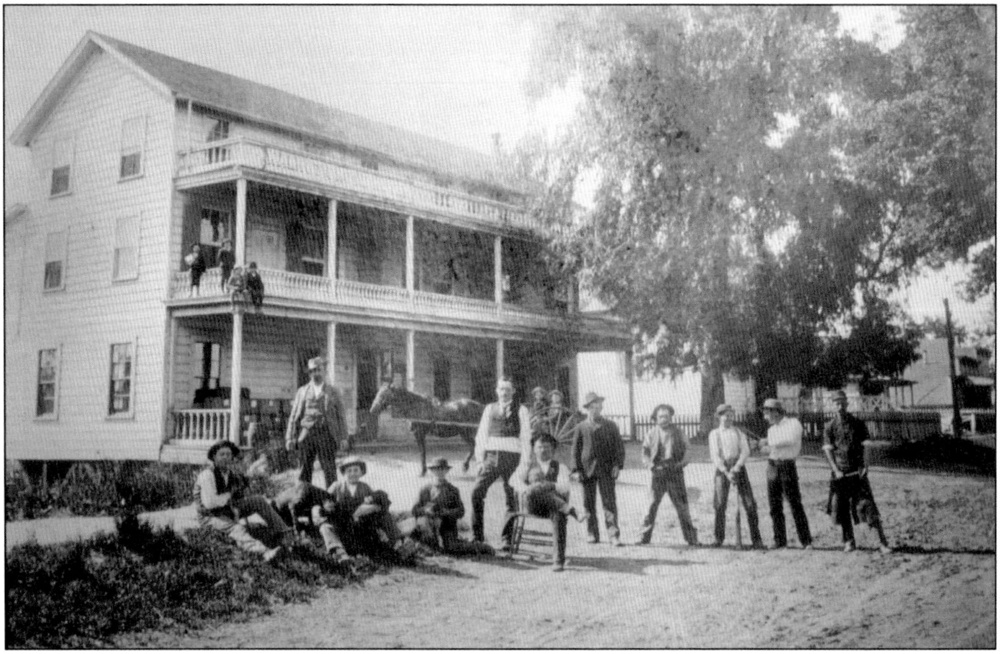

The original two-story, double-balcony Walnut Grove Hotel, constructed by the Sharp family in the 1890s and seen here in 1902, was a very common style reminiscent of other hotels in the delta. The hotel was moved from the levee road to Dixie Lane and was eventually torn down. Its original site on the levee road is now occupied by a liquor store. (SRDHS.)

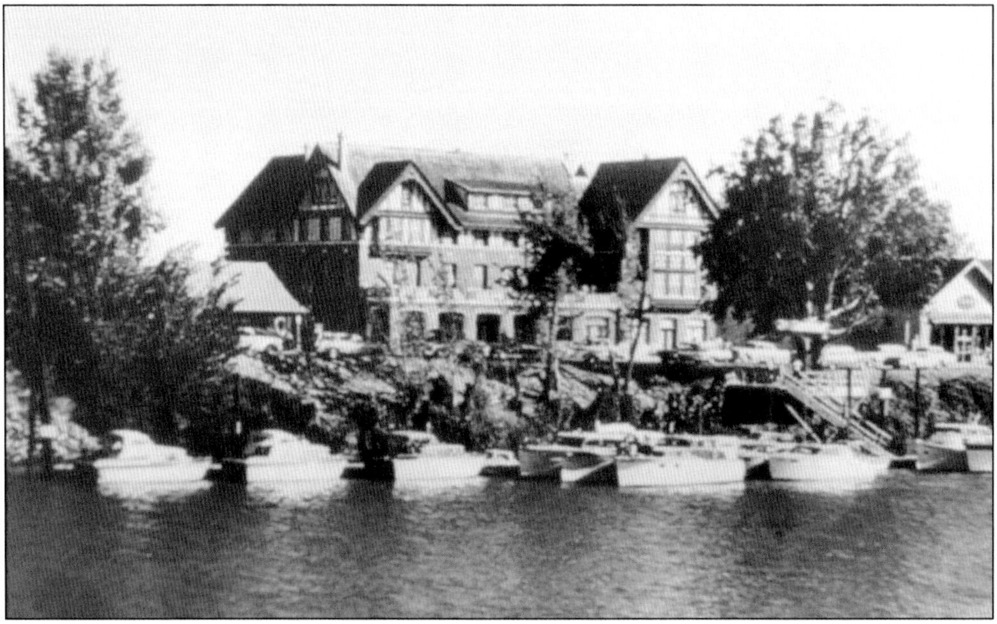

A new Walnut Grove Hotel was built on the same site as the earlier one. Its Tudor Revival design gave it the appearance of belonging in Europe rather than in the Sacramento River delta. The three-story hotel, complete with a full basement, was built in 1918 by Alex Brown at a construction and furnishing cost of $120,000. In 1961, father and son Toad and Tad Crofoot, from Texas, purchased the lodging, renaming it the Boon-Dox Hotel. (SRDHS.)

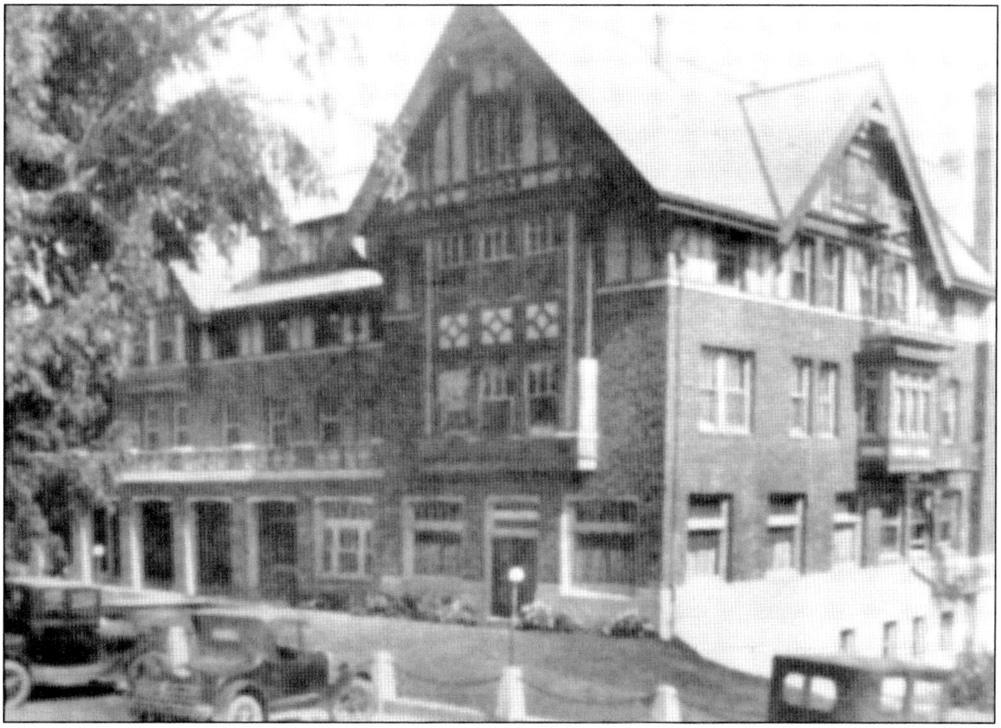

The Boon-Dox Hotel was just one of many fine hotels in the Sacramento River delta. Both the Boon-Dox and the hotel in Hood had more European-style architecture, which greatly differed from the hotels of the same era in Rio Vista, Isleton, and Ryde. (SRDHS.)

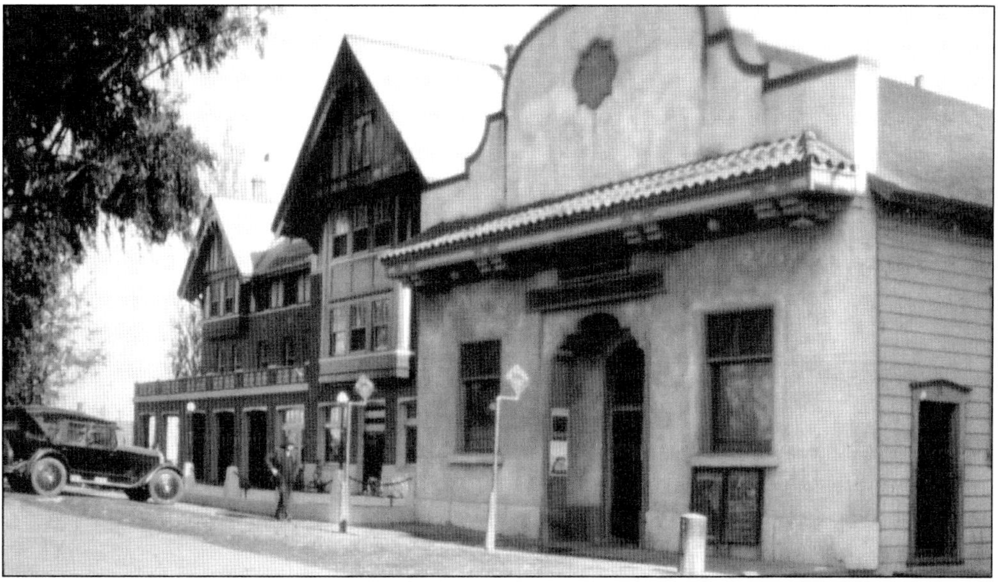

This is a seldom-photographed view of the Walnut Grove Hotel taken from downriver. The Mission Revival building on the right is the Lufkin Store and Public Hall, built in 1885. The front of the building housed a general store and later a post office, while the public hall was entered through a door on the right side of the building. The hotel was destroyed by fire, and the Lufkin building was most recently occupied by an automotive parts store. (SRDHS.)

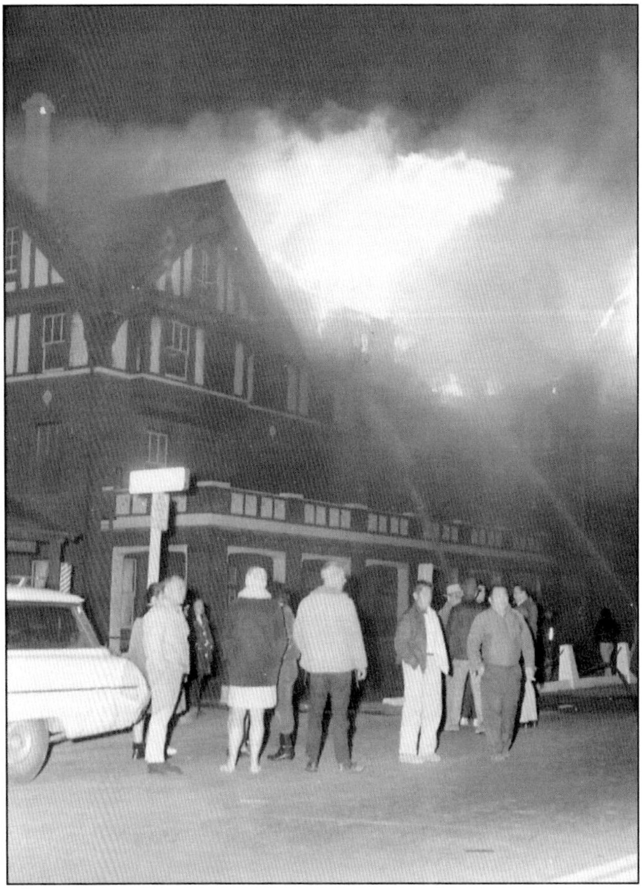

Many area fire departments responded to help extinguish the fire that eventually destroyed the Boon-Dox Hotel on October 21, 1969. The hotel had become one of the most well-known establishments in the delta. Frank Sinatra Jr. was almost certainly the most famous entertainer to have performed at the hotel. (RVM.)

Tracks were completed to Walnut Grove by the Southern Pacific Railroad in March 1912. The line, originally named the Sacramento Southern Railroad and originating at the Sacramento riverfront at I Street, was initially intended to extend as far as Antioch but never made it that far. Eventually, tracks were laid out to Isleton, crossing the Georgiana Slough north of Isleton. The Walnut Grove station (pictured) opened in 1912. (SRDHS.)

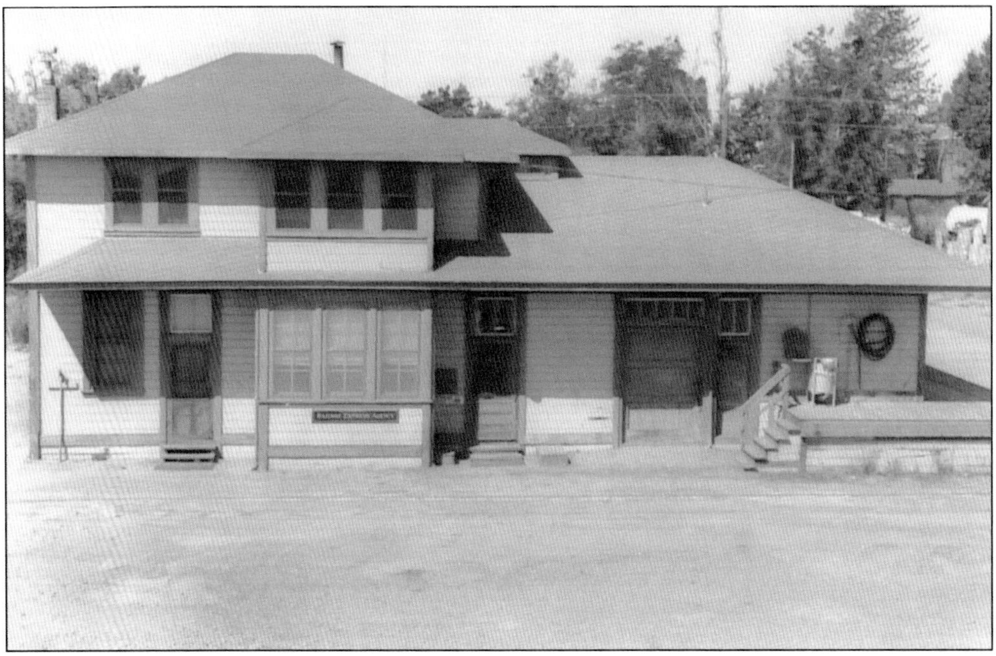

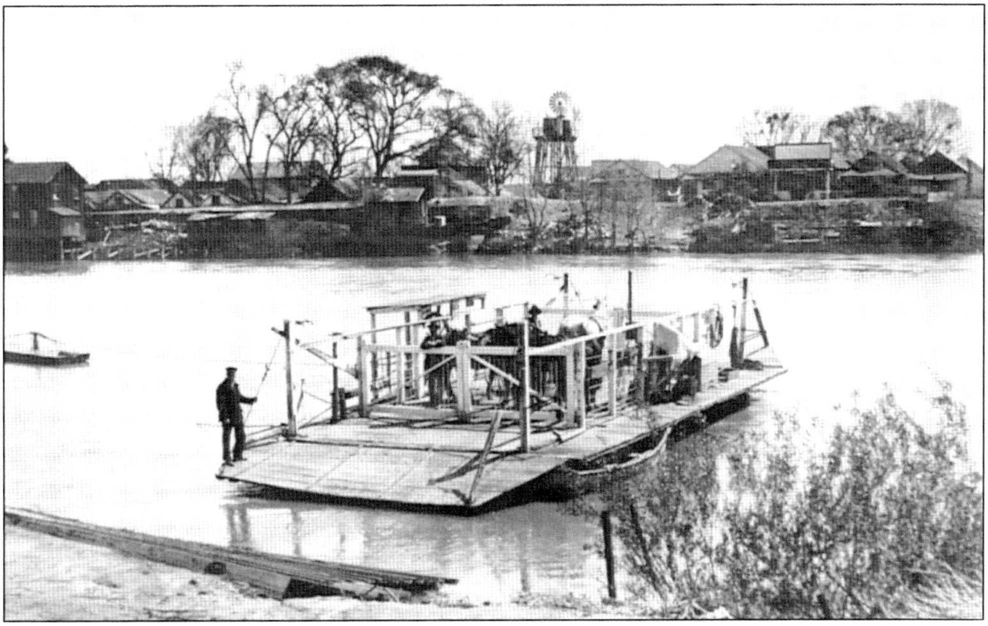

As more settlers arrived in Walnut Grove, the town expanded to the west side of the Sacramento River, thus creating the only delta town to be on both sides of the river. A ferry service operated for many years between the two parts of town, connecting Tyler Island with Grand Island. The ferry was discontinued when the original Walnut Grove Bridge opened in 1916. (SRDHS.)

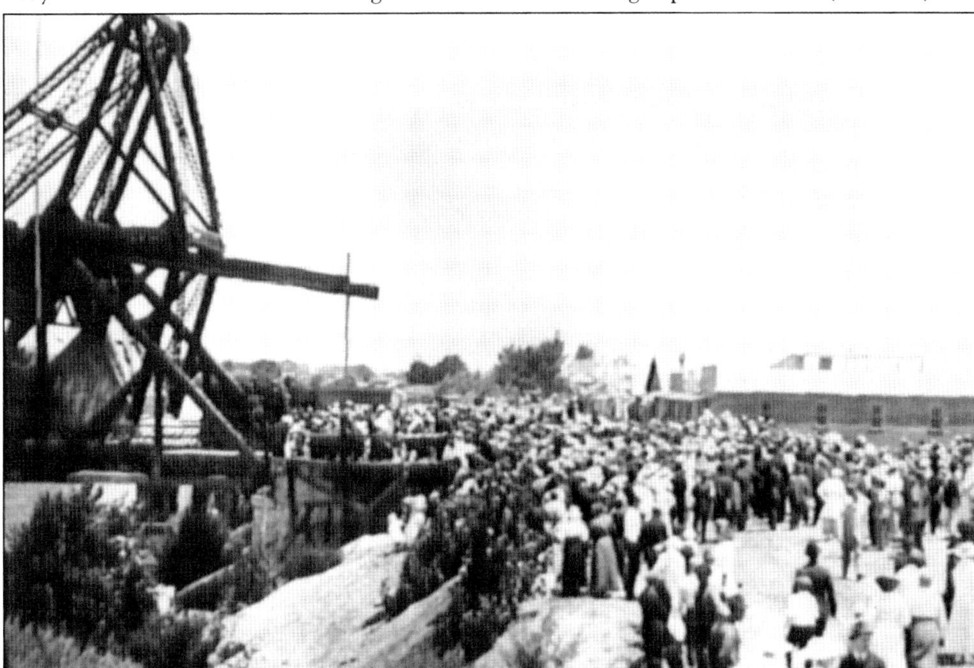

As with the grand openings of all the bridges in the Sacramento River delta, large crowds of local citizens attended the grand opening of the original Walnut Grove Bridge in 1916. As transportation and roads improved, bridges were constructed to replace the ferries that had previously transported locals around the area. (SRDHS.)

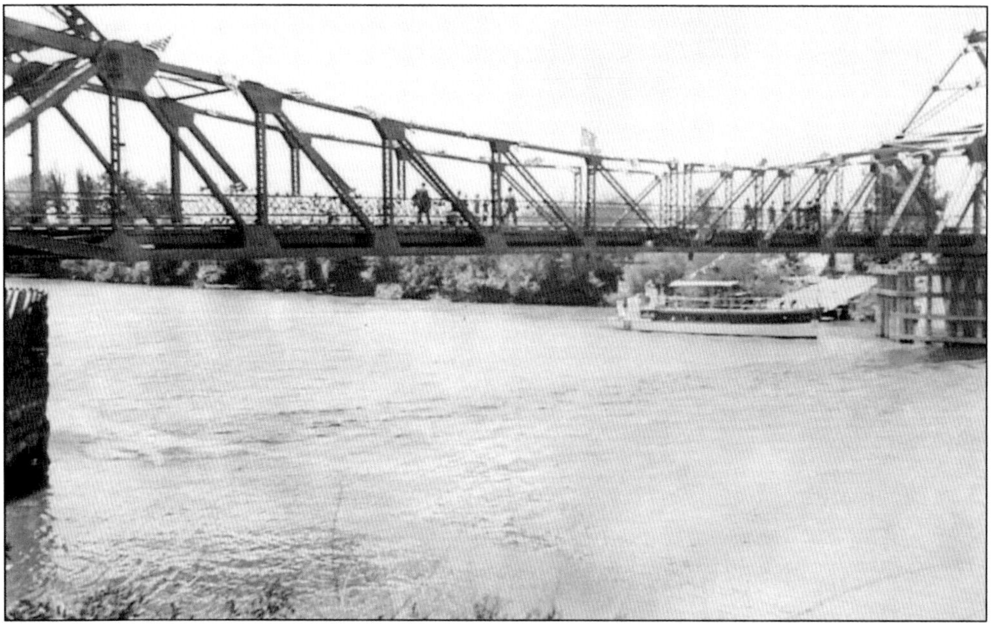

The original Walnut Grove Bridge was the first cantilevered counterweight bascule drawbridge built west of the Mississippi. It was officially opened by the 23rd governor of California, Hiram Warren Johnson, who traveled with various dignitaries to Walnut Grove on the gubernatorial yacht, seen here under the bridge, for the grand opening. (SRDHS.)

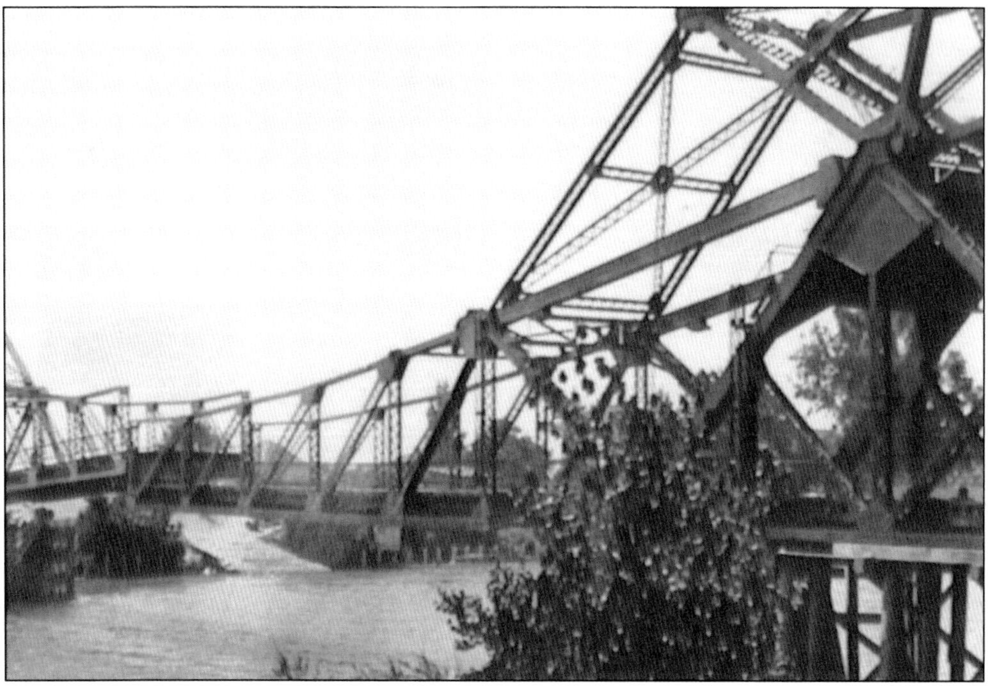

A new double-leaf bascule span bridge was constructed at Walnut Grove in 1952. The old bridge had issues with weight restrictions, so a new, almost identical span was built approximately 100 feet upriver. In 1993, the operator's building was lifted off the bridge and replaced with a new one. (SRDHS.)

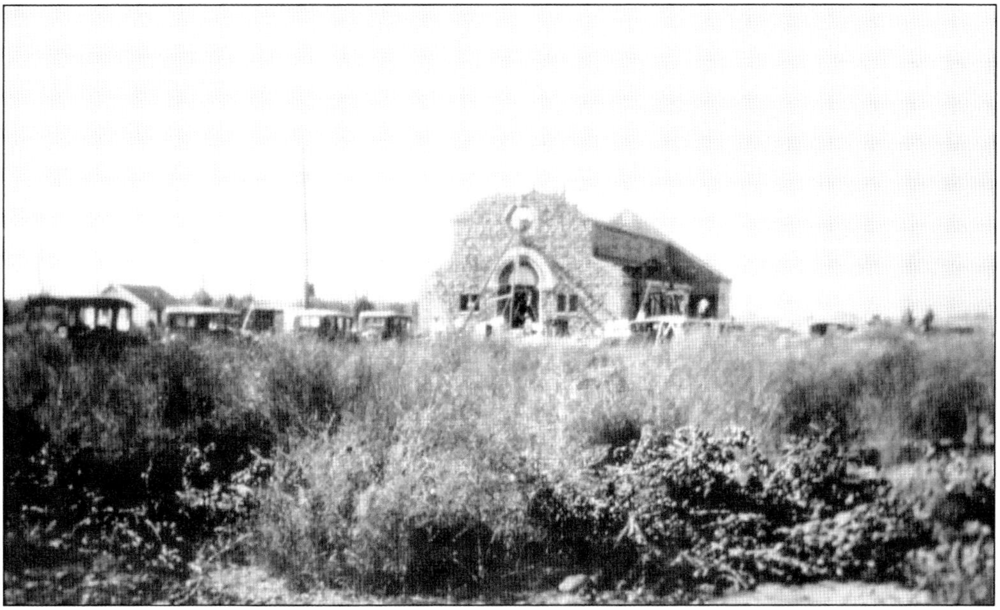

St. Anthony's Church was the first of three churches established on the west side of town. The local Catholic parish was established in 1881, replacing mission chapels in Ryde and Vorden. The church, designed by Harry J. Devine of Sacramento, is seen here during its construction in 1930–1931. Bishop Robert Armstrong of the Sacramento Diocese performed the dedication of the church, which is still in operation on Walnut Avenue. (SRDHS.)

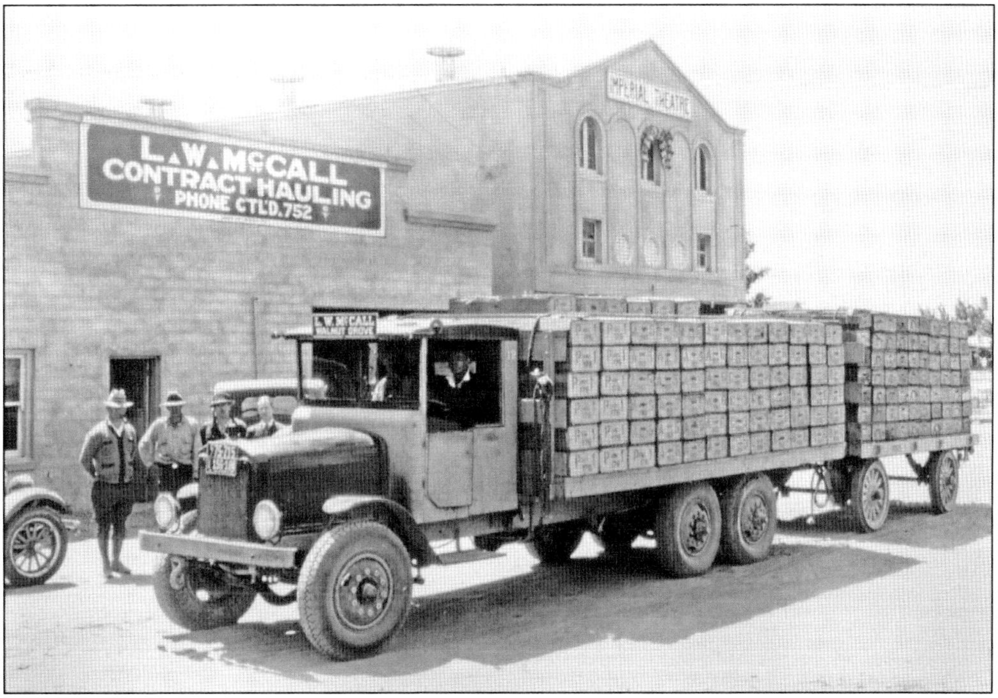

L.W. McCall Contract Hauling and the Imperial Theatre are seen here in 1935. As the canneries prospered and the bridges and roads became better, contract hauling became an essential business, necessary for the transportation of fruit and produce from the area canneries. (SRDHS.)

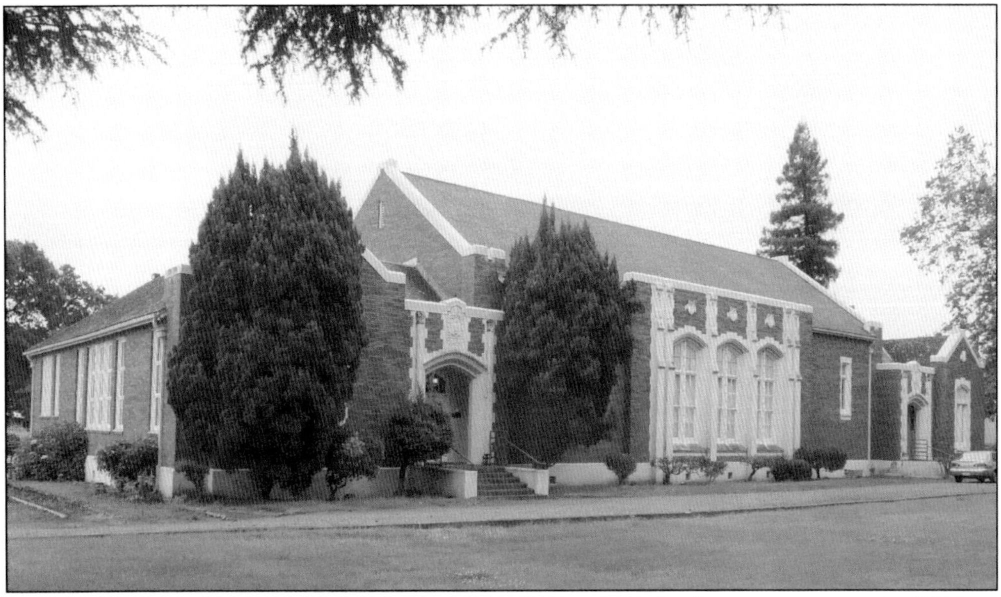

The Jean Harvie School was an elementary school named for the longtime principal of Walnut Grove School. It was built between 1924 and 1926 and held its first graduation exercises in 1926. In 1942, the school closed and the students were transferred to a newer local schoolhouse so the building could be used for wartime services. After the war, the school was reopened for early primary grades. Eventually, the school was closed, citing the Field Act of 1930. Jean Harvie is seen below in her senior picture for the Rio Vista Joint Union High School yearbook, *Netherlands*. (Above, SRDHS; below, RVM.)

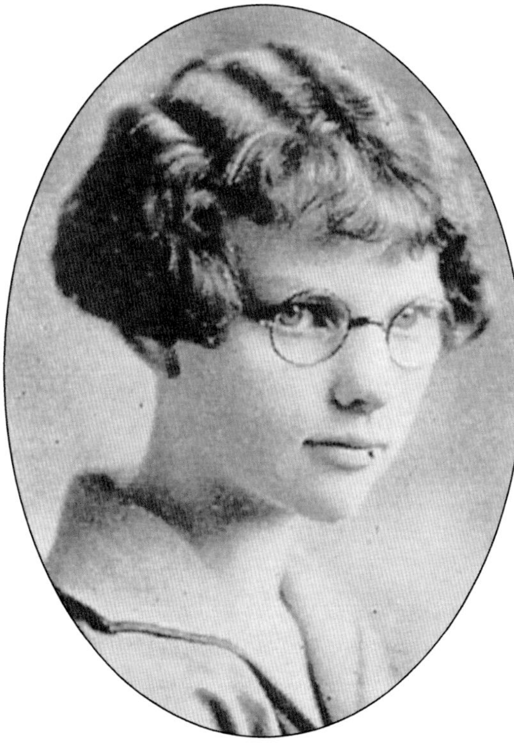

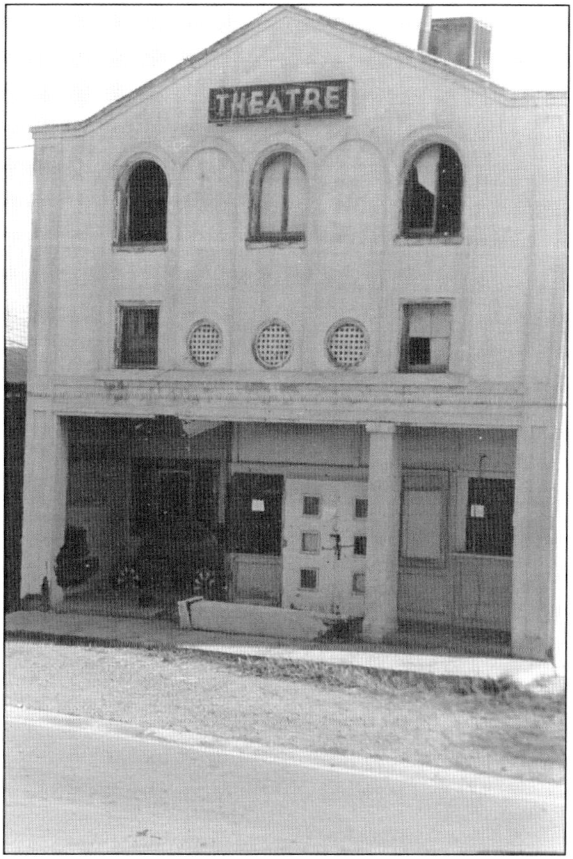

The Imperial Theatre was built in the 1920s on Market Street and continued to operate as a theater through the 1960s. It was later renamed the Grove Theatre, but many referred to it simply as the Walnut Grove Theatre. It is seen here after it fell into disrepair, which it was in for many years. (SRDHS.)

The Cross Delta Channel Gates, located between Walnut Grove and Locke, connect the Sacramento River with Snodgrass Slough and the Mokelumne River system. It is a man-made channel, and even though they are commonly referred to as "locks," they are actually gates. This image was taken during the construction of the gates in 1951. (SRDHS.)

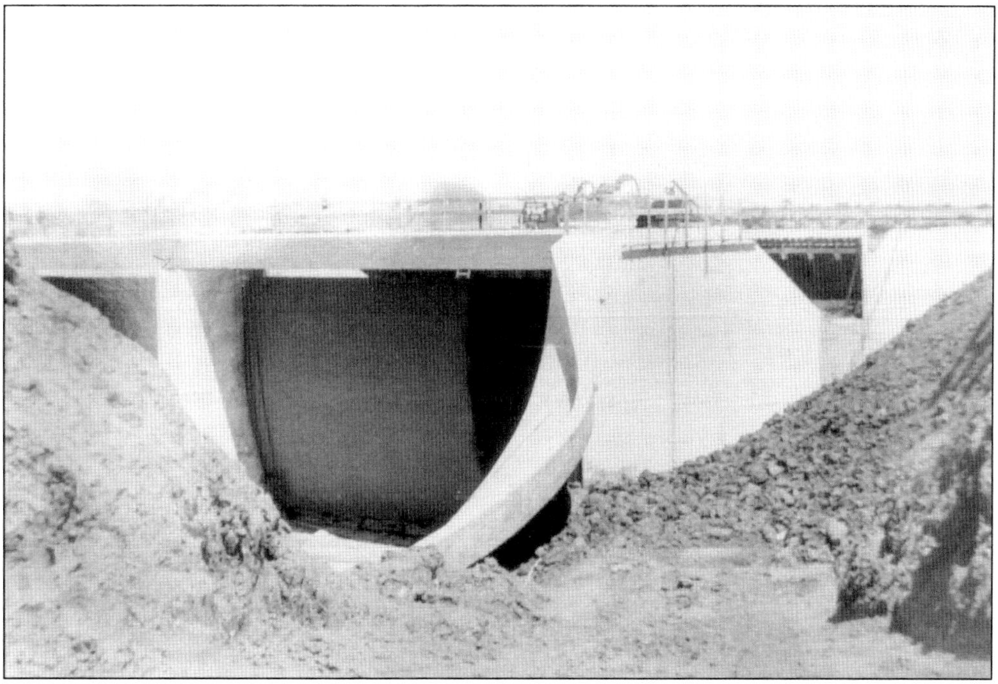

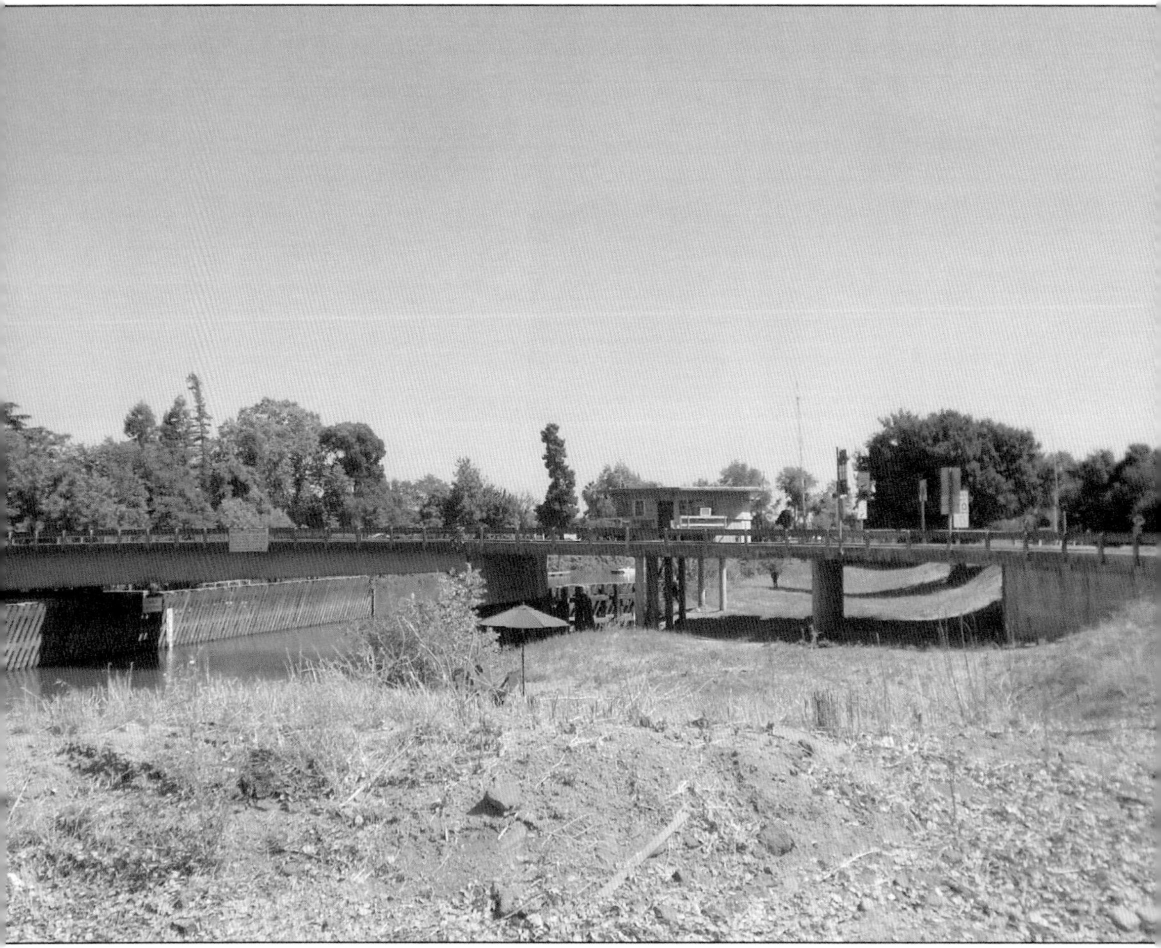

The current 1962 bridge crossing Georgiana Slough, just downstream of Walnut Grove, replaced a swing-arm bridge that was built in 1900 in a similar style to the Tyler Island Bridge. The old bridge's westerly ramp, just north of the new span, is still visible today and is often used as a parking place for fisherman and visitors. The American Institute of Steel Construction named the new bridge the "Most Beautiful Movable Steel Bridge Completed in 1962." (Author's collection.)

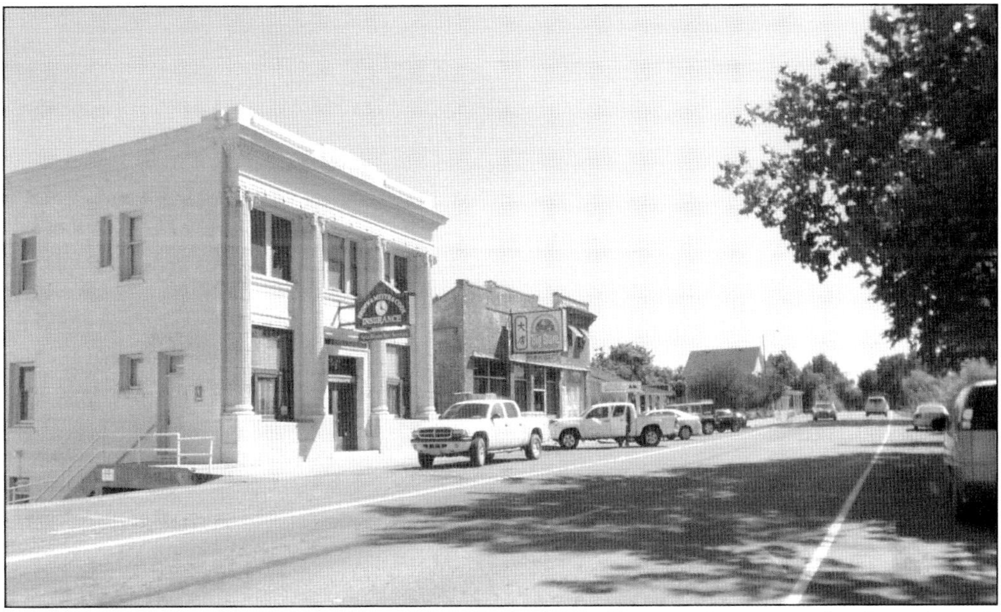

The Bank of Alex Brown was chartered in 1913 and incorporated as a state bank, with both commercial and savings departments. When it came time to name the bank, John Brown chose to name it in honor of his father. The business was conducted for the first three years out of the Alex Brown general merchandise store. In 1916, this building was erected to accommodate the growing bank. (SRDHS.)

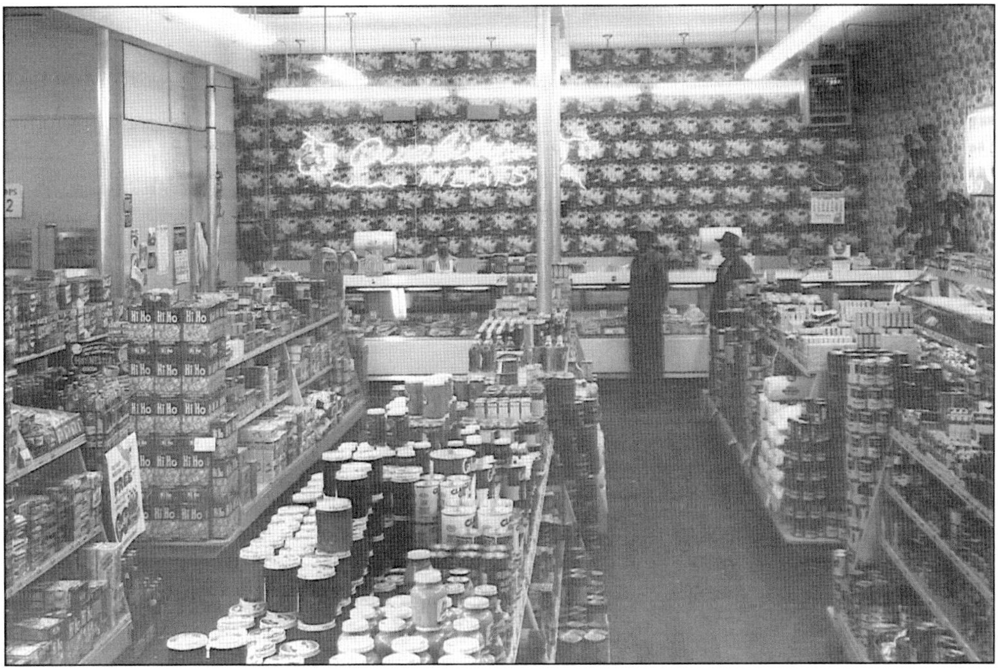

Commonly known as the Big Store, the building southwest of the former Bank of Alex Brown was first constructed by Brown to be his general store after the 1915 fire. In the late 1940s, the Lee family purchased the general store from the Browns and changed the name to the Big Store. This 1950s photograph shows an elegantly decorated and well-stocked business. (SRDHS.)

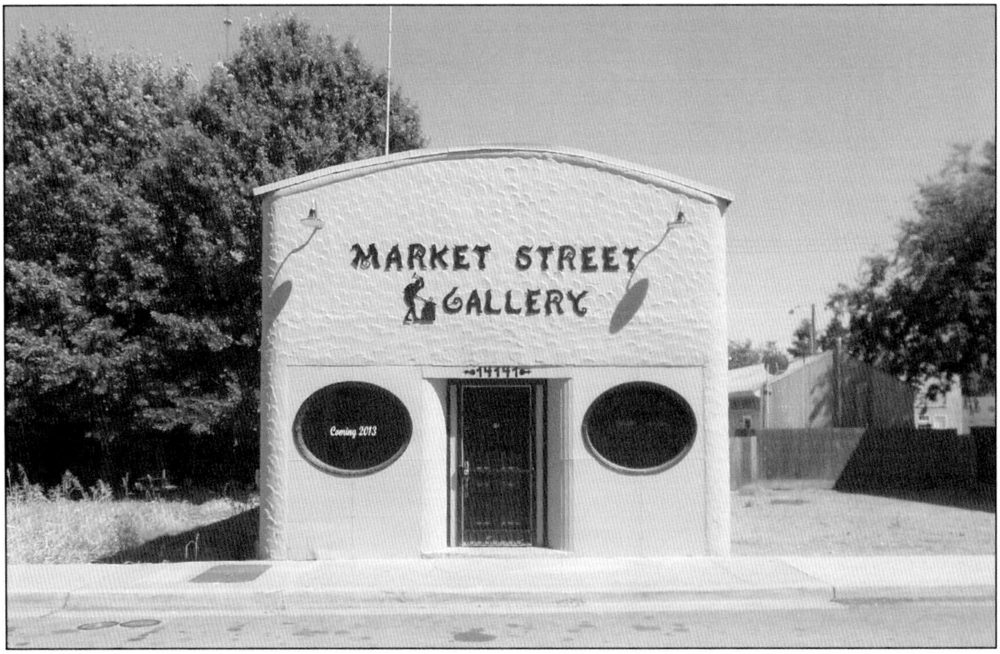

This unique single-story building is commonly referred to as the Porthole because of its windows. It was constructed by William Schauer of Noah Adams Lumber Company in 1937, during the reconstruction process after the big fire of 1937. It was later the home of Sam's Bar. (Author's collection.)

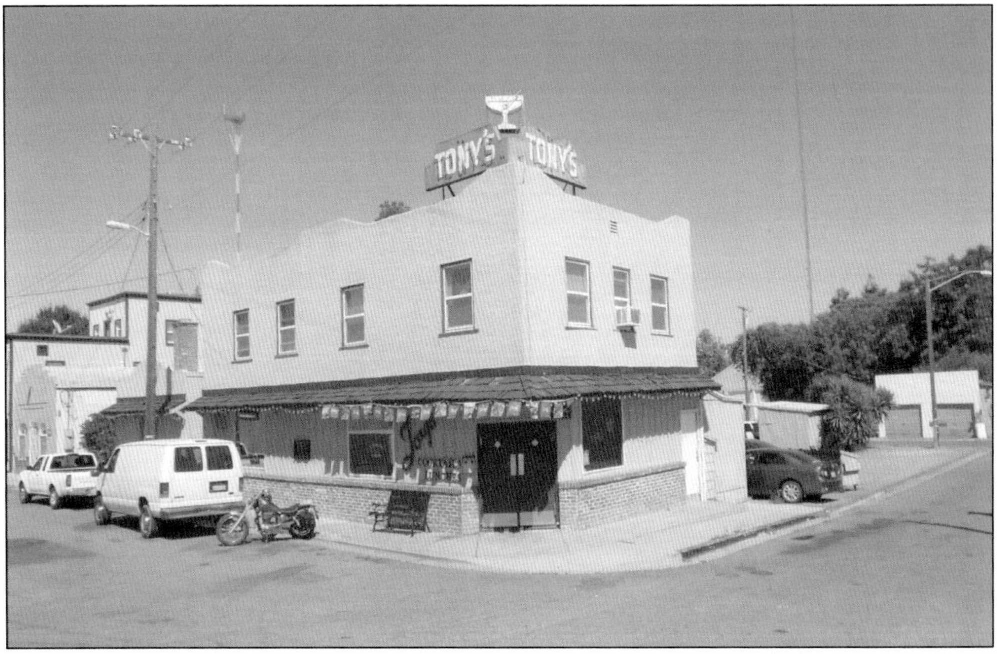

This late-1930s building was constructed during the reconstruction period after the fire of 1937 by William Schauer of the Noah Adams Lumber Company, and designed by the firm's architect, Mitch Landis. The two-story section has always been a restaurant and saloon, while the single-story section was once a barbershop. (Author's collection.)

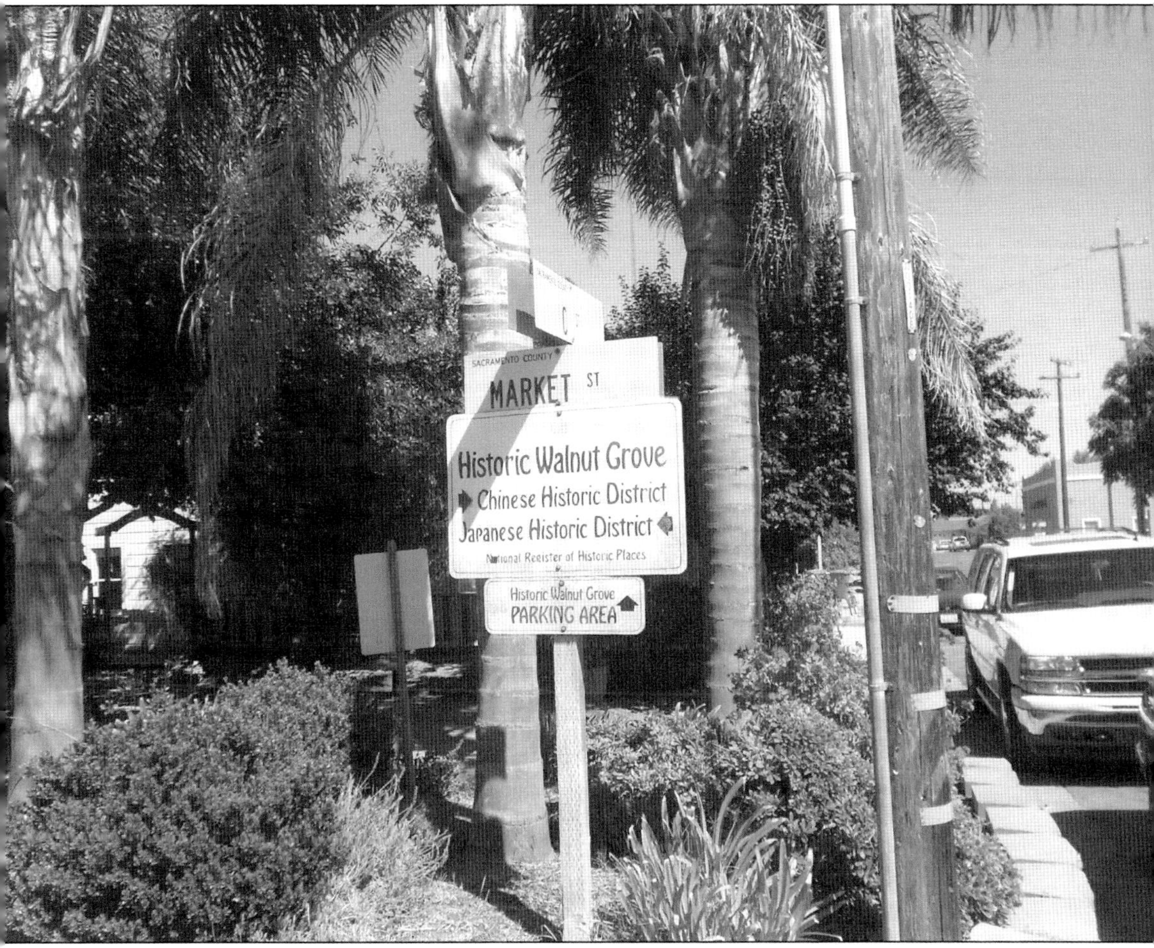

The Chinese and Japanese districts are divided by C Street, with the Chinese section to the northeast and the Japanese section to the southwest. A fire on October 7, 1915, destroyed the original Chinatown, after which many Chinese relocated to Lockeport (Locke). In 1937, a second fire destroyed much of Chinatown, but Japantown was saved and eventually expanded. The Chinese section was divided into two sections by immigrants from Sze Yap and Xiangshan (now Zhongshan), China. Unfortunately, the two groups, speaking different dialects of Chinese, could not coexist, and after the fire, only the group from Xiangshan relocated to property owned by the Locke family. (Author's collection.)

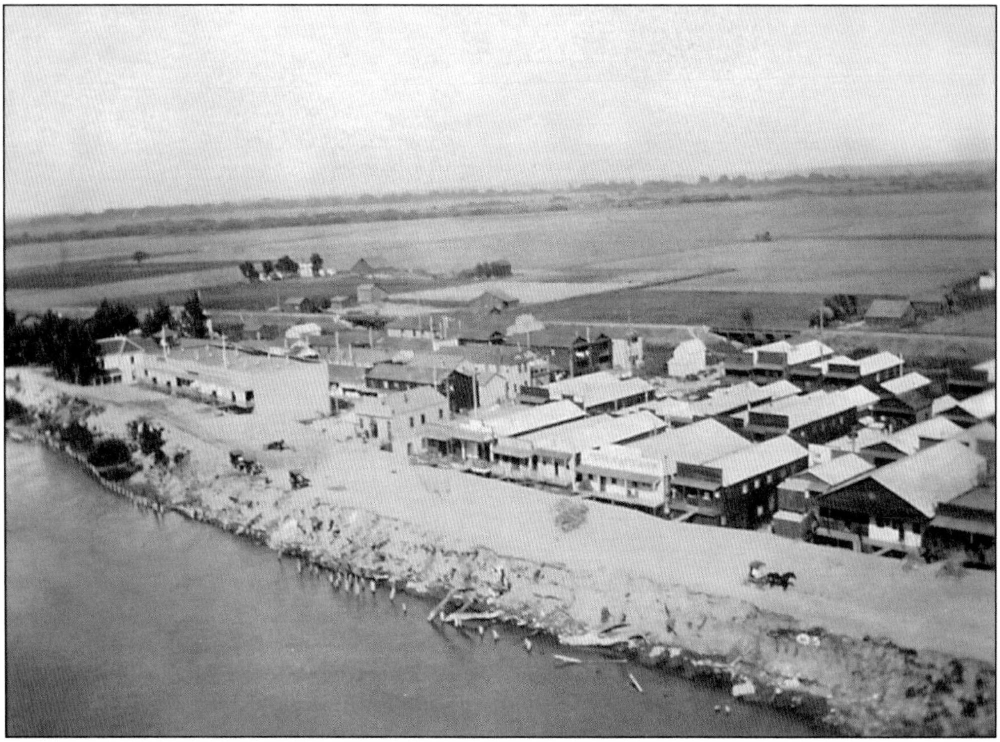

This aerial photograph of Walnut Grove's Chinese and Japanese section shows the dirt levee road in the era when horse-drawn buggies shared the roads with early automobiles. (RVM.)

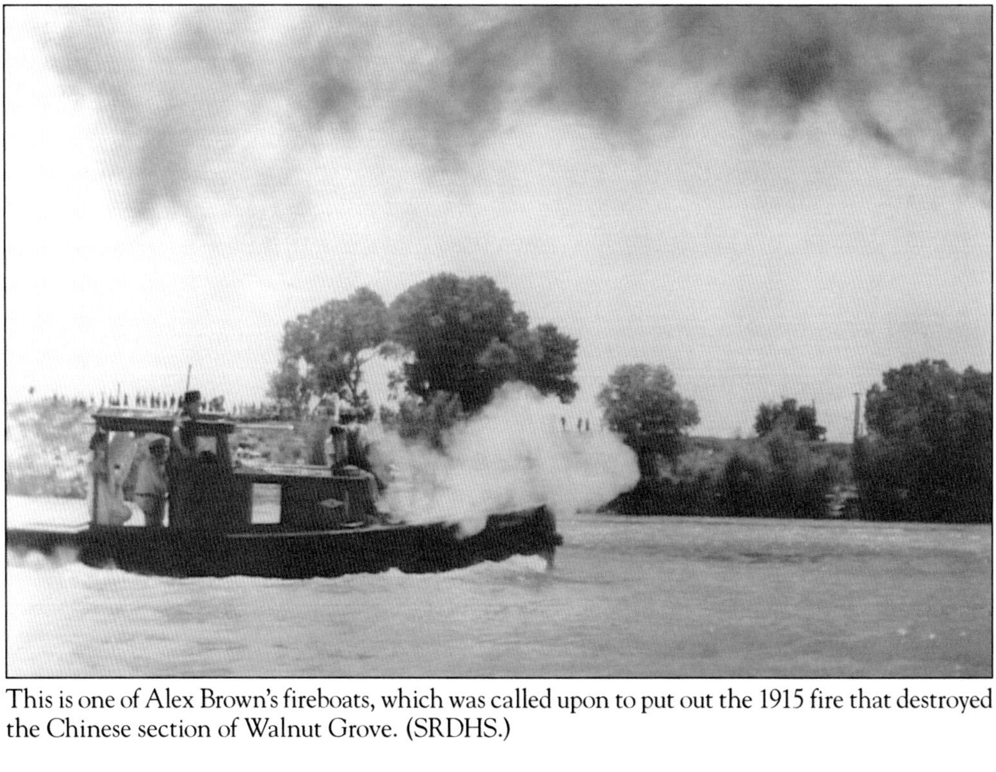

This is one of Alex Brown's fireboats, which was called upon to put out the 1915 fire that destroyed the Chinese section of Walnut Grove. (SRDHS.)

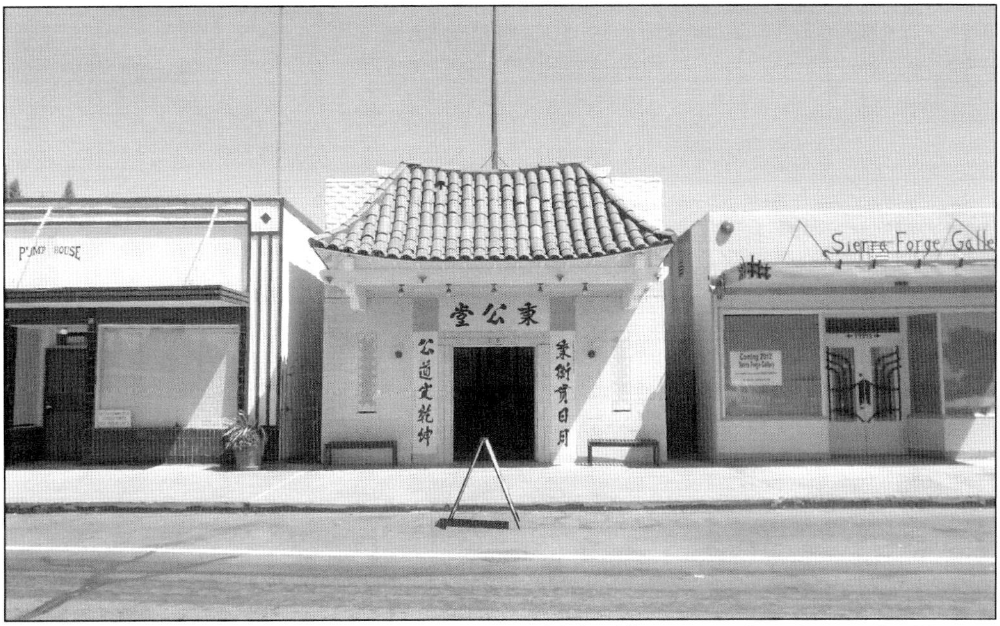

Considered by many to be one of the most recognizable buildings in Walnut Grove, the Chinese Freemasons Hall was built in 1938. Like so many structures in Walnut Grove, it was built during the reconstruction period following the 1937 fire. Prior to the fire, a joss house was located on the site. (Author's collection.)

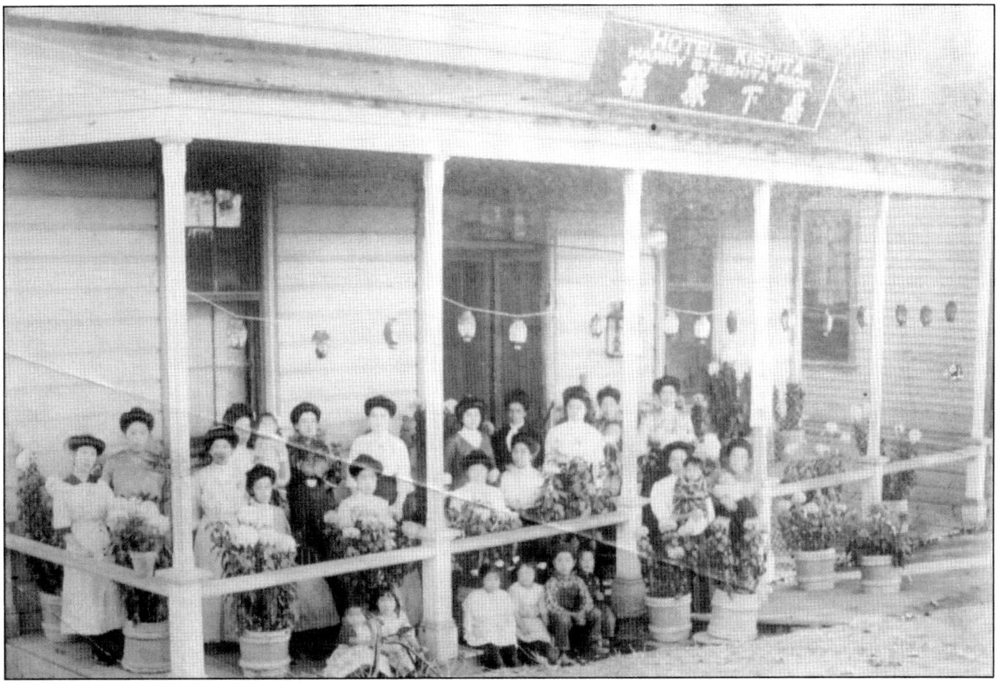

The Hotel Kishka was one of the earliest Japanese hotels in Walnut Grove. The Japanese first arrived in the delta in the 1880s and initially settled within existing Chinatowns. Eventually, they created their own districts in both Walnut Grove and Isleton, with very few Japanese settling in Rio Vista, Ryde, Courtland, Hood, Clarksburg, or Freemont. (SRDHS.)

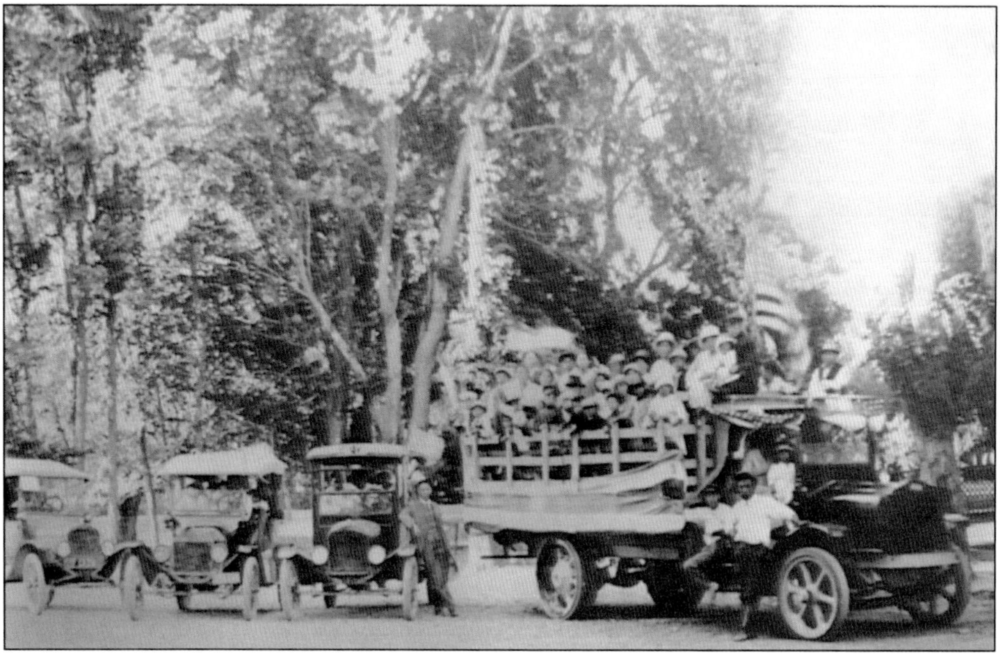

Before World War II, the Japanese Association of Walnut Grove hosted cultural events throughout the year. Quite often, the association would bring Kabuki dancers and other traditional cultural performances to events, which were often held at the motion picture theater in Walnut Grove. This photograph was taken at a Fourth of July celebration in the late 1920s. (SRDHS.)

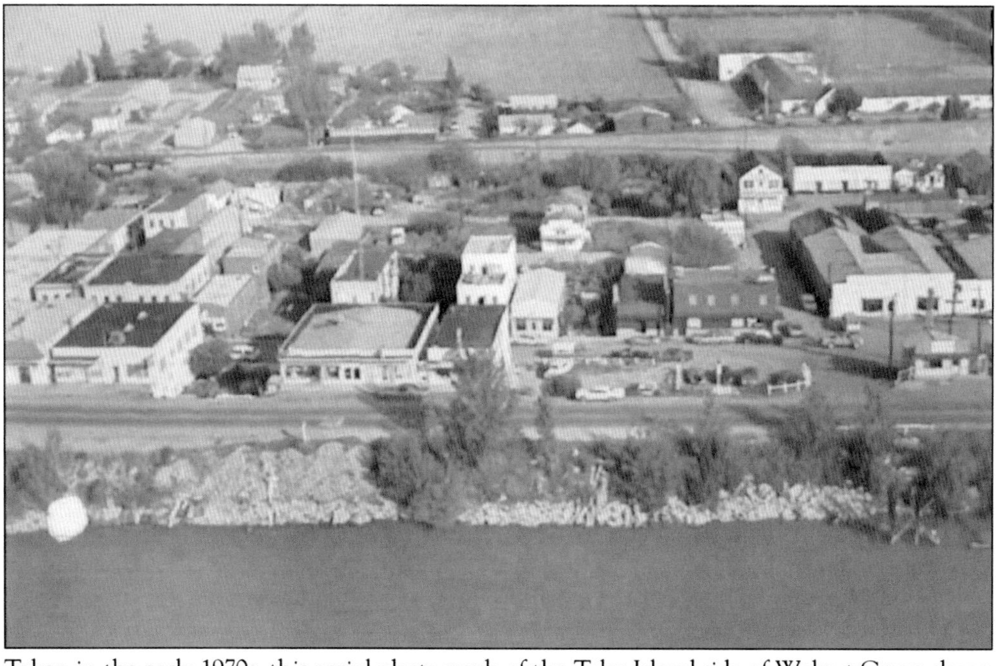

Taken in the early 1970s, this aerial photograph of the Tyler Island side of Walnut Grove shows that very few changes have occurred there in the last four decades. This image clearly shows the location of the Southern Pacific Railroad line, Walnut Grove School, and the many buildings unique to Walnut Grove. (SRDHS.)

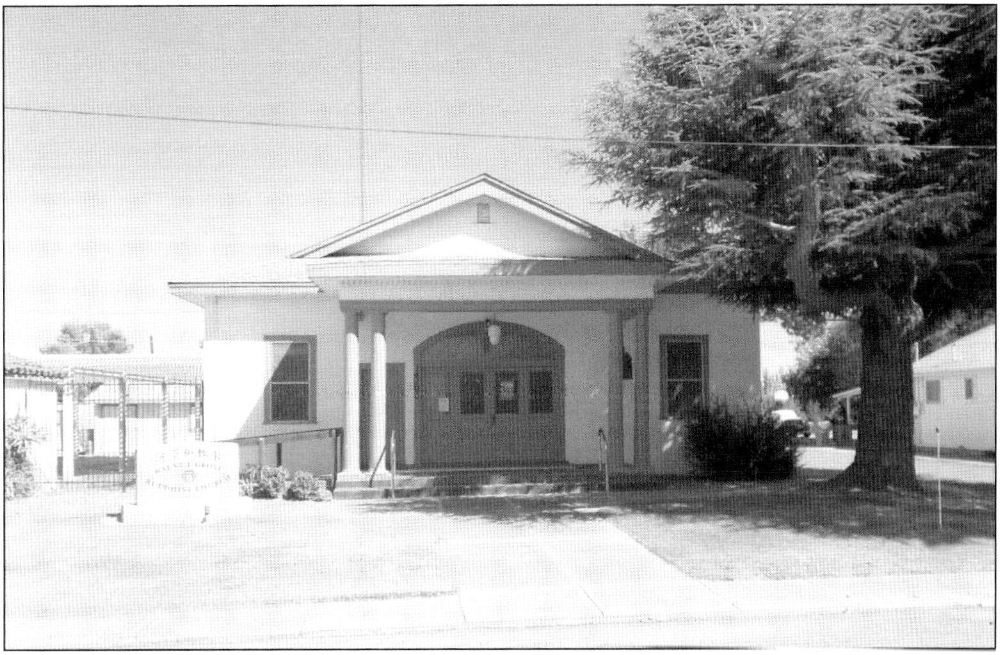

The Buddhist church in Walnut Grove was established in 1927. Only the delta communities of Walnut Grove and Isleton had Buddhist churches. However, the one in Isleton closed during World War II. Every year since 1954, the Walnut Grove Buddhist Church has sponsored a bazaar that is anticipated and enjoyed by many. (Author's collection.)

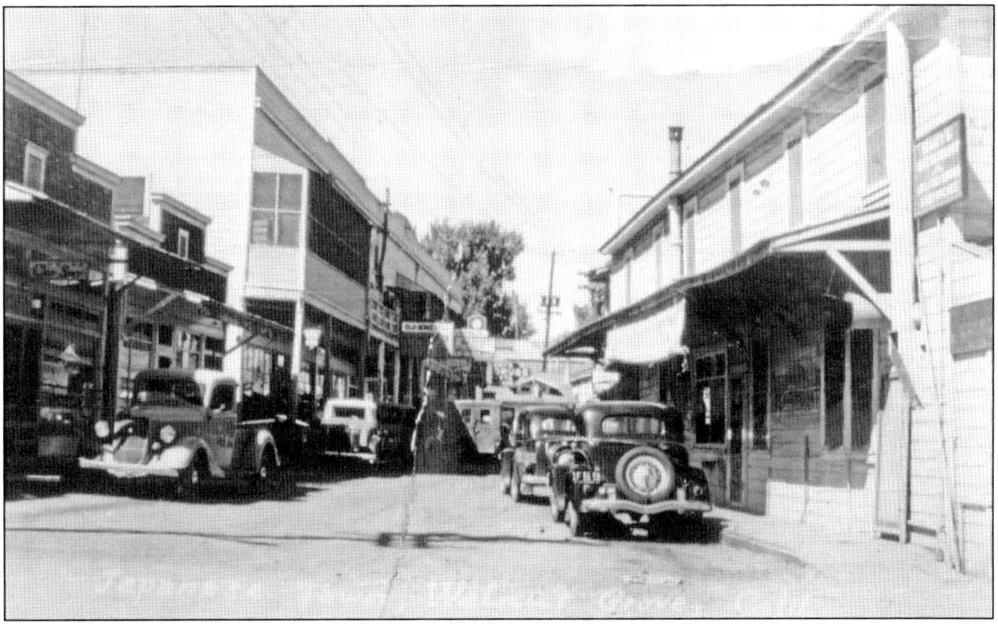

This photograph looks northeast towards the Japanese section of Walnut Grove in 1930. After the devastating fire of 1915, the Japanese section expanded. It was located between C Street and the rail fill, but eventually expanded to the other side of the fill. The 1937 fire destroyed everything south of C Street to Bridge Street, the Chinese section. The Japanese section escaped unharmed. (SRDHS.)

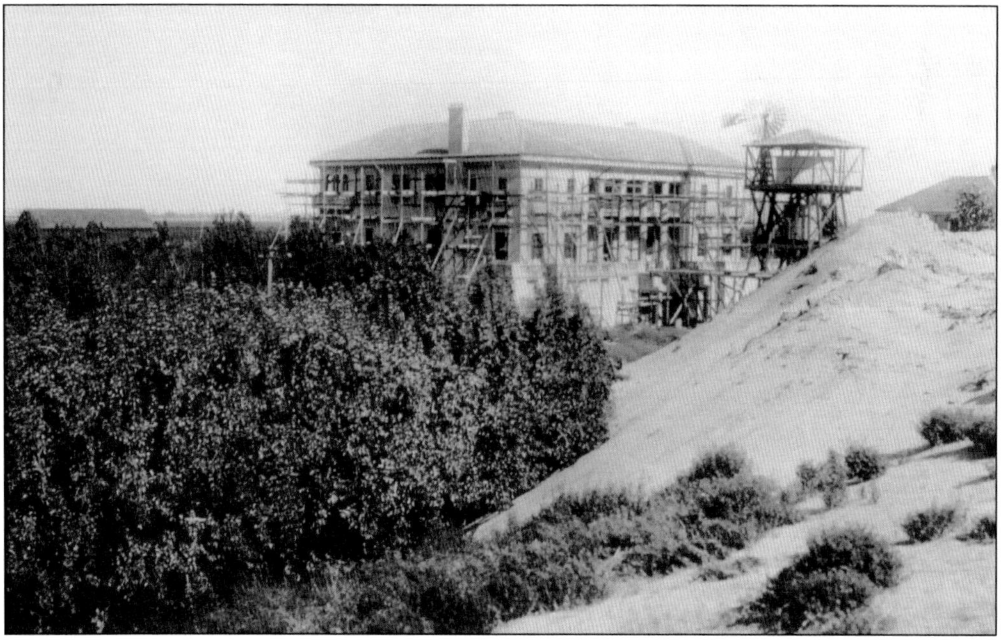

The Louis William Myers home, more commonly known as the Grand Island Mansion, was designed by San Francisco architect John W. Dolliver in 1914. Construction began in 1918 and was completed in 1923. Unfortunately, Myers passed away in 1922 and did not see the completion of his home. The final cost for the four-story, 24,000-square-foot, 58-room Mediterranean-style mansion was a reported $340,000. (SRDHS.)

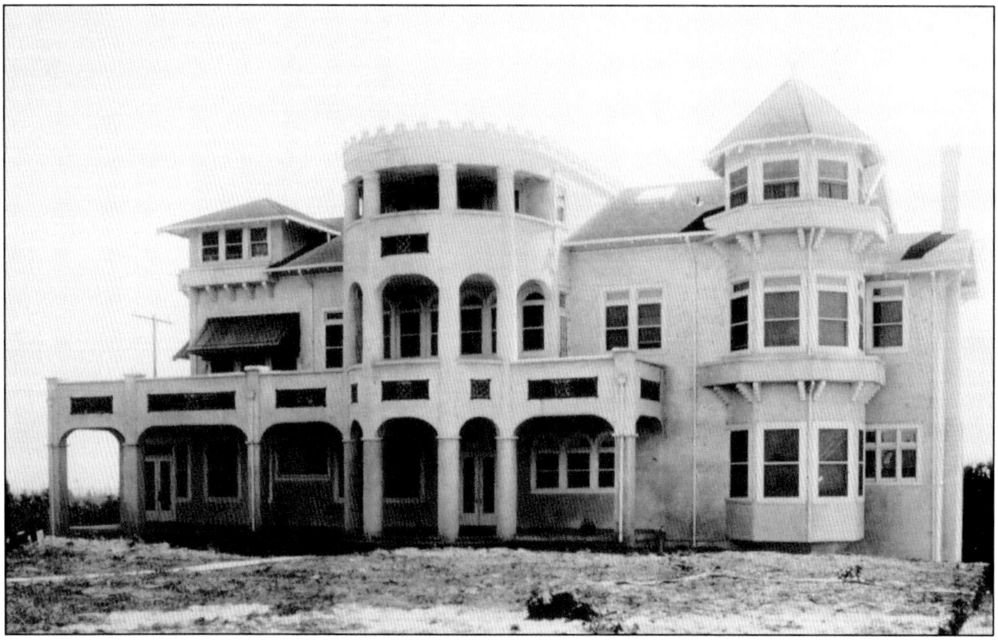

The William J. Smith home, known to many as "the Castle," was built when Smith hired Rio Vista builder Henry Mortensen to remodel an 1880 house on Grand Island. The remodeling began in 1917 and was completed in 1919, creating a four-story, 21-room house. Due to high taxes and the Great Depression, the home was torn down in the mid-1930s. (SRDHS.)

Five

Locke

The Locke family—brothers George, Clay, and Lloyd H.—owned property on the Sacramento River northeast of Walnut Grove. Making their livings through farming, the families constructed a wharf, a packing shed, and a warehouse where they could process their produce and ship it to San Francisco by steamship. In 1913, Tin Sin Chan and Wing Chow Owyang approached the Lockes and struck a deal to lease some property from them adjacent to the warehouse and packing shed. The two men then erected buildings to serve the needs of the Chinese who where working as laborers in the area.

The two Chinese men named the steamship stop Lockeport. After a fire destroyed Walnut Grove's Chinatown and Japantown, in October 1915, a group of Chinese merchants from Walnut Grove, led by Bing Lee and including Chan Hing Sai, Tom Wai, Chan Dai Kee, Ng So Hat, Chan Wai Lum, Chow Hou Bun, and Suen Dat Suin, met with the Locke brothers regarding the possibilities of establishing a Chinese community on their land. A deal was struck to clear nine acres of orchard for the town, but since California's 1913 Alien Land Act prevented Asian immigrants from owning land, the Locke family leased the property to the Chinese.

After receiving approval from the Locke brothers, the delegation of Chinese immigrants obtained a loan from their tong, and the construction of several buildings was commissioned across from the warehouses on the levee road. The name was shortened to Locke, and the community began to grow. On May 6, 1971, Locke was added to the National Register of Historic Places by the Sacramento County Historical Society because of its unique status as the only town in the United States built exclusively by Chinese for Chinese. In 1990, it was further designated a National Historic Landmark District. In 1977, the town was purchased from the Locke heirs by a Hong Kong–based developer and then resold in 2002 to the Sacramento Housing and Redevelopment Agency. In 2004, the agency allowed the sale of the property to its longtime residents.

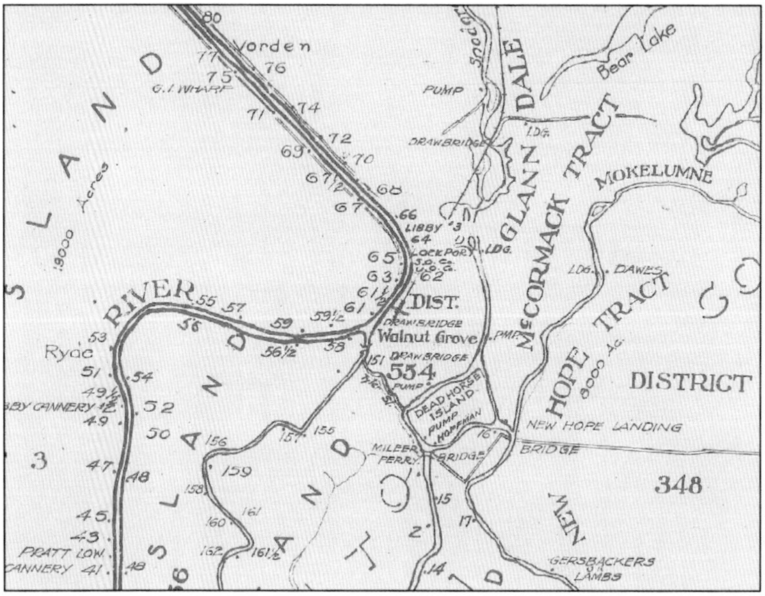

Lockeport was established in 1913 and was shortened to Locke in 1916, after nearby Walnut Grove's Chinatown was destroyed by fire. Locke is half a mile upriver from Walnut Grove on upper Tyler Island. This section of a 1922 map is one of few that identifies it as Lockeport rather than Locke. (RVM.)

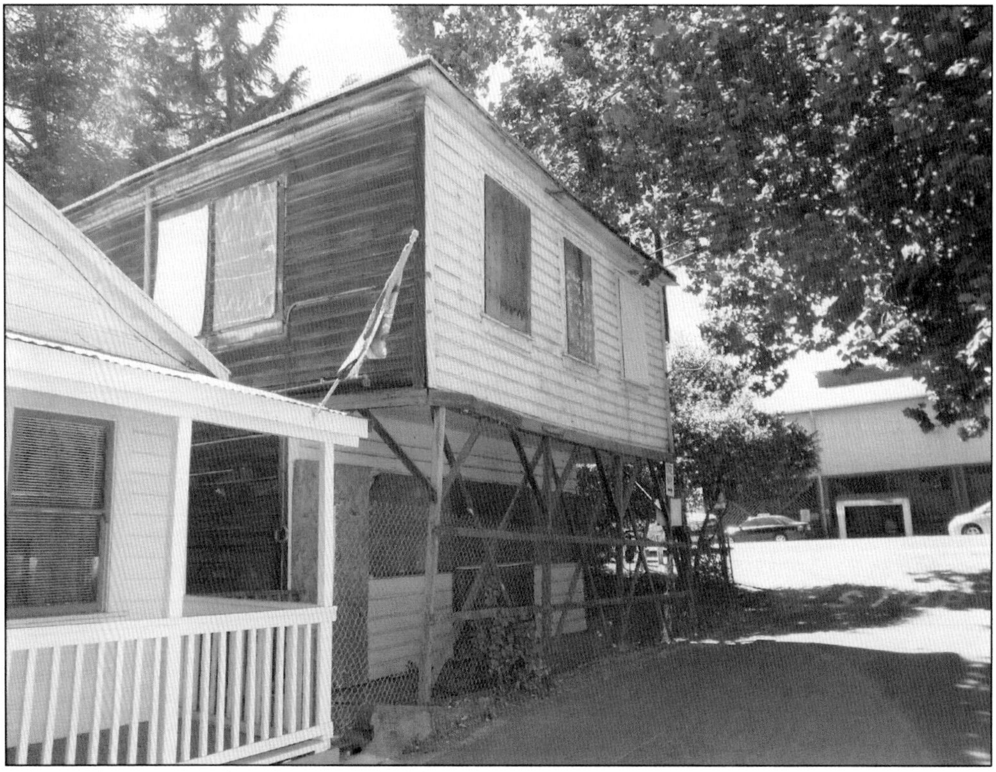

The Lockeport Hotel is the second-oldest structure in Locke. The three-story building was constructed in 1912 by the Owyang family. The bottom floor was the Owyang family residence, the middle floor was a restaurant operated by the family, and the top floor served as a hotel. (Author's collection.)

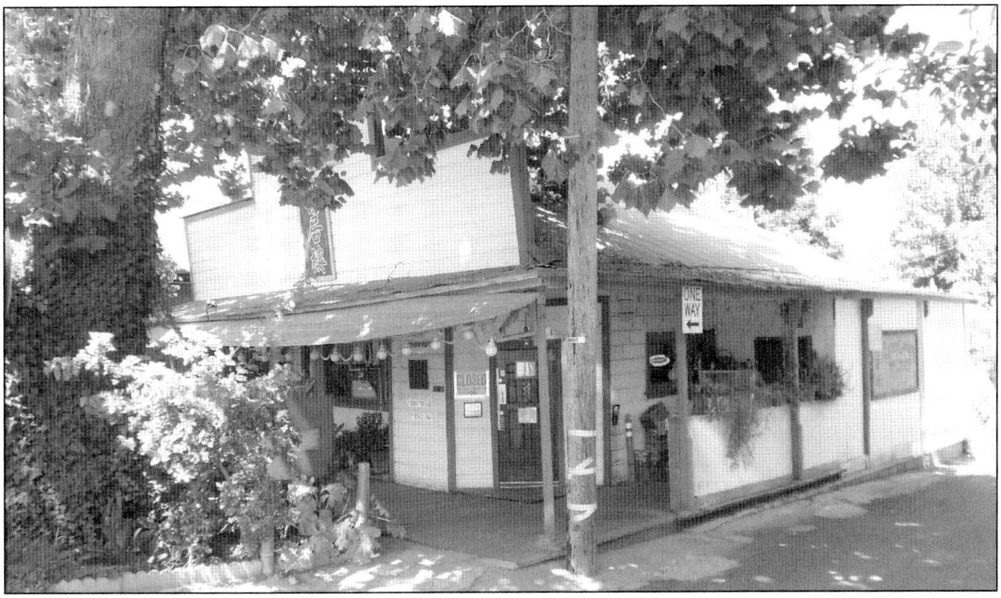

This recent photograph shows the first building in Lockeport, a 1912 saloon and gambling hall built by Tin Sin Chan (or Chan Tin-Sen). It is one of several structures predating the establishment of Locke in 1916. The building is known to most as the Locke Garden Restaurant. (Author's collection.)

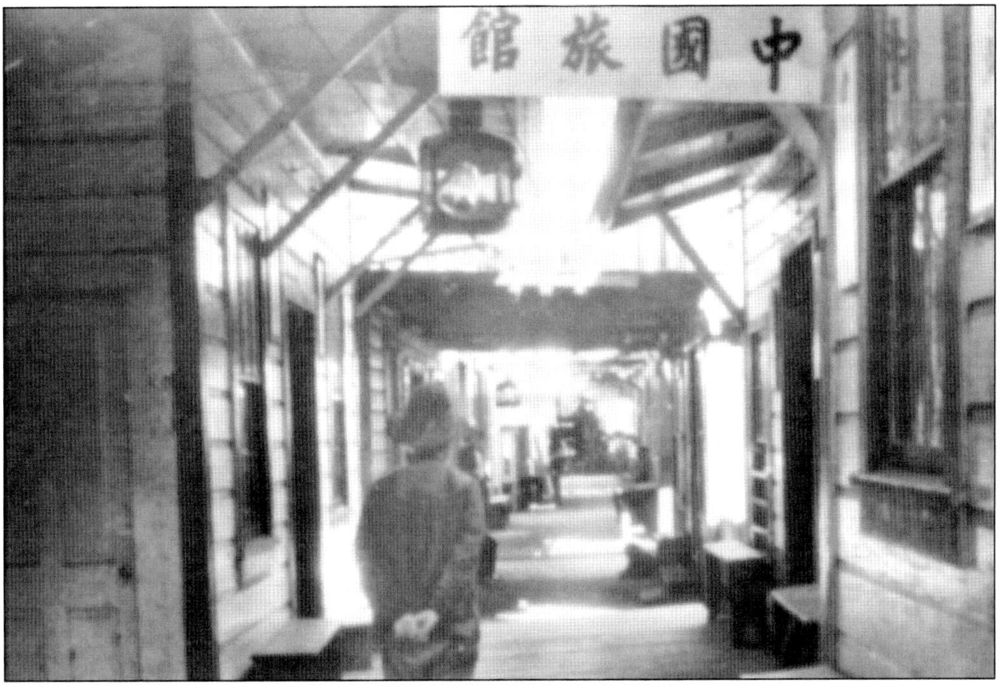

The primary Chinese social groups in the delta were the tongs. The people from Xiangshan made up the Jan Ying Association; the Kuomintang (KMT) represented the National Party of China; the Chee Kung Tong, a branch of the Triad Society of China, supporters of Dr. Sun Yat-sen; and the Bing Kung Tong. This image, taken in 1925, depicts one of the alleyways in Locke during the evening hours. (SRDHS.)

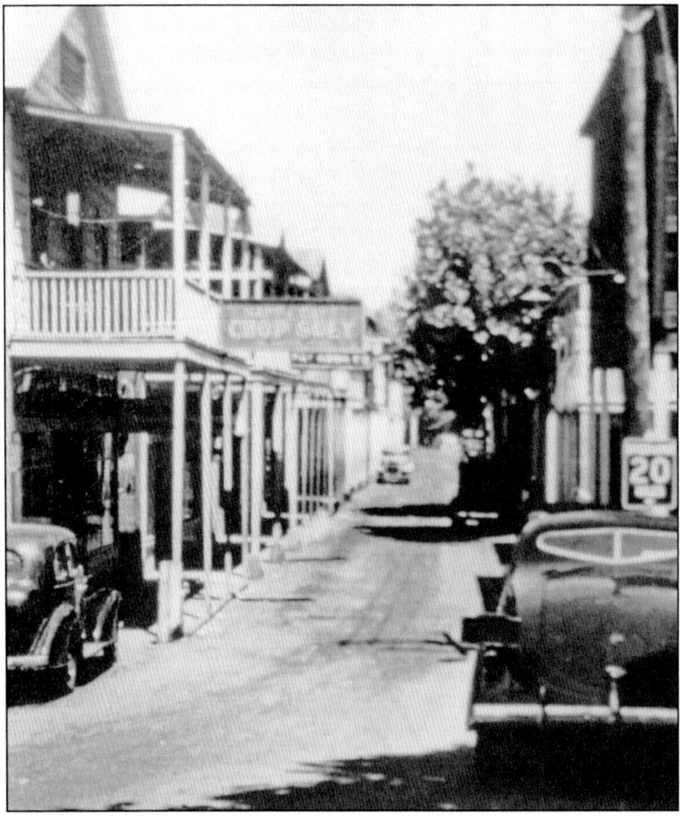

The Chinese who settled Locke were from the Pearl River delta in Guandong Province, China. Sun Yat-sen, the "father of modern China," who was also from the region, was embraced when he visited the Sacramento River delta in 1909 and 1910. During those visits, he drew large crowds in delta towns, including Courtland, where he sought refuge from his political rivals while rallying support and raising funds for a revolution in China. The photograph at left of Main Street in Locke was taken in 1939 from the intersection of Main and River Streets. The image below shows the same view in the present time. (Left, SRDHS; below, author's collection.)

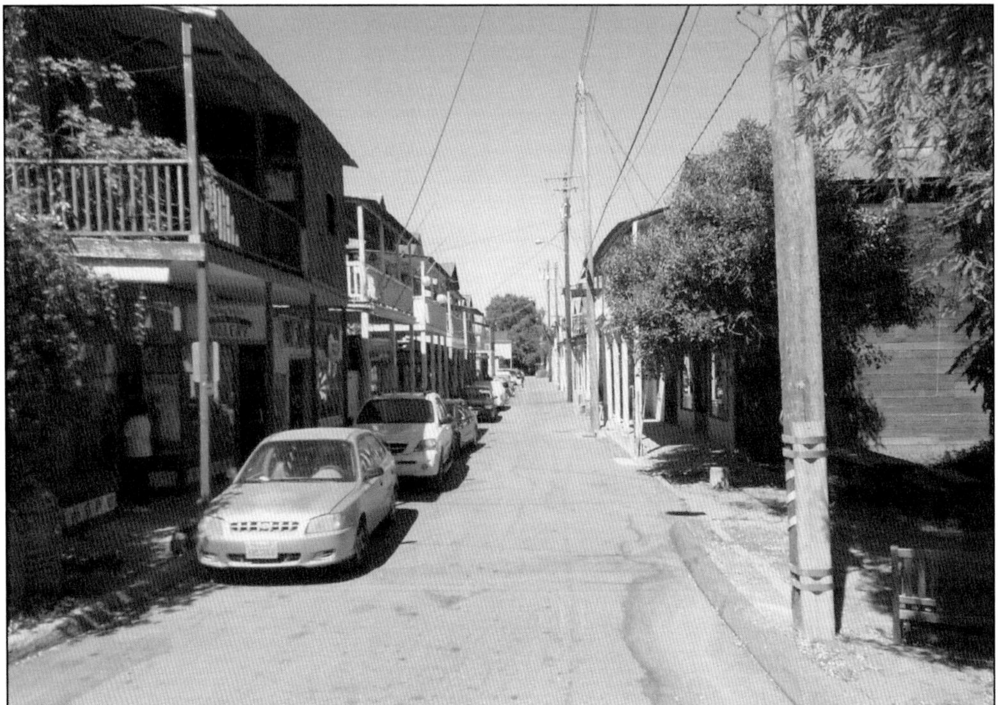

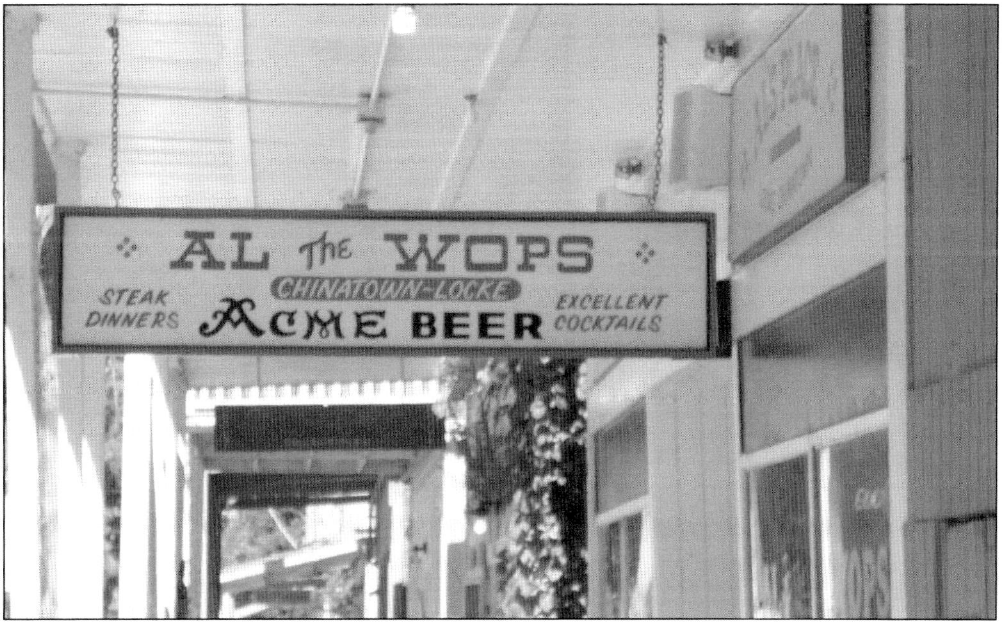

This building was originally constructed in 1915 by Lee Bing and three partners. In 1933 or 1934, Al Adami of Rio Vista leased the bar, making it the only non-Chinese business in town. Bing's son Ping Lee eventually sold the business to Adami in 1941, the year Adami changed the name to the infamous Al the Wops. After that, the restaurant became a delta legend. (Author's collection.)

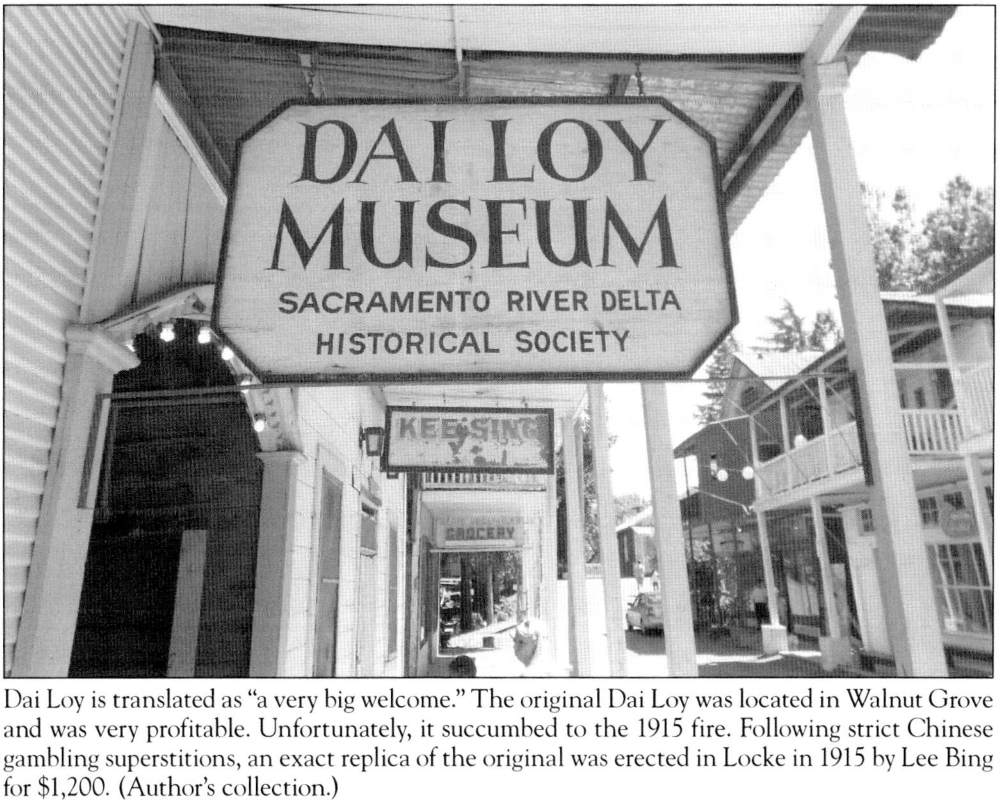

Dai Loy is translated as "a very big welcome." The original Dai Loy was located in Walnut Grove and was very profitable. Unfortunately, it succumbed to the 1915 fire. Following strict Chinese gambling superstitions, an exact replica of the original was erected in Locke in 1915 by Lee Bing for $1,200. (Author's collection.)

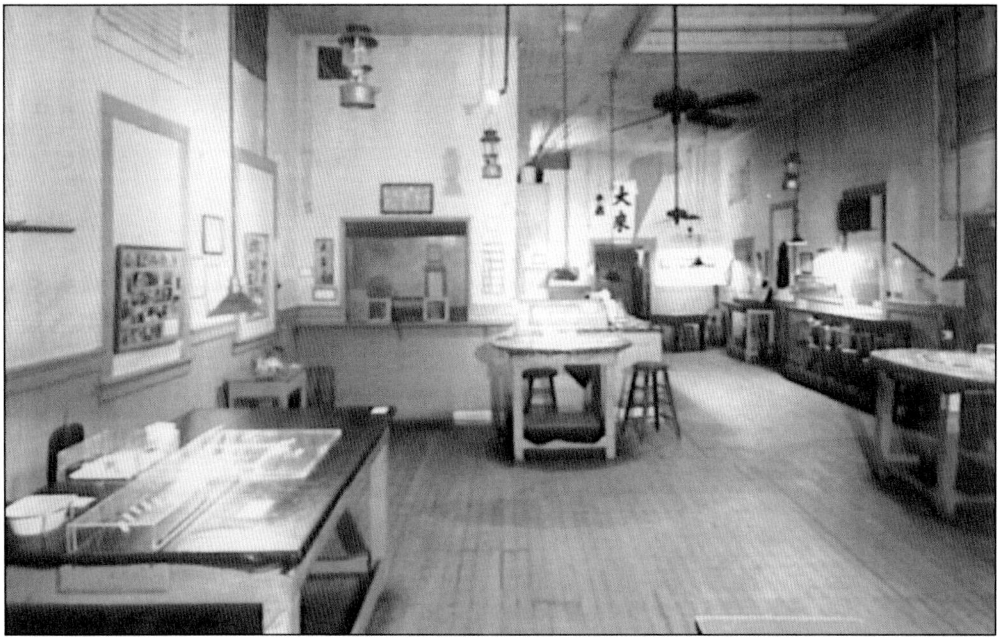

This photograph shows the interior of the Dai Loy Museum. There were five gambling houses operating in Locke by the 1930s. Games played included fan-tan, dominoes, pai gow, "dow ngow," and lottery, and in later years, blackjack and craps. The Dai Loy was in operation from 1915 until 1950, when Sacramento County officials closed it down. (SRDHS.)

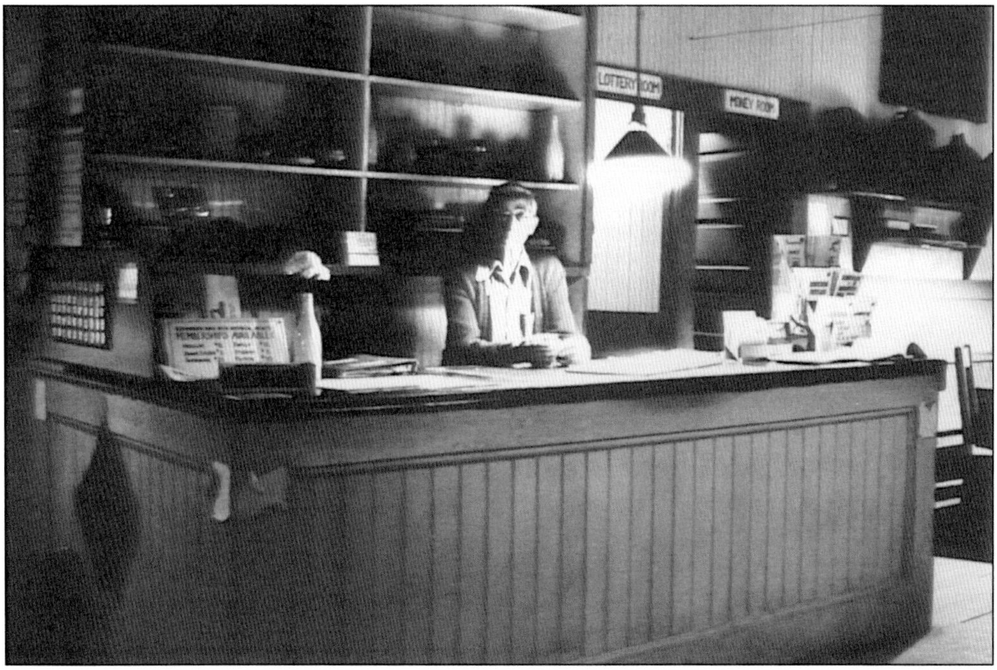

Longtime delta resident Clarence Pratt volunteers as a docent at the Dai Loy Museum in Locke. Initially, the gambling facilities catered exclusively to the Chinese, and on occasion, to East Indians. Eventually, the Japanese were allowed, followed by the Filipino laborers who were new to the region, and lastly, Caucasians. Locke became the mecca for gambling in the delta. (SRDHS.)

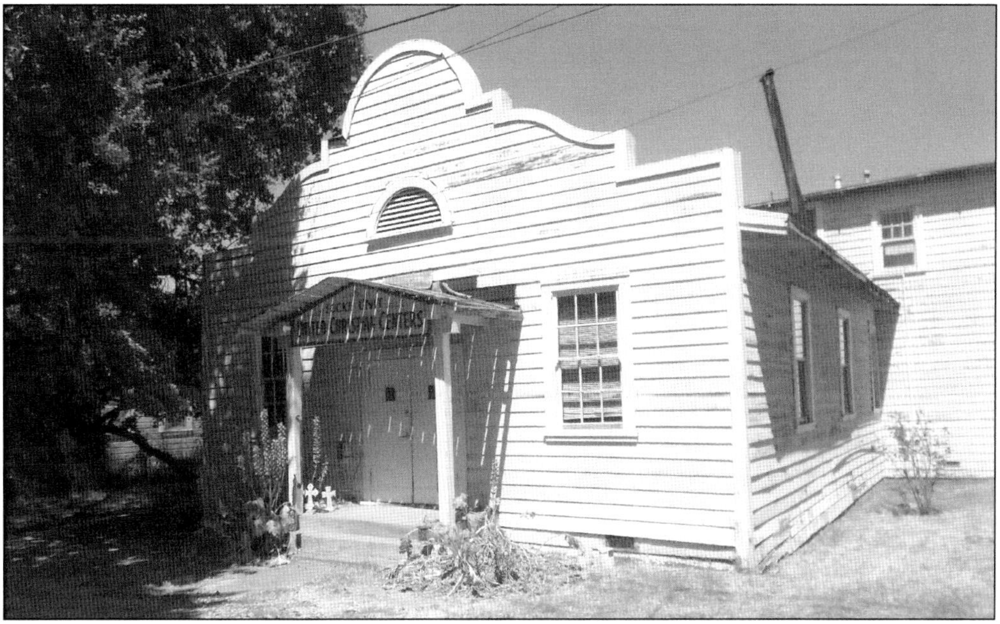

Nestled among residences on Key Street is the Locke United Christian Center. It was initially built in 1926 as Baptist Mission Church and carries the distinction of being the only building specifically erected as a church in Locke's history. It was no surprise that the largest contributors to the church were the local gambling halls. (Author's collection.)

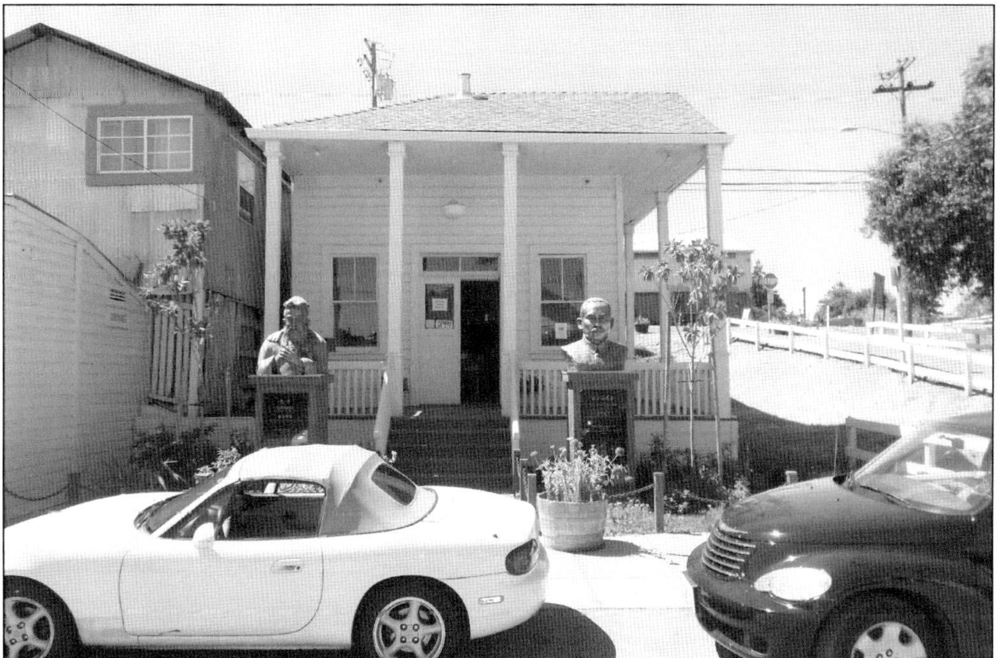

The Chinese School was built in 1915 with funds from the Kuomintang (KMT), the Chinese Nationalist Party founded by Sun Yat-sen. The building was first used as a meeting hall and branch office for the KMT and as a community hall for Locke. In 1926, it became the school, teaching the Chinese language to local children. (Author's collection.)

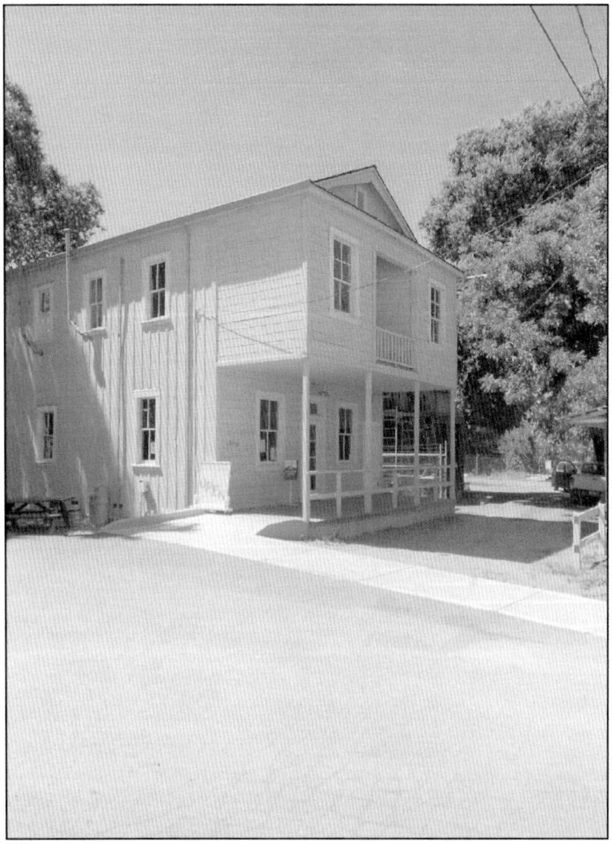

The Locke boardinghouse is an exhibit and research facility operated by California State Parks and the Locke Foundation. The building is at the T intersection of Locke and Main Streets. Jack Ross, who owned the service station and garage on the levee adjacent to the boardinghouse, purchased the building in 1926. (Author's collection.)

The Star Theatre (below) was a Chinese-owned movie theater in the silent film era. The theater was on the top floor, and a gambling hall occupied the downstairs. The building was also been used as a Chinese opera, brothel, and gambling den. Because of its architecture, it stands out as one of the most recognizable buildings in Locke. (Author's collection.)

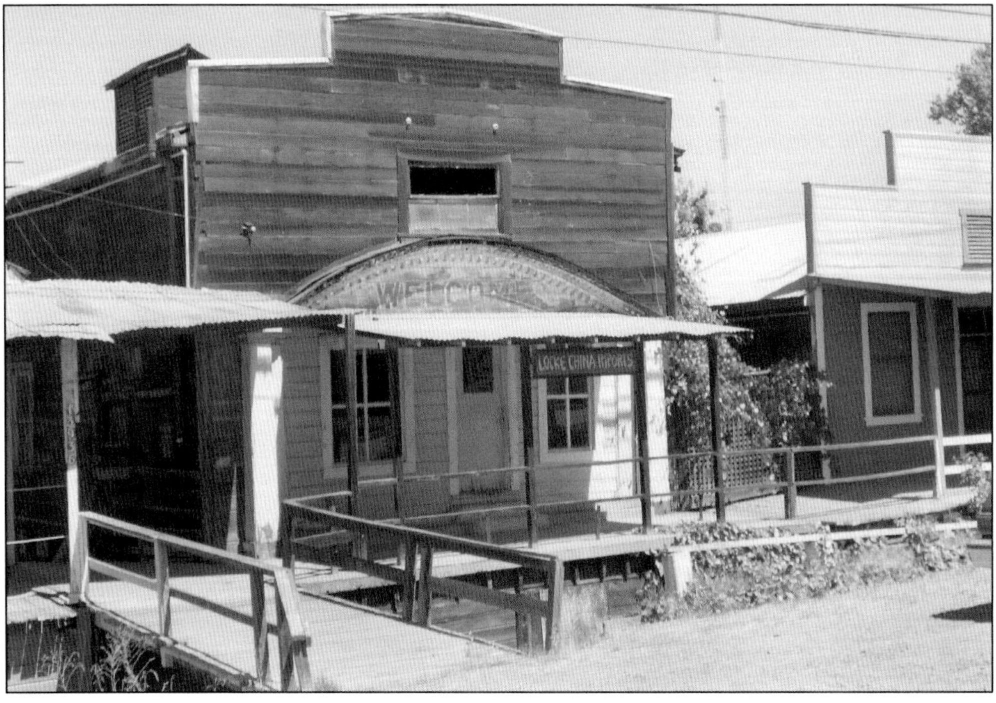

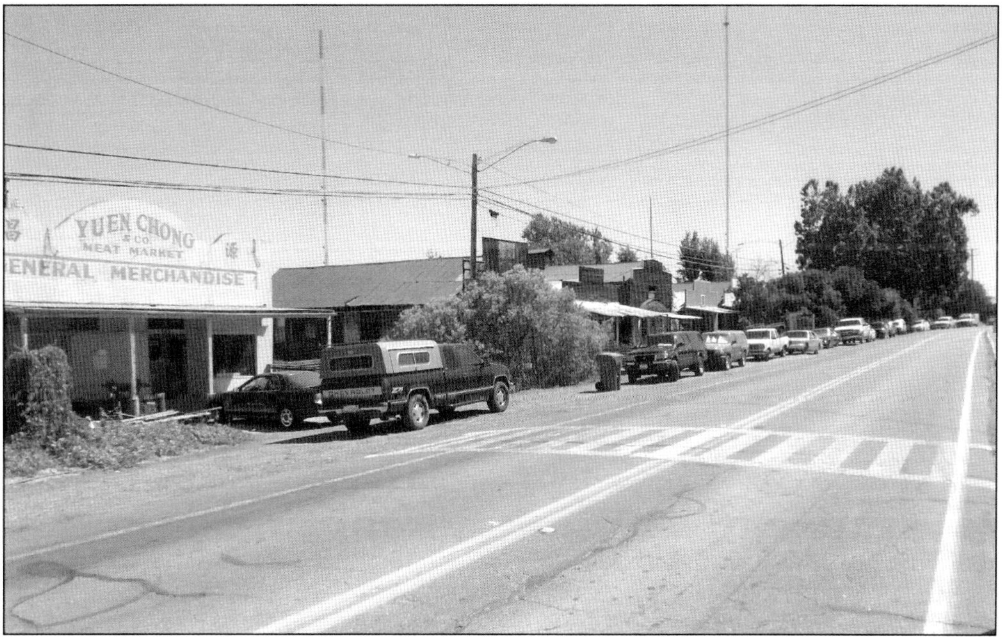

This is a current view of the Locke storefronts facing the Sacramento River. From left to right are buildings historically known as Yuen Chong market; Wah Li, a gambling house and drugstore; Gambling Hall, a soda fountain; Star Theatre; Owyand Tin Git, an ice cream shop; Victory Club, a gambling hall and speakeasy; and Original Kee Sing, a Japanese barber. (Author's collection.)

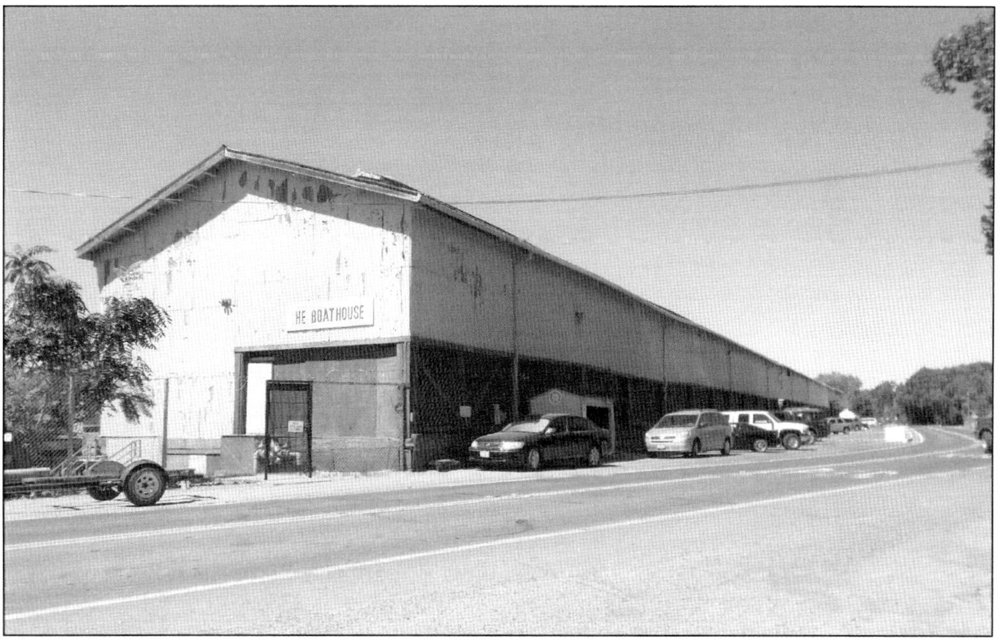

The boathouse was originally the Southern Pacific Railroad warehouse, with a spur from the main track leading to it. Over the years, it has been rented and occupied by American Fruit Company, Lambert Packing Company, California Packing Corporation, Earl Fruit Company, Simonds & French, and Scobel & Day. (Author's collection.)

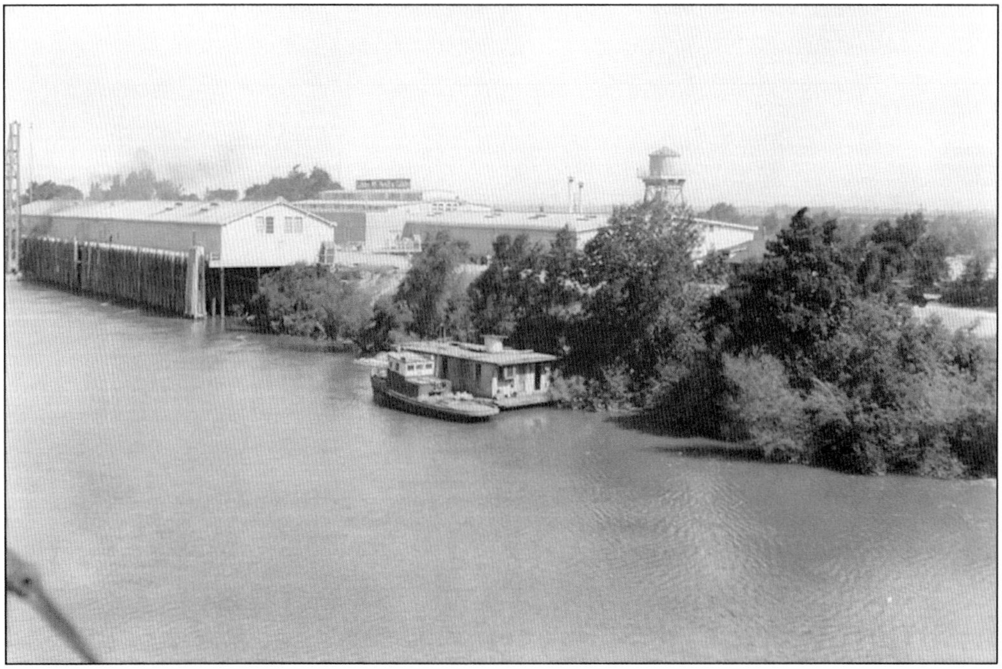

Because of Locke's location, surrounding land, and access to the water and railroad, several canneries and packing sheds were established there. A quarter mile upriver, the Sacramento River Association had a large packinghouse, which was later taken over by Libbey, McNeil & Libbey. A shook box factory hanging over the river across from the cannery was also owned by Libbey. (CSL.)

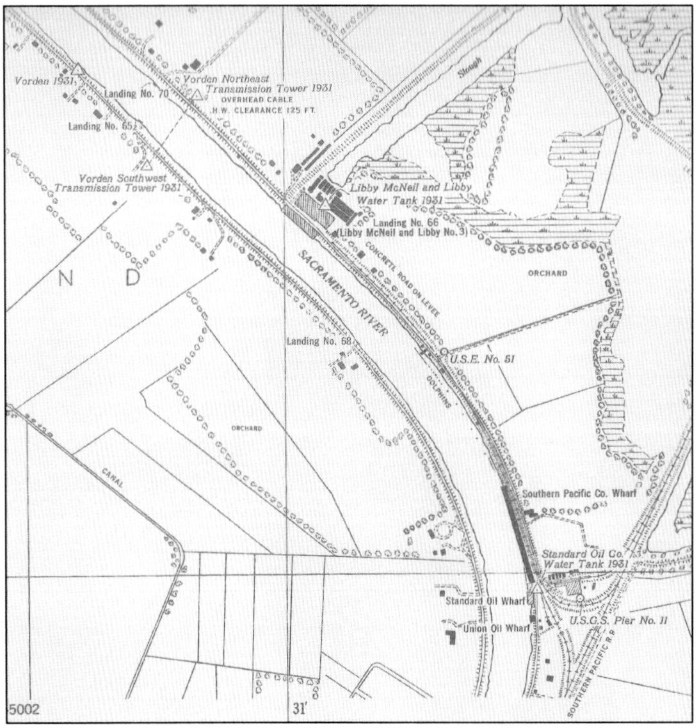

In the 1920s, the community of Locke boasted several boardinghouses, gambling halls, brothels, and bars, two slaughterhouses, a flour mill, six restaurants, nine grocery stores, a theater, a hotel, and a lodge. It believed that during that era the permanent population was around 600, but approximately 900 visitors would arrive on the weekends. (RVM.)

Six

THE FORGOTTEN TOWNS

The majority of the towns and communities on the banks of the Sacramento River survived, but some were not so lucky, among them Vordon, Paintersville, Onisbo, Webster, and Emmanton. For some of them, photographs and maps verify their existence, while some only receive a brief mention in history books.

Vorden was located approximately two miles upstream from Locke and began its life as Trask's Landing, named after Charles Frederick Trask. In 1868, Trask inherited 220 acres, which he farmed for about eight years before the San Francisco Union Savings Bank repossessed it, along with the majority of the acreage in the newly formed Pierson district. Trask left the delta around 1876. In 1878, the bank in San Francisco sent one of its employees, P.J. van Loben Sels, to make improvements on the levees. He eventually purchased some of the land, and in 1890, changed the name from Trask's Landing to Vorden, after the name of his hometown in the eastern Netherlands.

Armstead Runyon established the settlement of Onsibo, located opposite the head of Steamboat Slough, in 1849. Runyon named the town after an Indian chief. A post office was established in 1853, and a schoolhouse with a Masonic hall on the second floor was erected in 1860. But with the founding of Walnut Grove and Courtland and the transferring of the community's post office to Courtland in 1867, Onsibo was soon no more.

Webster, established in 1849, was a settlement located on the eastern bank of the Sacramento River, for which little information is available. It was approximately 10 miles downstream from Sacramento, near the site of Freeport. There is a reference to the settlement on an 1850 map of "the Sacramento River from New York of the Pacific to Boston." It is indicated as Webster or Russian Embarcadero. Paintersville was founded by Levi Painter in 1854 when he purchased 123 acres on the banks of the Sacramento River. He constructed a wharf, making the town accessible by water, and subsequently built warehouses, a general store, a hotel, and a saloon.

The community known as Emmaton, approximately six miles south of Rio Vista at the northern end of Sherman Island, was founded by J.M. Upham in 1871. Upham began to build up the community, adding a wharf, a hotel, a general merchandise store, a lumberyard, and two grain and hay warehouses. Floodwaters destroyed the town in the winter of 1878. Efforts to rebuild did not succeed, but the site has since been occupied by farmhouses, a labor camp, and packing sheds.

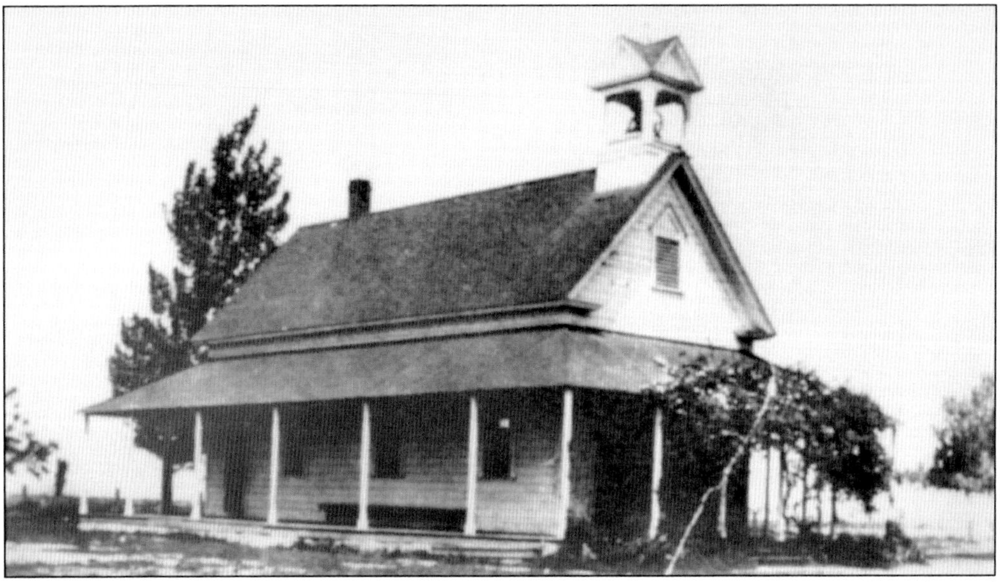

The one-room Vorden schoolhouse was located at what would become the junction of Vorden and Herzog Roads, in the Pierson district. The simple wooden building with a gabled roof and belfry was a typical design for the era. The school operated from 1904 to 1920 and offered instruction from kindergarten through eighth grade. (SRDHS.)

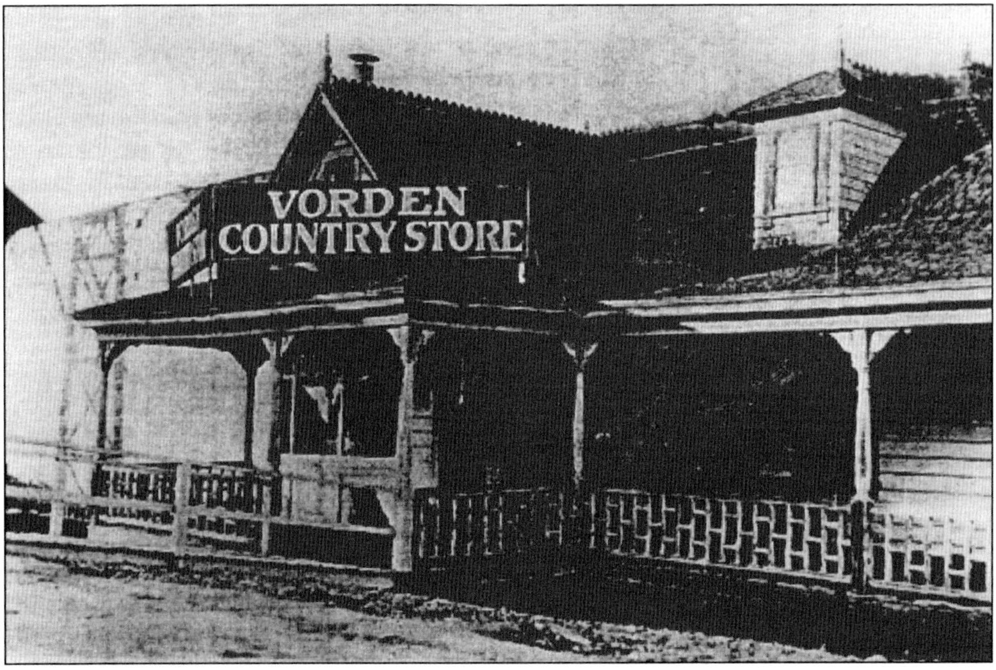

Vorden Country Store was on the levee, in front of the Del Monte cannery, facing the Sacramento River. For many years, a man named Shirley Hall owned and operated the store. Hall's establishment also provided overnight room and board for riverboat travelers. Eventually, Hall relocated to Courtland and operated the Red & White store. (SRDHS.)

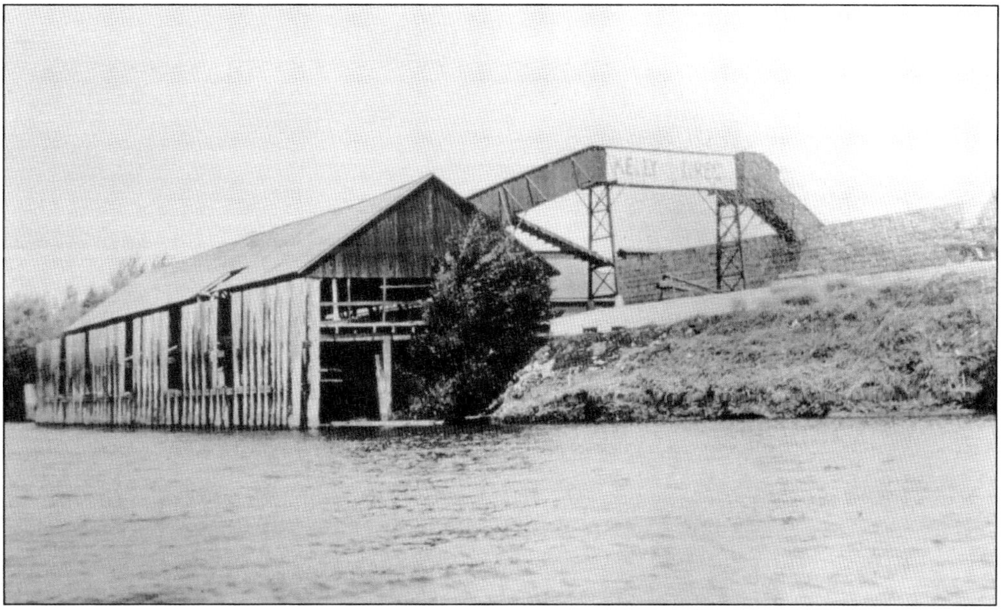

Like most towns on the Sacramento River delta, Vorden had a cannery, run by Del Monte and seen here along with one of its warehouses. The asparagus cannery was said to employ as many as 200 Chinese workers during the busy season. (SRDHS.)

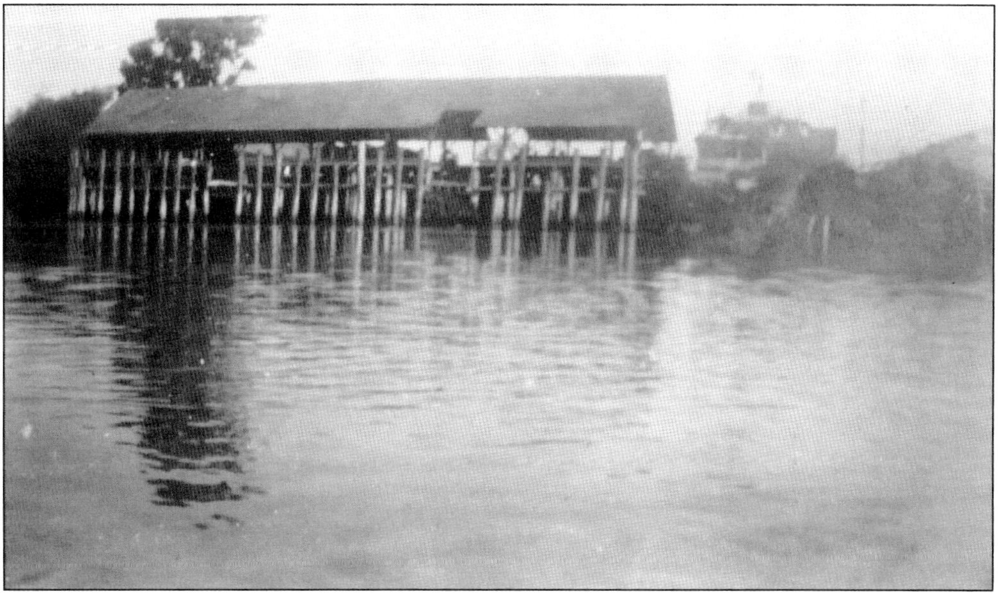

In its glory days, the community of Vorden boasted a wharf, a post office, the Vorden Hotel, the Del Monte cannery, two grocery stores, a school, a Catholic church, several dairies, a tavern, and the Glanvale Creamery. Eventually, the cannery closed, the post office consolidated with Locke, and both the church and the school closed. Fine homes and other buildings were abandoned and fell into poor condition; they eventually either collapsed or were torn down. (SRDHS.)

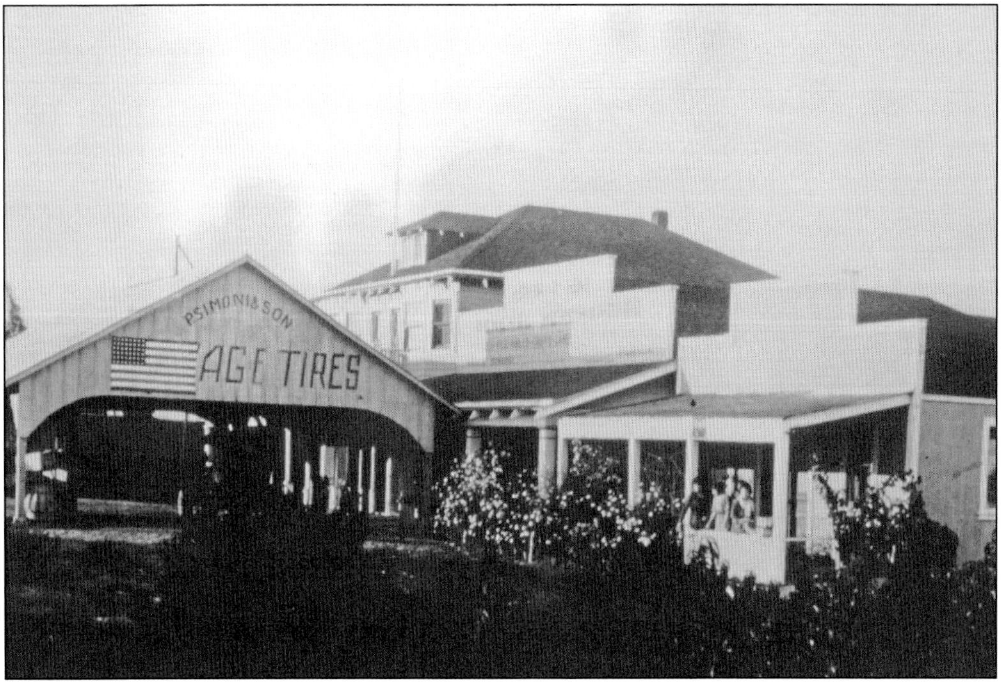

Rio Simoni arrived in Vorden and erected a fine two-story building. His family lived on the second floor and he ran a saloon on the main floor. The building was moved from the riverfront across to the other side of the levee. In 1913, Simoni built a grocery store and hotel and a pole shed. (SRDHS.)

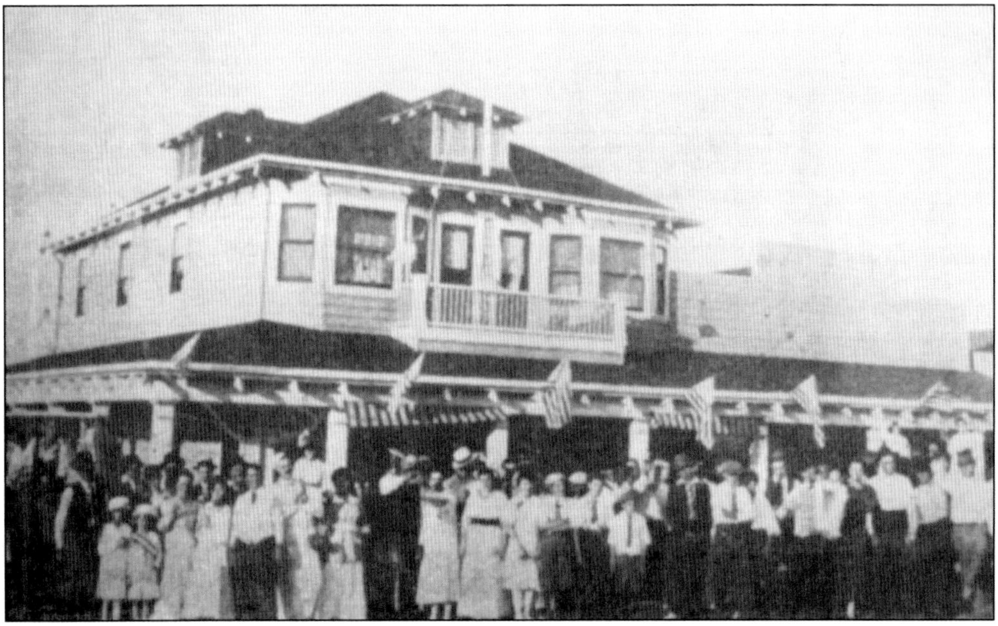

The Vorden Hotel was built by Rio Simoni in 1913 at the corner of the levee road (now River Road) and Vorden Road. The hotel had eight rooms for rent on the second floor and a bar and general merchandise store on the main floor. Here, townsfolk celebrate the Fourth of July in 1906. (SRDHS.)

This enlarged section highlights a 1931 map that is one of the last to mark Vorden as a community. It is apparent in the map's details that several buildings still existed at the time of its compilation. Travelers through the delta and many current residents do not realize that what is now just a T in the road where Vorden Road meets the highway was once an actual town. (RVM.)

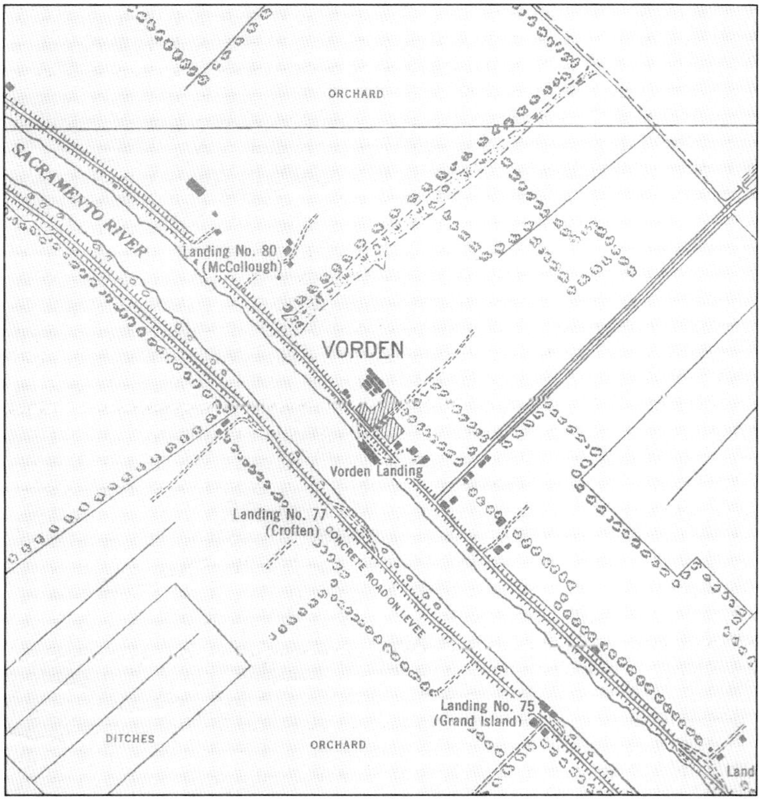

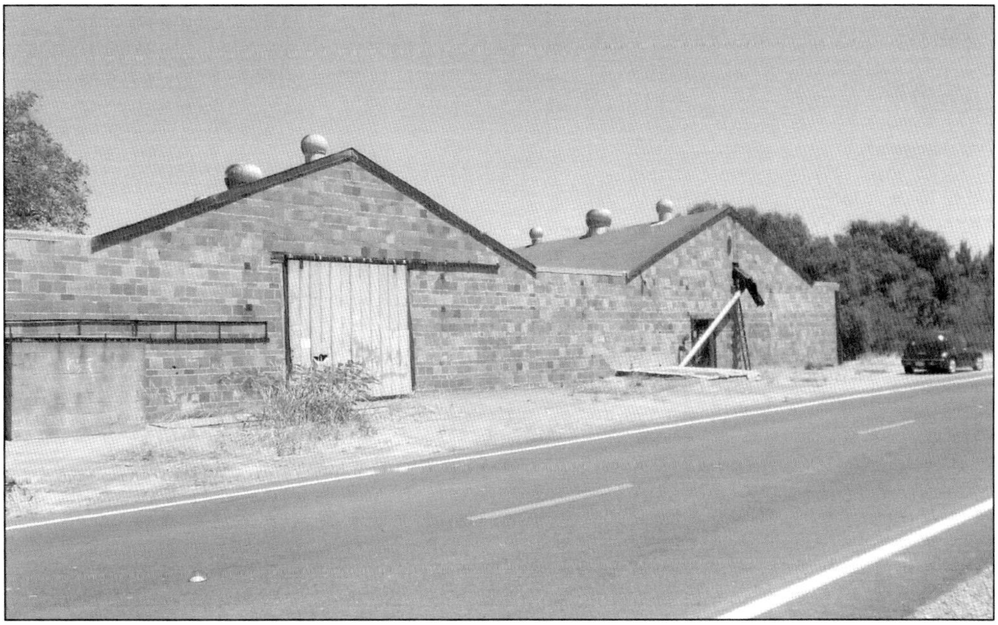

Nestled along the banks of the Sacramento, and in some cases a short distance inland, are the abandoned buildings that serve as reminders of the years when the canneries were the main sources of employment in the delta. This abandoned brick warehouse is near the former community of Vorden. (Author's collection.)

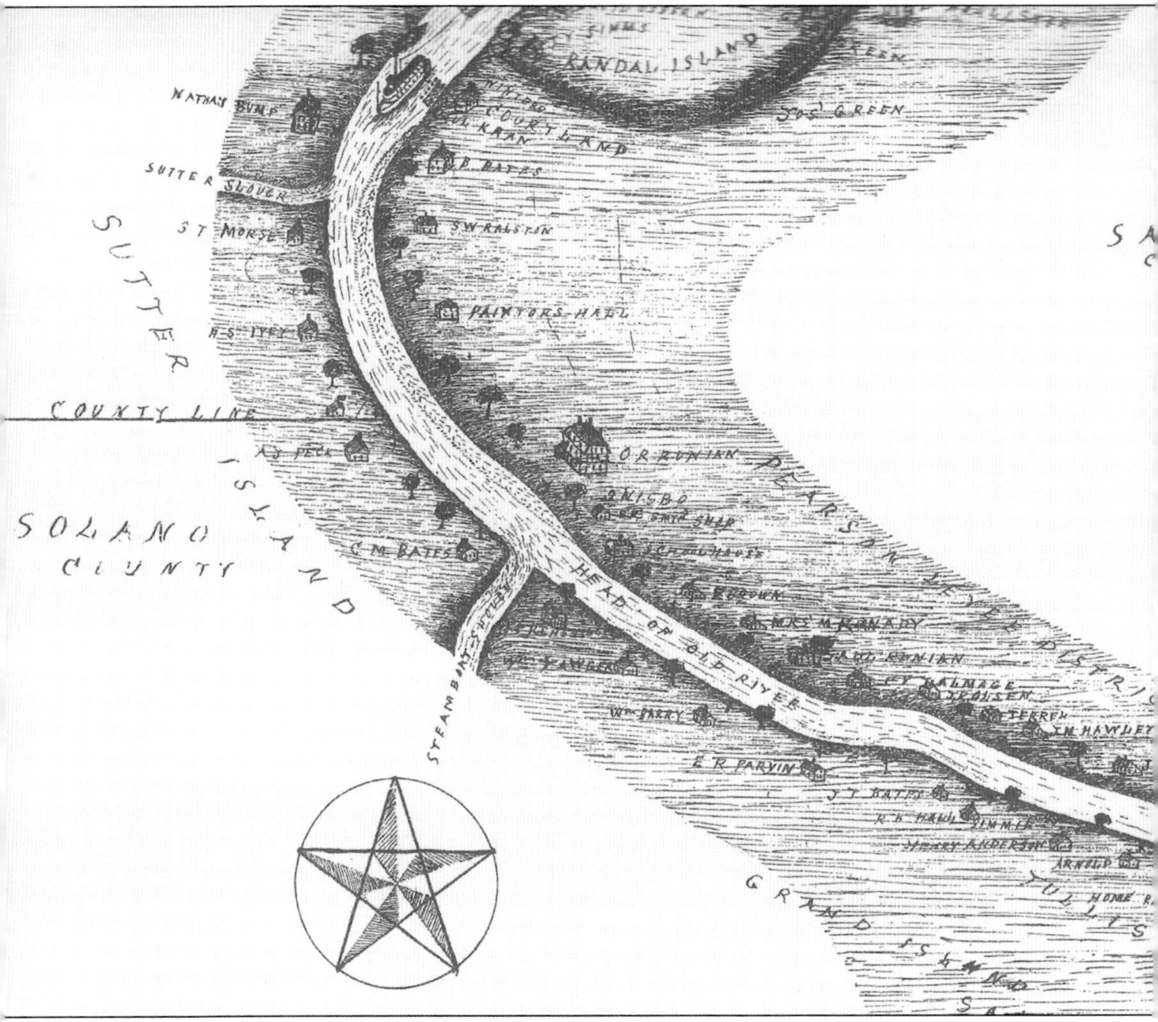

There are conflicting dates as to the establishment of the short-lived community of Onsibo. One story states that it was founded by Armstead Runyon and named after a local Indian chief who died on his ranch on October 24, 1862. The other states that the speculative town was established in 1849. Either way, the settlement was a mile or two south of Courtland and was only in existence until 1868. (RVM.)

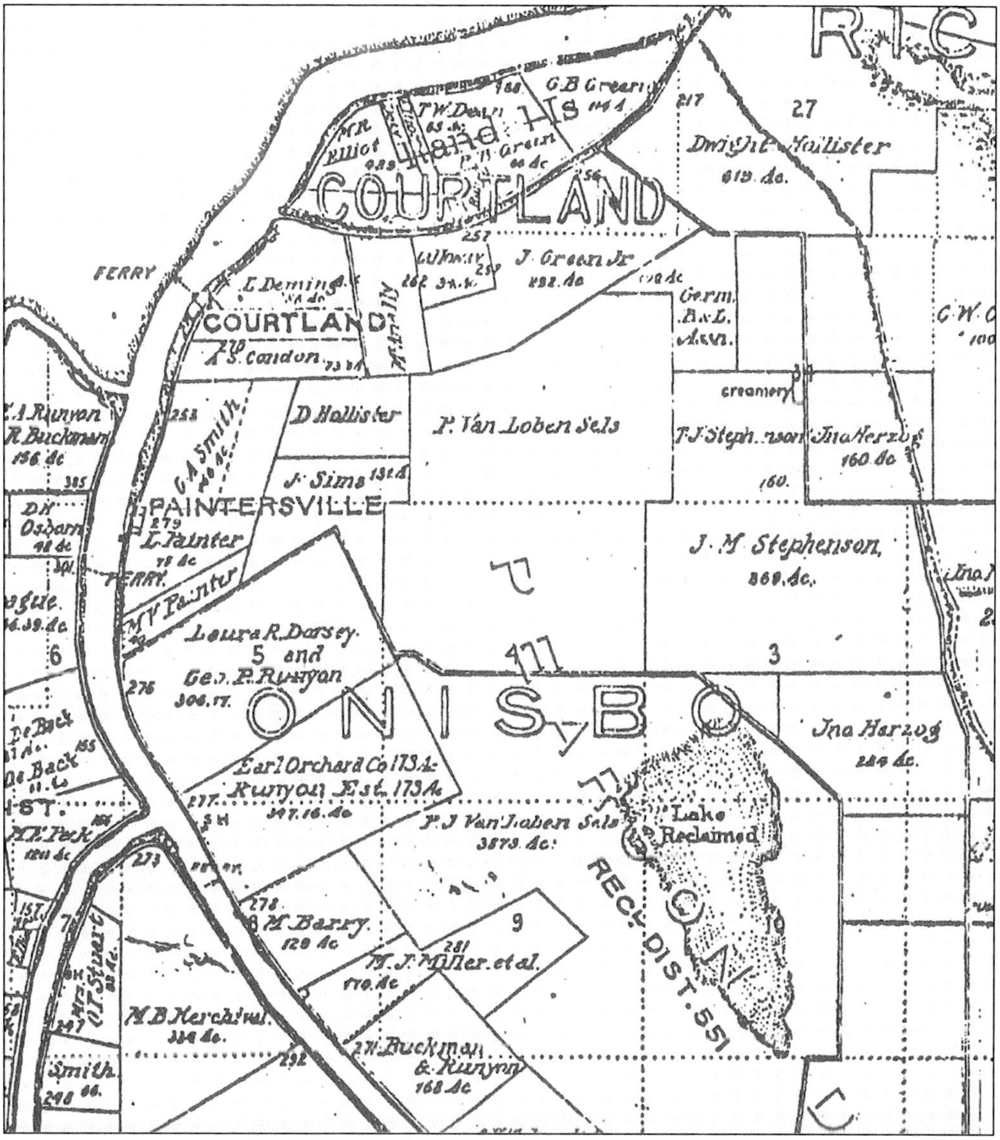

This enlarged section of a 1903 map shows Courtland and Paintersville as well as a portion of the Pierson district. (RVM.)

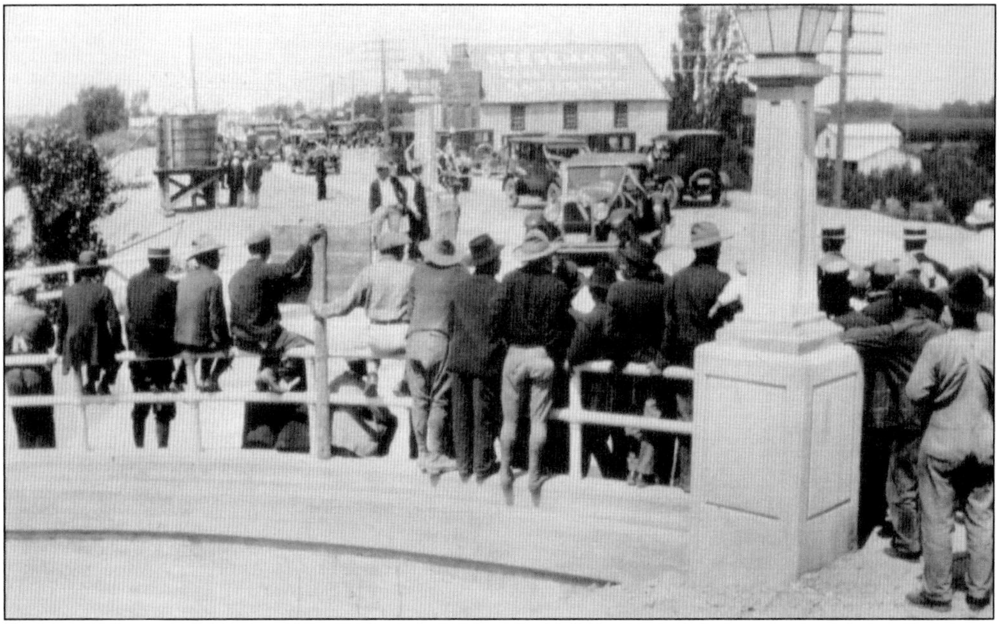

The Paintersville Bridge, with its double-leaf bascule design, was built in 1923 by the Strauss Bascule Bridge Company of Chicago. It is about the only thing that remains to keep the former town's name alive. The bridge is seen here at its dedication ceremony in 1923. (SRDHS.)

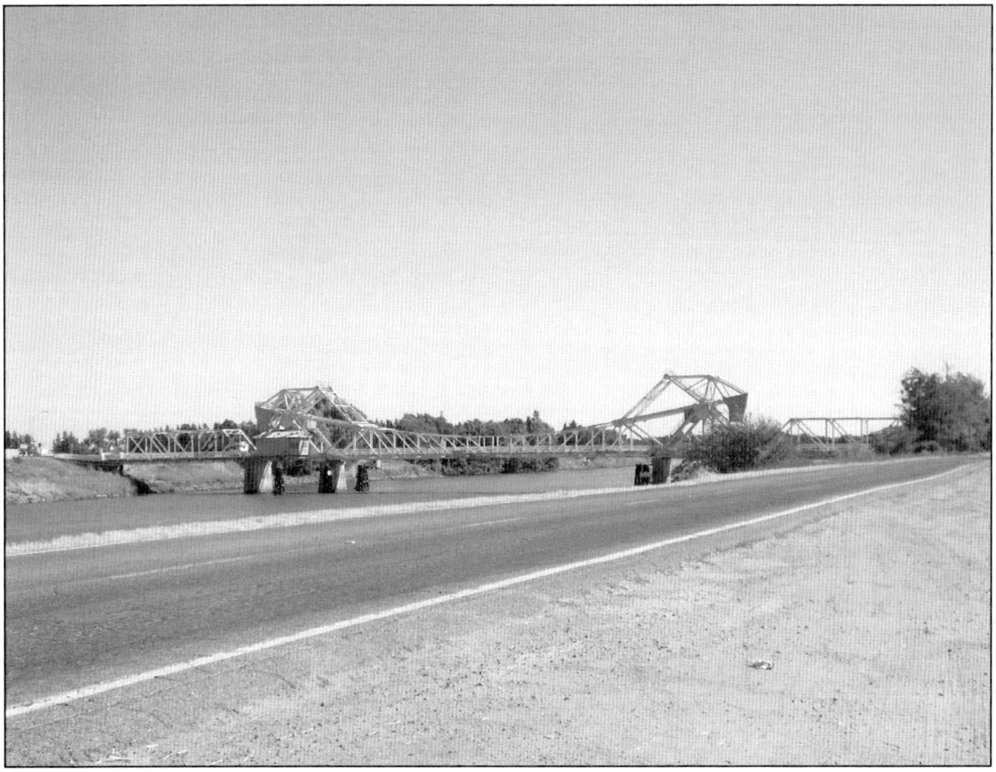

The Paintersville Bridge was the third of four bridges in the Sacramento River delta designed by Strauss. It is seen here in 2012. (Author's collection.)

Seven

COURTLAND

The community of Courtland was founded in 1870 by James V. Sims, a native of London. Sims's humble beginnings seem to be shrouded with inconsistencies. One story suggests that he was born in Illinois in 1828 and headed for California in 1851, in the company of six other gentlemen. In this account, he did not have enough money to pay for the entire journey, so at a point in the trip he stopped, and it was said that he kept a lodging house for a short time in order to earn enough money to continue his trek to California. When he arrived, the only possessions that he owned were the few blankets he carried. That first summer, he found odd jobs and was said to have walked to Auburn and Newcastle, in Placer County, for a job whipsawing.

The story that holds more weight, however, is that Sims was a native of London, England, and born in 1832. In 1845, Sims's father journeyed across the Atlantic to Canada to find a new life. Shortly after arriving and settling down, the elder Sims sent for his wife and son, James. That same year, James joined the now famous Stevenson's Regiment, which fought in the Mexican War (1846–1848). After serving four years, Sims left the Army; he was then 17. Like many newcomers to California during those years, Sims got gold fever and decided to try his hand at gold mining, first heading to the Mokelumne River in Calaveras County. He then went into partnership with several gentlemen and began mining on the American River. Together, the men were making around $80 a day; with his share, Sims invested in land. After a period of time, the partners did not feel they were making enough money, and each went his own way. Altogether, Sims continued to mine for nearly 20 years before deciding on a change in life. When he arrived in the delta in 1870, Sims purchased 100 acres and became one of the earliest grape growers in the delta. He also ventured into the profitable pear market. Sims was ahead of his time, with his ability to assess the potential value of the land in the delta.

When Sims decided to create a town on his property, he chose to name it after his son, Courtland. Sims was the founder of the settlement and the owner of the land it sat on, but many other prominent men were instrumental in the town's foundations, including Benjamin Bates and Capt. Albert Foster. The supervisor for the California Navigation Co., Captain Foster constructed a wharf measuring 182 feet by 50 feet at a cost of $6,000. Once the wharf was completed and a post office was petitioned for, the community began to grow by leaps and bounds, as general merchandise stores, blacksmith shops, saloons, and hotels were all built quickly.

Famed steamships like the *Chrysopolis* and the *Yosemite* and later the *Modoc* and the *Apache* made daily stops. Before long, Courtland was a thriving community surrounded by fertile soil for planting and farming.

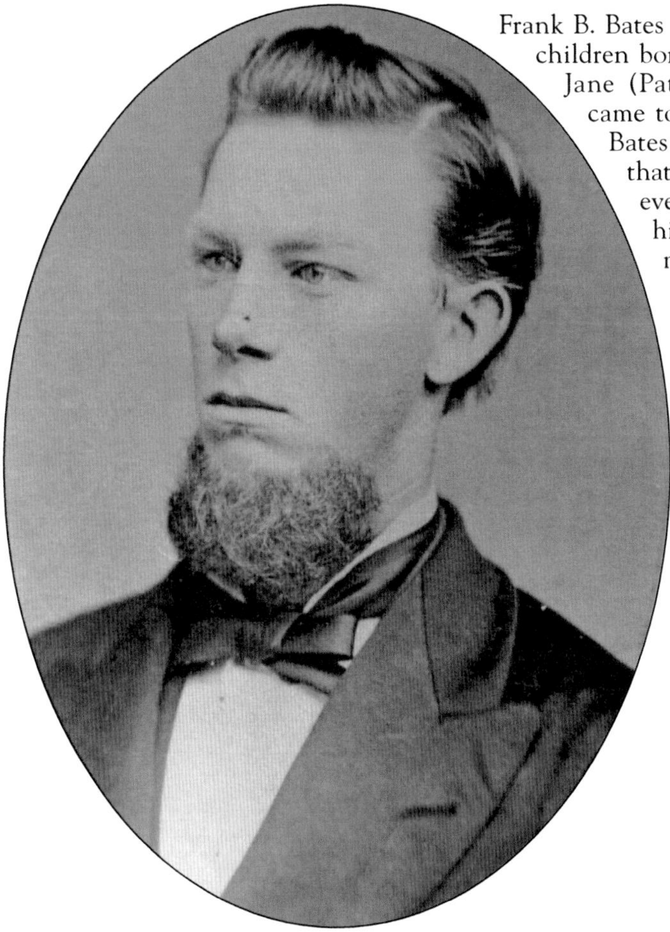

Frank B. Bates was born in 1855, one of five children born to pioneers Benjamin and Jane (Patton) Bates, who originally came to the area in 1849. The elder Bates owned the 128 acres of land that Courtland still sits on. Frank eventually inherited a portion of his father's estate and devoted the majority of it to fruit orchards and vineyards and some of it to the community. (SRDHS.)

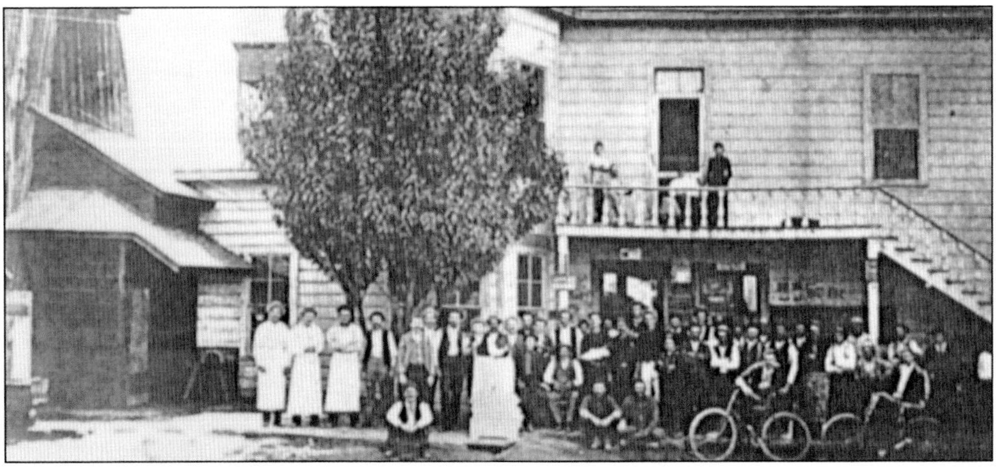

Local businessmen stand by the stage depot and Wells Fargo office in 1897. This photograph was likely taken the same day and from almost the same place as the photograph on the facing page. (SRDHS.)

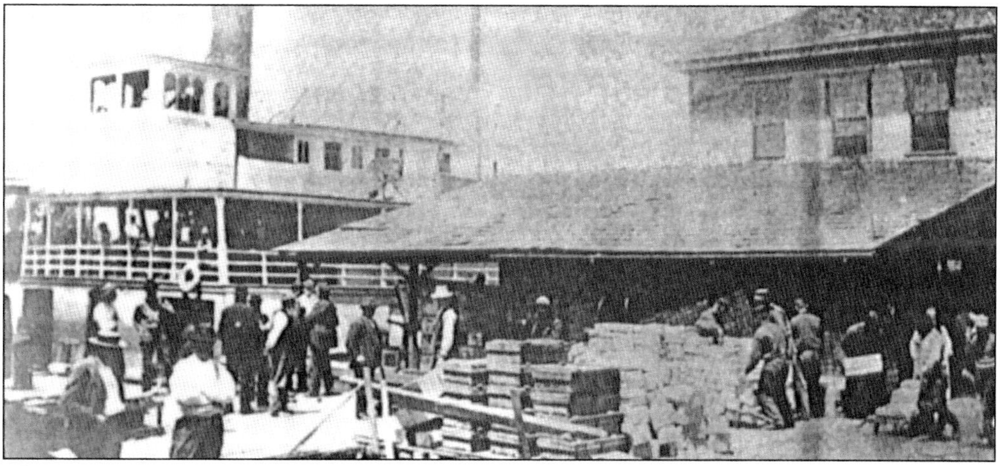

This 1897 scene of the Courtland wharf shows lots of activity as a steamship is being loaded with shipments of fruit. The wharf, measuring 182 feet by 50 feet with two 25-by-60-foot stores, was constructed for a combined total of $6,000. The wharf quickly became the hub of the community, as more and more fruit was shipped out of Courtland. (SRDHS.)

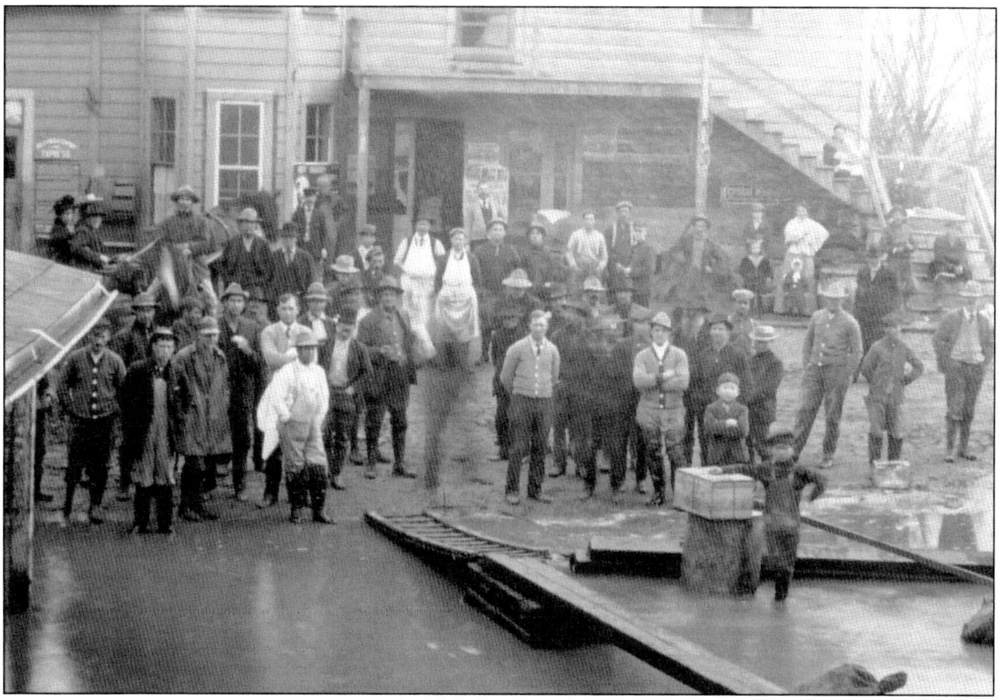

A group of Courtland residents has gathered in front of the Bauer, Miller & Newbert store during the flood of 1907. The communities of Rio Vista and Isleton were also inundated with water during the flood. (SRDHS.)

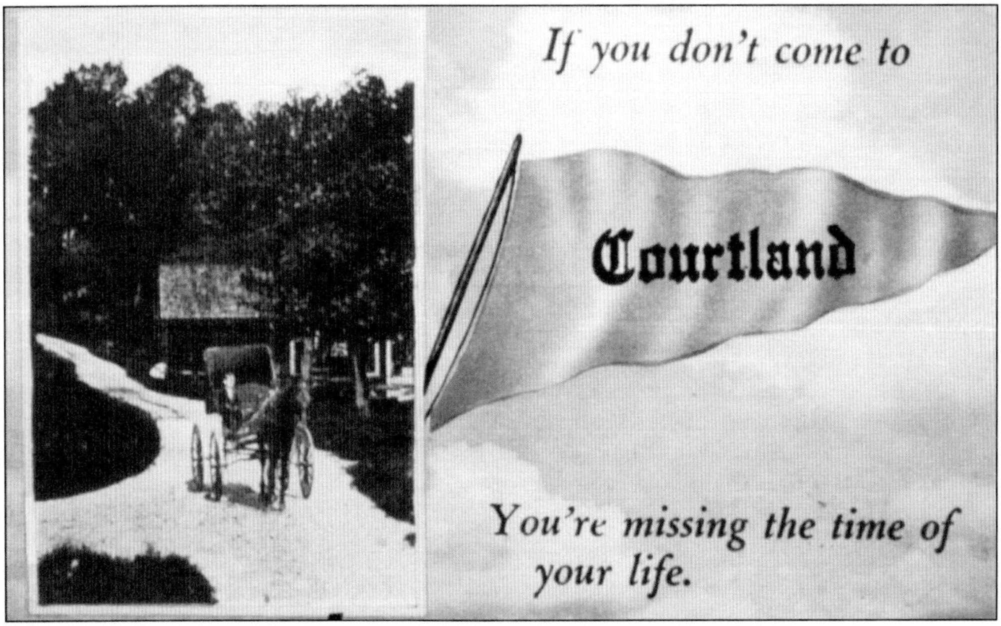

These stylish postcards, created using a standard template containing the town name and a catchy sentiment, were very popular in the early 1900s. Similar cards were made for both Rio Vista and Emmanton. (SRDHS.)

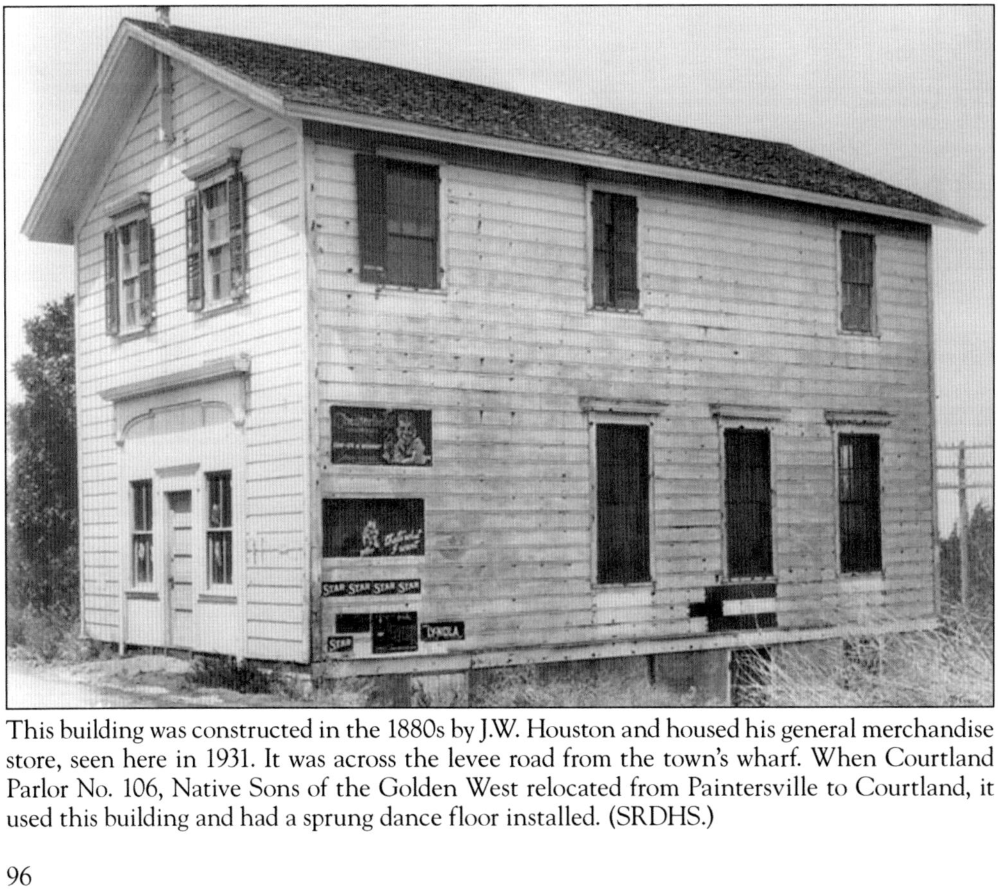

This building was constructed in the 1880s by J.W. Houston and housed his general merchandise store, seen here in 1931. It was across the levee road from the town's wharf. When Courtland Parlor No. 106, Native Sons of the Golden West relocated from Paintersville to Courtland, it used this building and had a sprung dance floor installed. (SRDHS.)

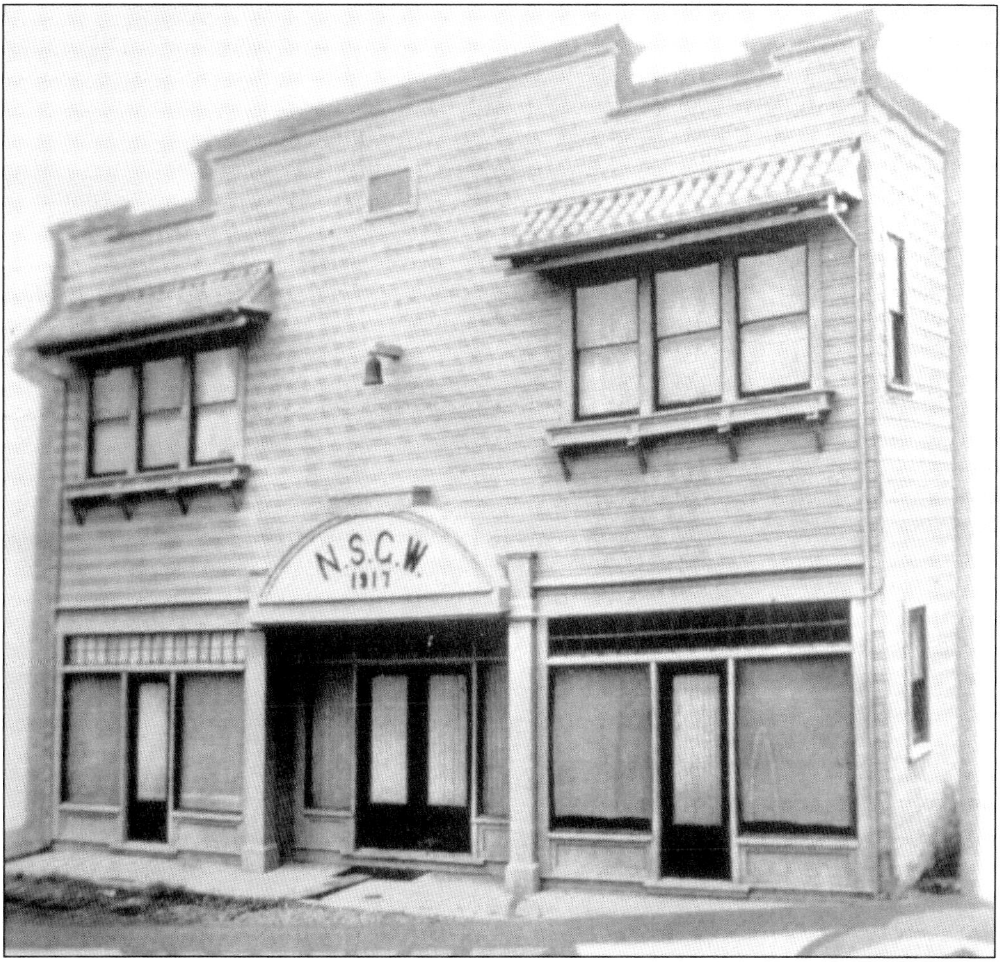

Courtland Parlor No. 106, Native Sons of the Golden West (NSGW), was chartered on June 10, 1887. This meeting hall, on the corner of Sequoia Avenue and Riverside Avenue, was the third location used by the local Courtland branch of the NSGW and was eventually torn down in 1962. Due to lack of membership, the organization relocated to Elk Grove in the 1950s. (SRDHS.)

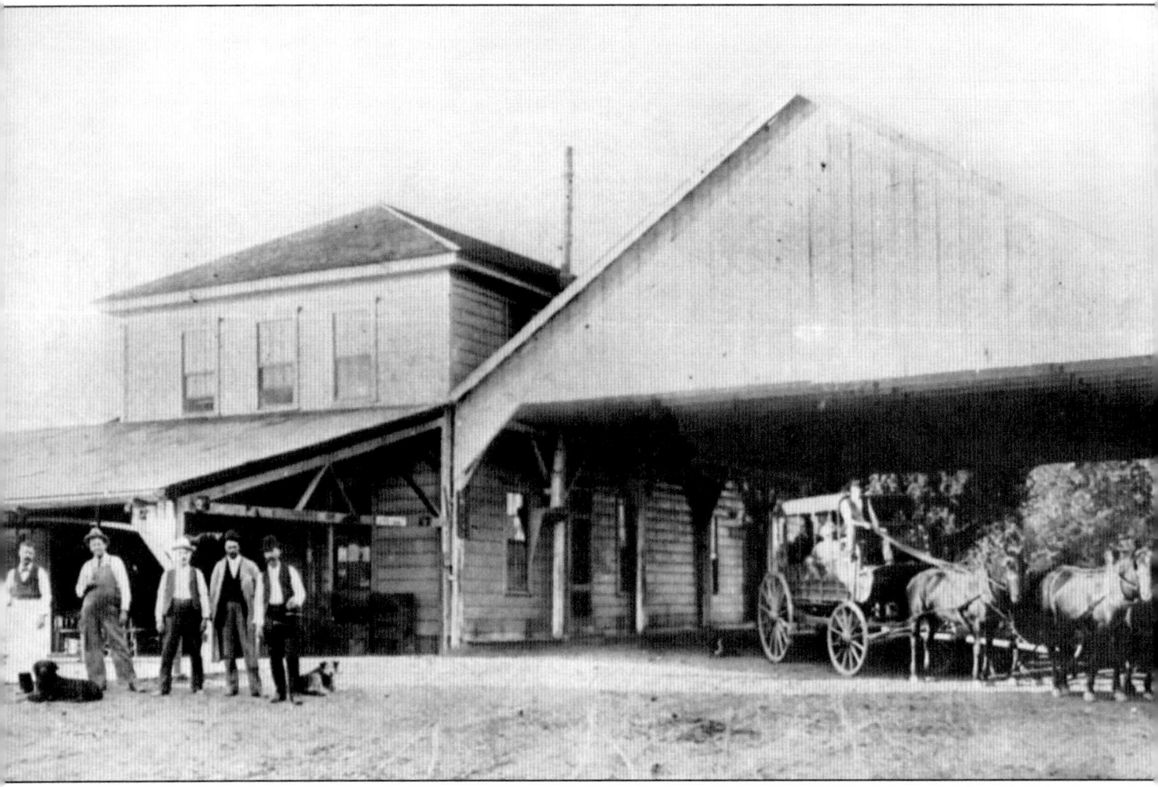

This image of the back of the Courtland Hotel was taken on September 9, 1899. The shed was built so the horses of weary travelers and townsfolk had a place to take refuge from the weather. J.W. Houston was a former Sacramento County assessor who moved to Courtland and owned the hotel, wharf, livery stable, and general merchandise store. He also held the positions of express agent, postmaster, telegraph operator, and insurance agent. (SRDHS.)

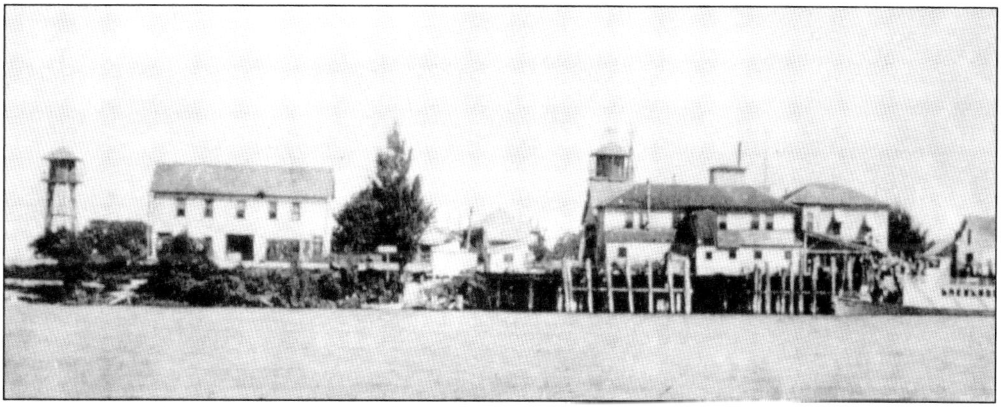

This photograph of Courtland was taken from the across the Sacramento River shortly after the levee was raised. The building on the left is the Courtland Hotel. During the harvest season, a variety of fruits and vegetables was shipped from the Courtland wharf aboard steamships to San Francisco, including pears, peaches, plums, beans, and celery. (SRDHS.)

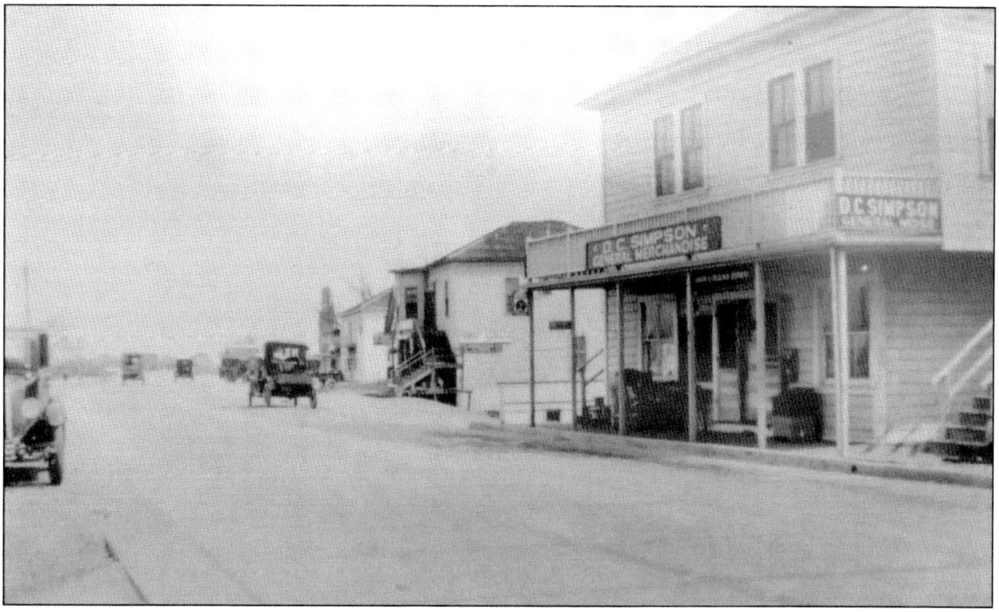

This view looks northwest down the levee road (River Road) towards D.C. Simpson General Merchandise before 1920. The building was originally constructed as an IDES (Irmandade do Espírito Divino, "Fraternity of the Divine Spirit" in Portuguese) hall on the second floor, with apartments on the main floor. The IDES gave up the building when it was moved across the levee, at which time Simpson opened his store on the ground floor and converted the upstairs into apartments. In the 1930s, the building became a Red & White store and was operated by Shirley Hall. The building was destroyed by fire in 1984 while undergoing renovation to become a private residence. (SRDHS.)

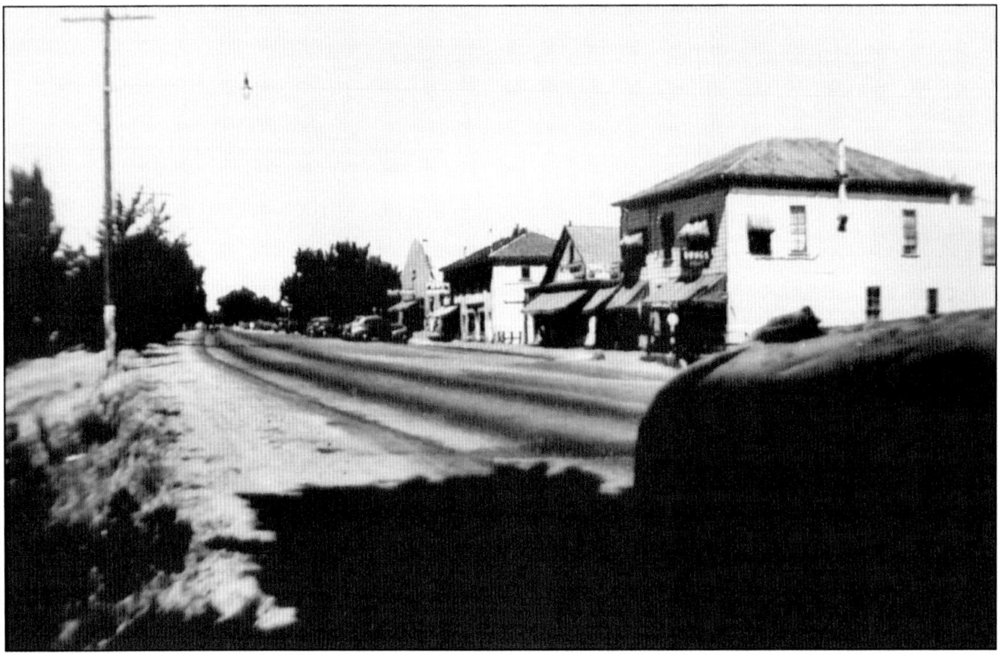

This view, also looking northwest down the levee road (River Road), was taken in the 1940s. The building on the far left is the Miller & Jackson general merchandise store, which is now Courtland Market. (SRDHS.)

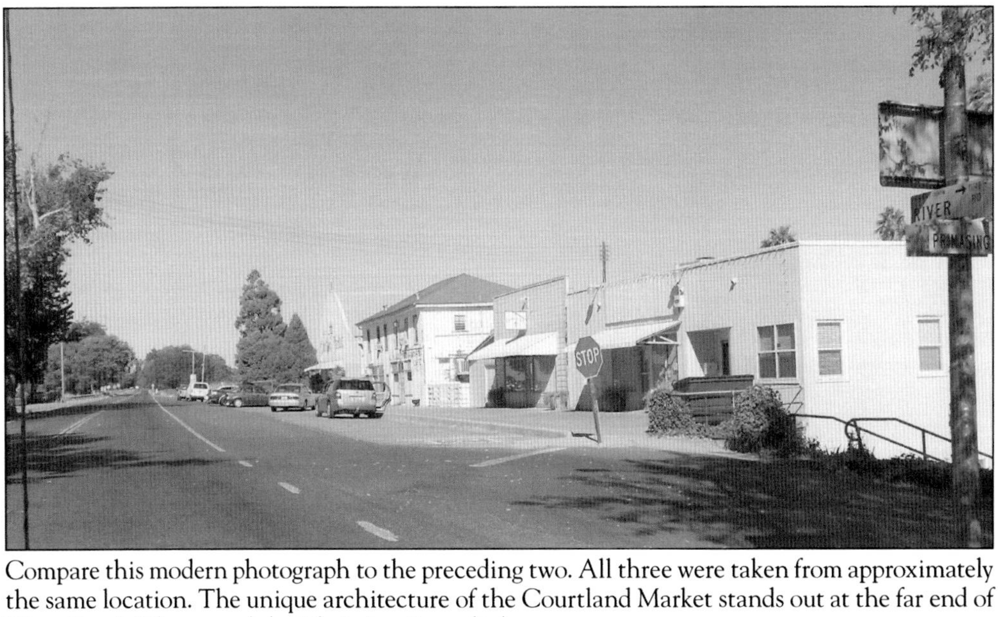

Compare this modern photograph to the preceding two. All three were taken from approximately the same location. The unique architecture of the Courtland Market stands out at the far end of River Road. (Photograph by Christina Pezzaglia.)

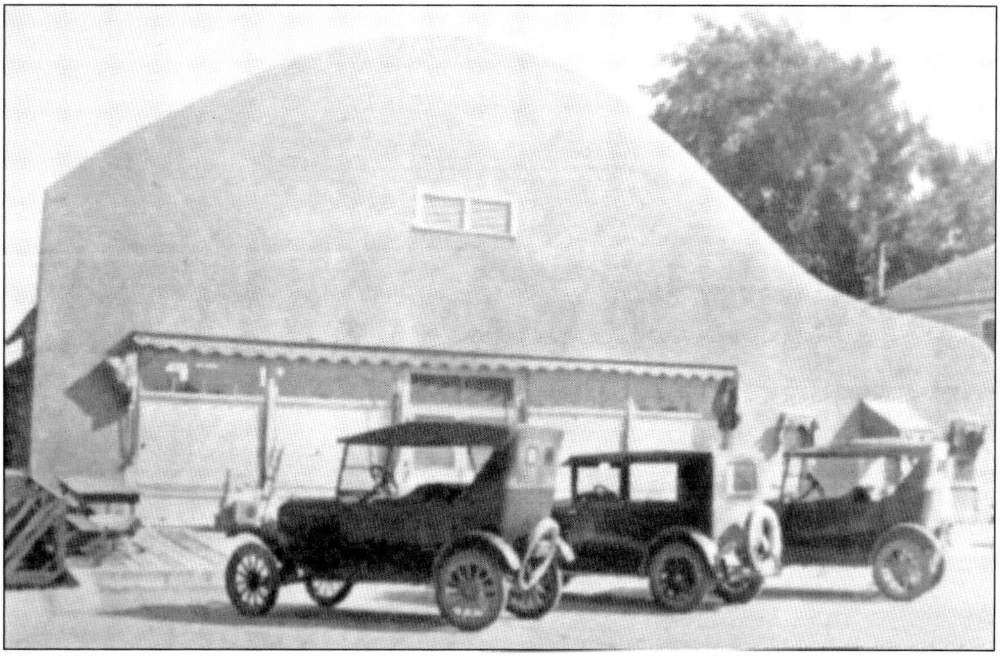

Now the Courtland Market, this is the most recognizable building in Courtland. It opened as Miller & Jackson's general merchandise store in 1925, when this photograph was taken. The store began as Bauer, Miller & Newbert, became Bauer, Miller & Jackson, and had settled as the partnership of Miller & Jackson by 1925. The store was a one-stop shop, carrying everything from clothing to hardware. (SRDHS.)

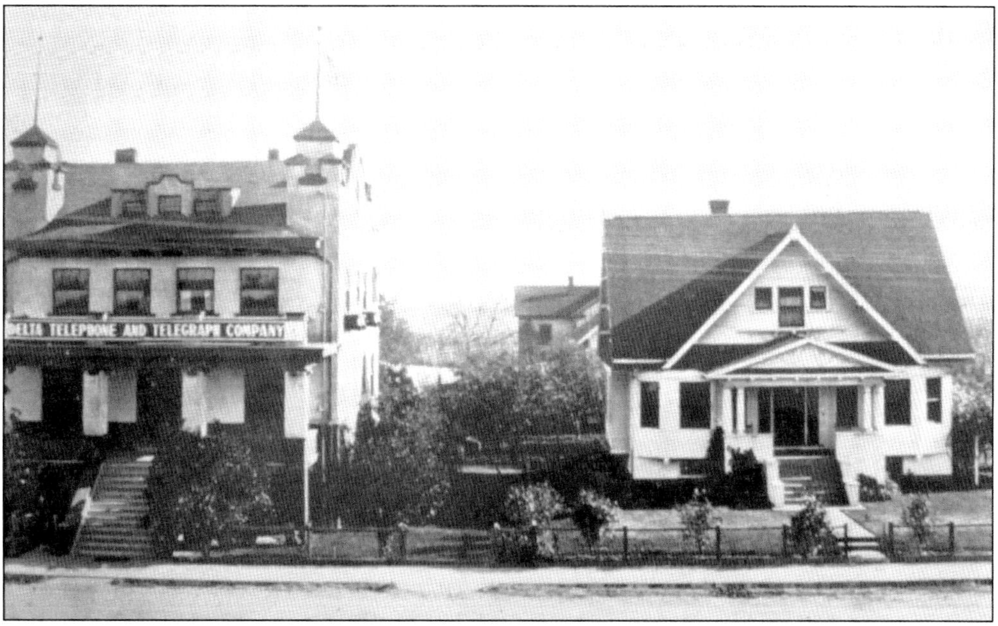

The Freeport Telephone Company was established in 1889 by a group of Freeport farmers. The name was changed to the New Freeport Telephone Company in 1901; and on April 26, 1917, it was changed to the Delta Telephone and Telegraph Company. In 1917, the office was moved to this building on Riverside Avenue in Courtland. (SRDHS.)

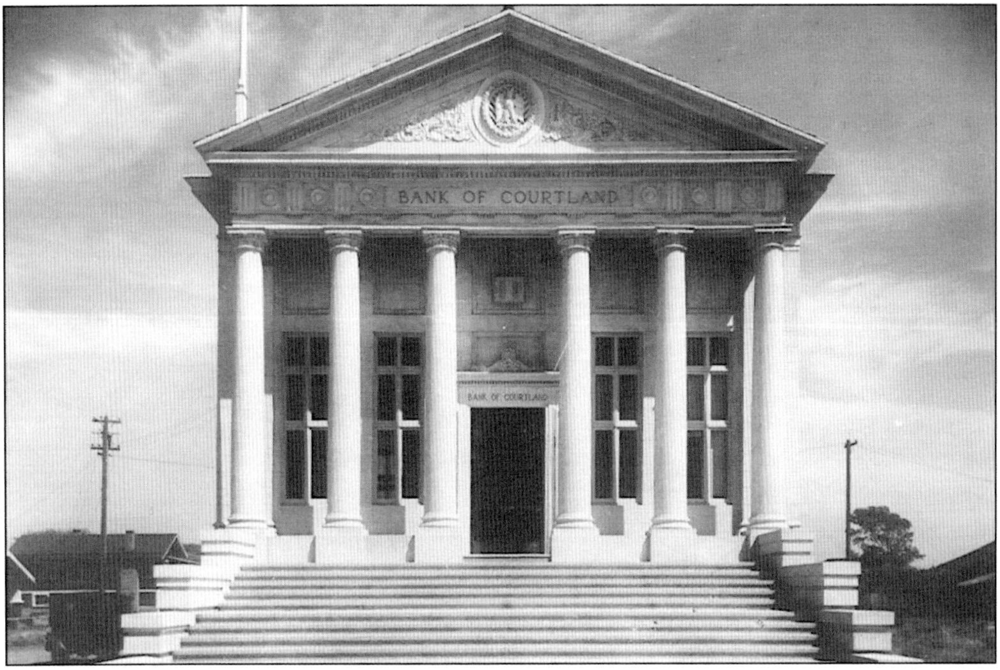

The Bank of Courtland, on the corner of Riverside and Sequoia Avenues, was chartered in 1919 with $65,000 in capital. Unfortunately, the bank went under after the stock market crash of 1929. Eventually, the Delta Telephone and Telegraph Company purchased and moved into this building in 1937. (SRDHS.)

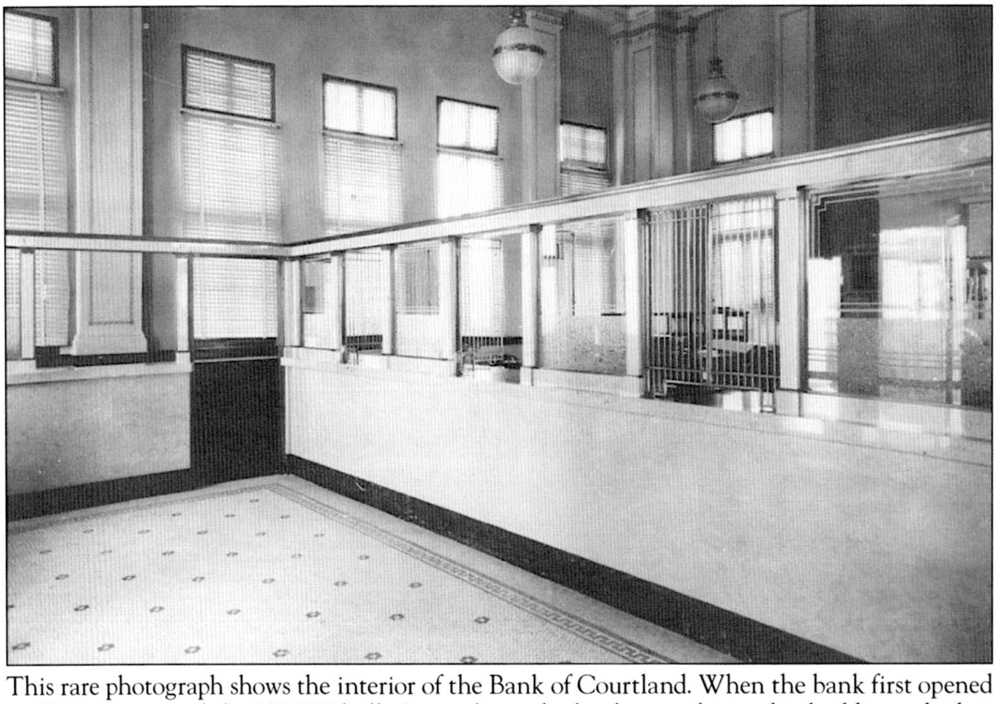
This rare photograph shows the interior of the Bank of Courtland. When the bank first opened in 1919, it occupied the NSGW hall. A year later, the bank moved into this building, which it constructed across the street. The stately lobby featured this mosaic tile floor. (SRDHS.)

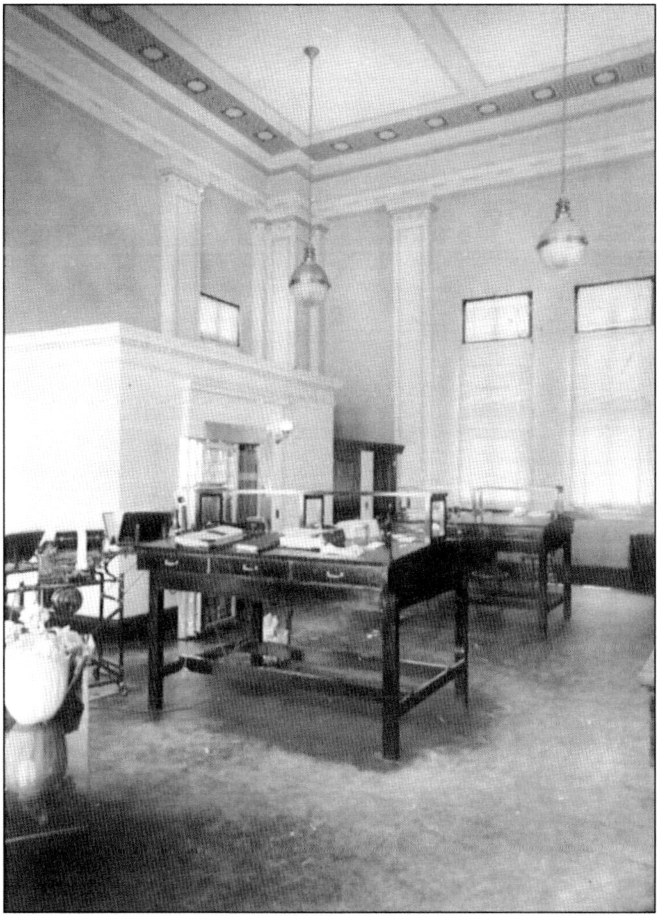

In 1937, the Delta Telephone and Telegraph Company purchased the former Bank of Courtland building. In 1952, the company boasted 1,786 stations and covered the delta from just north of Freeport to halfway south on Sherman Island as well as four counties—Sacramento, Yolo, San Joaquin, and Solano. This photograph shows the interior of the building when it was still owned by the bank. (SRDHS.)

Courtland Service Station, which sold Associated oil, was owned and operated by E.G. "Babe" Kirkland, who offered candy, ice cream, Menlo root beer, and other soft drinks in addition to gas and oil. The station was on the levee road at the northeast end of town. A Mobil service station operated out of the building in later years. (CSL.)

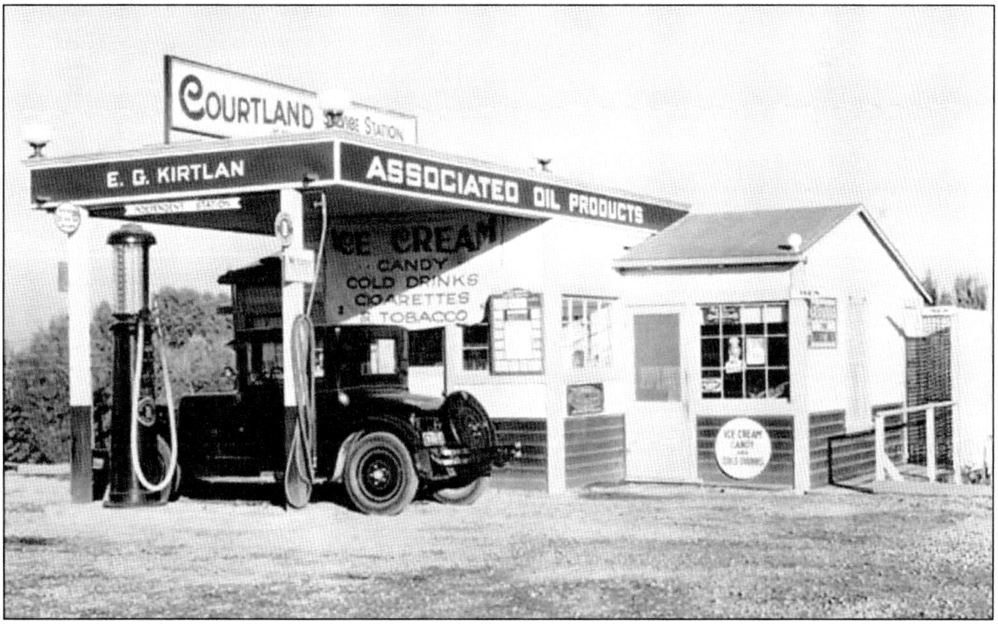

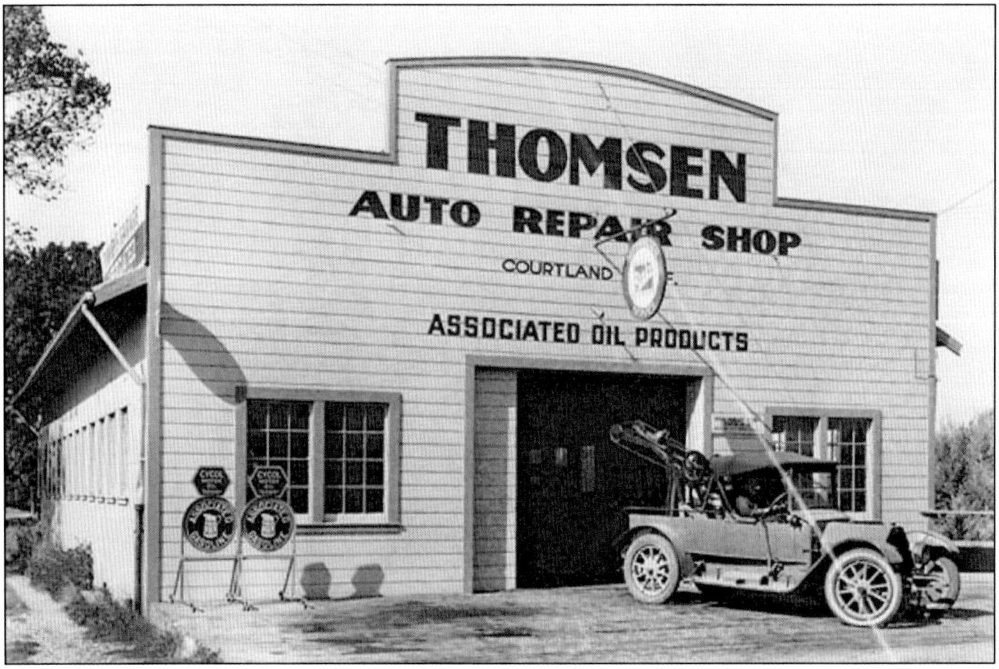

Garages such as this one appeared up and down the delta as automobile usage increased. As times changed and the mode of transportation moved away from the horse and buggy and towards the automobile, blacksmith usually became mechanics and a new era was born. (CSL.)

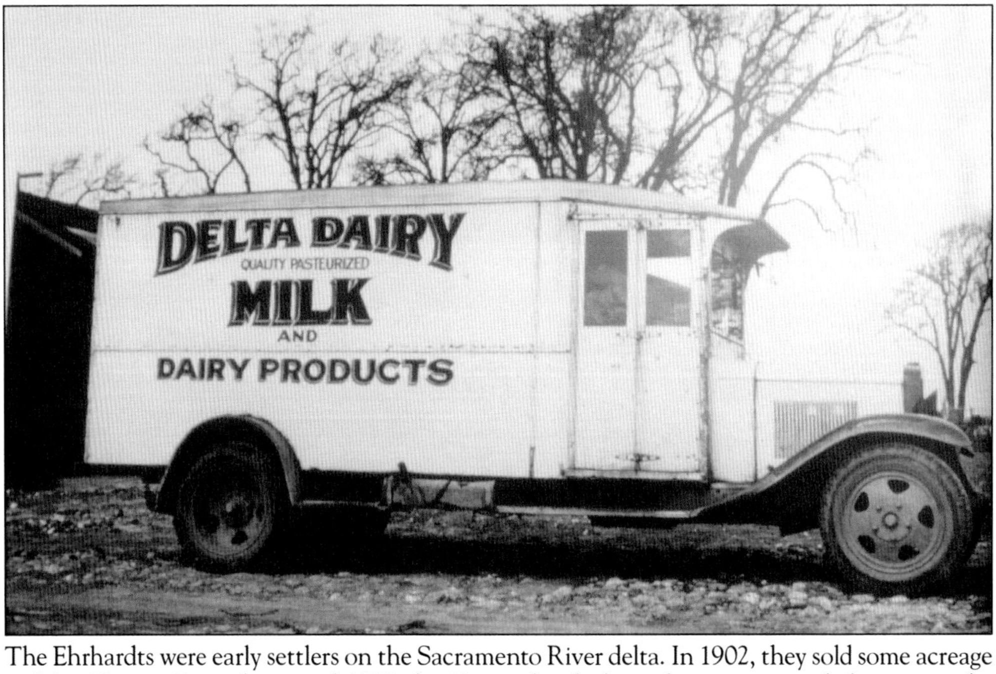

The Ehrhardts were early settlers on the Sacramento River delta. In 1902, they sold some acreage to John Herzog. From then until 1955, the Herzog family farmed row crops, and also operated a dairy from 1924 to 1955. In 1960, vineyards were planted, which are still producing today. The fourth generation of the Herzog family still resides on the land. This photograph of a Delta Dairy delivery truck was taken in the 1930s. (SRDHS.)

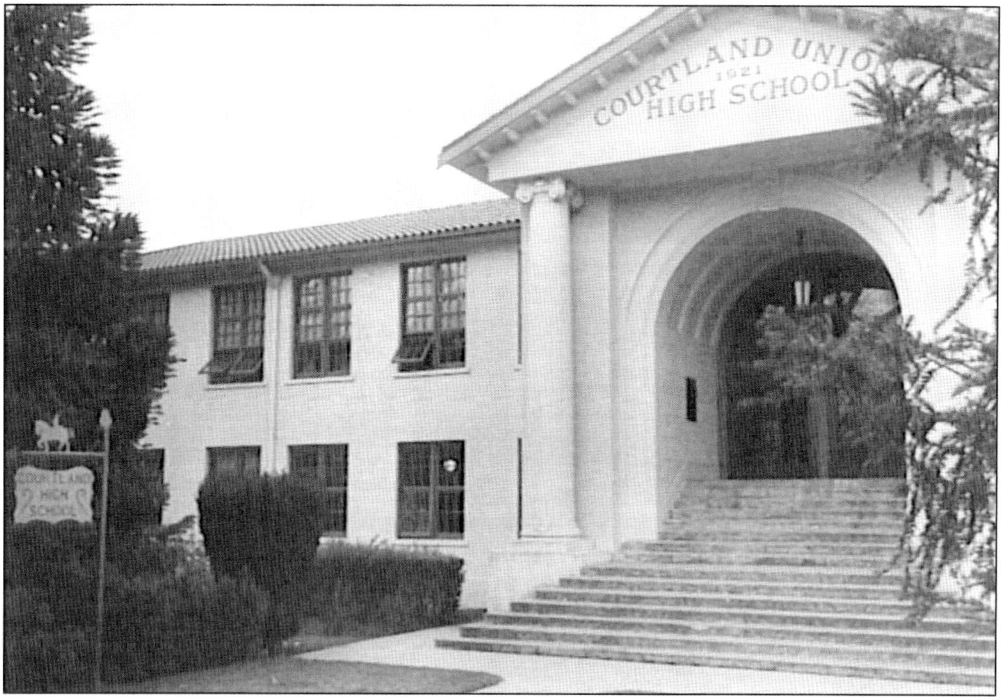

Courtland Union High School was completed in 1921. In 1915, several small school districts had been established in the delta towns. This was one of those schools, which were built to meet the needs of the community. The school grounds were designed by John McLaren, the longtime superintendent of Golden Gate Park in San Francisco. The school closed in 1966 when the River Delta Unified School District was formed. (SRDHS.)

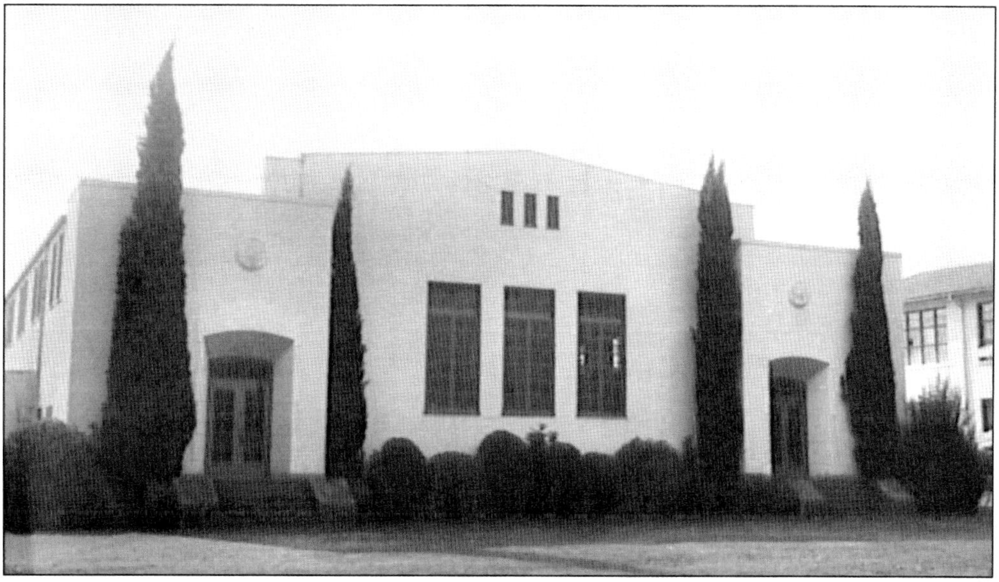

As the community grew, so did the school, and this gymnasium was eventually constructed for Courtland Union High School in 1930 and linked by a hallway to the main building. In the school's early years, the student body chose *La Perita* as the name of the school yearbook and the Charger as school mascot. (SRDHS.)

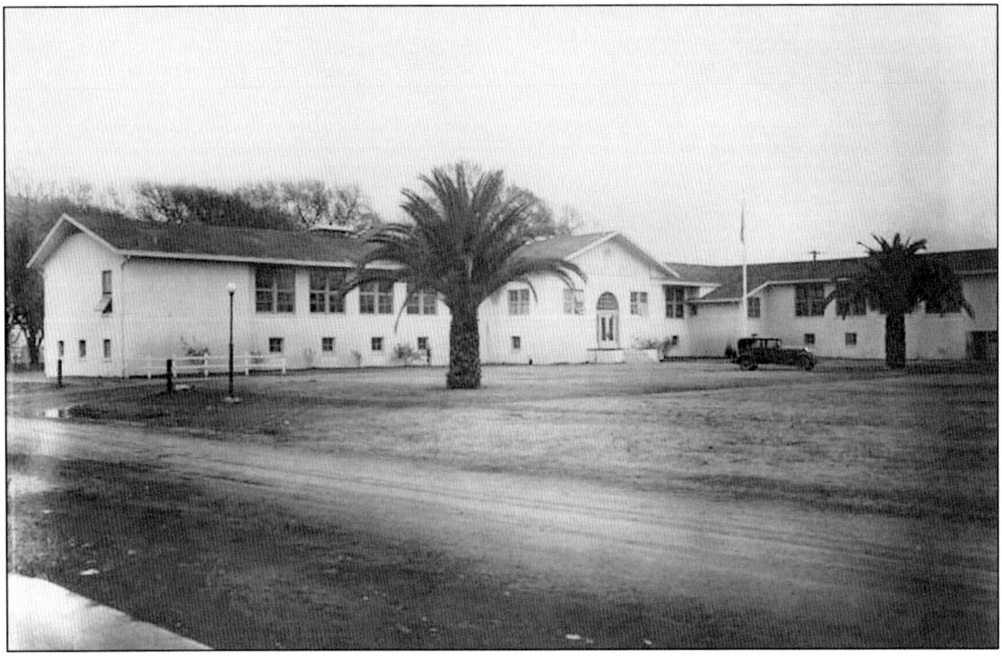

Bates Elementary School, named after early Courtland pioneer Benjamin Bates, opened in 1921 on Primasing Avenue. The towns of Rio Vita, Isleton, Ryck, Walnut Grove, Locke, Courtland, and Clarksburg all had grammar schools, while only Rio Vista, Courtland, and Clarksburg had high schools. (CSL.)

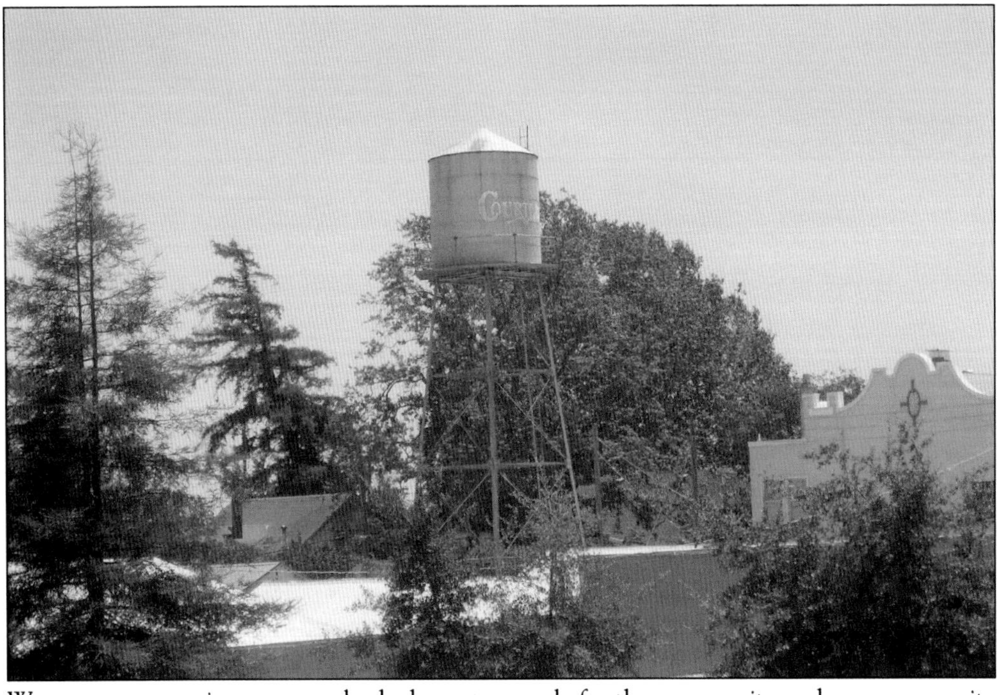

Water towers were important as both the water supply for the community and as a community marker for those on the Sacramento River. There are still water towers similar to this one in Locke, Ryde, Isleton, and at the Discover the Delta Center. (Author's collection.)

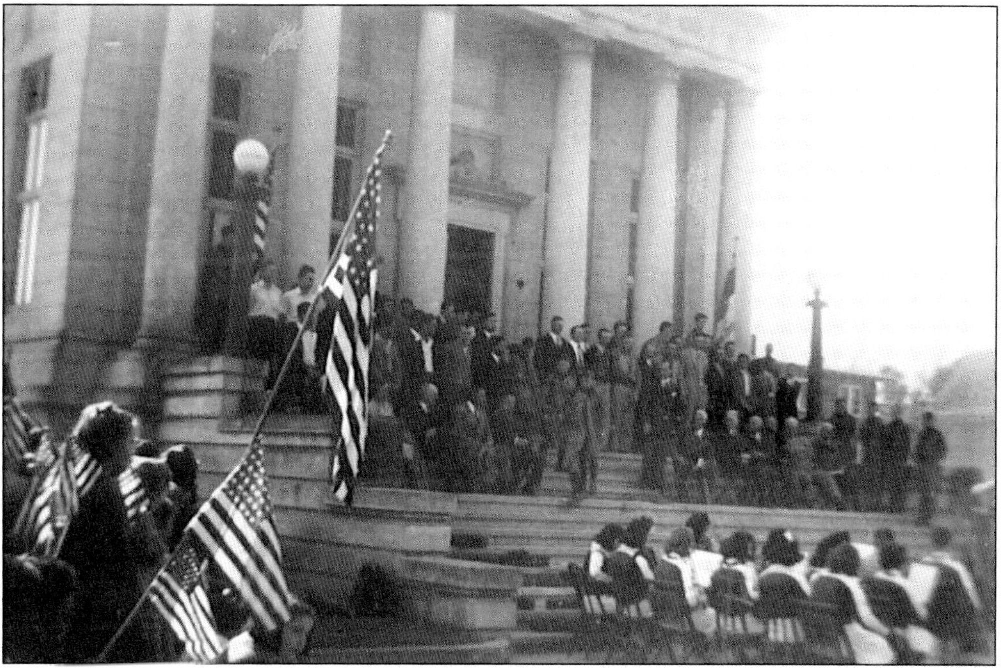

Practically the entire community of Courtland turned out on March 11, 1941, for a big send-off to 36 local men who were drafted into the military. Because the community was so small, everyone knew everyone, and the large crowd gathered on the steps of the Delta Telephone and Telegraph Company offices to give their family members and friends a patriotic send-off. (SRDHS.)

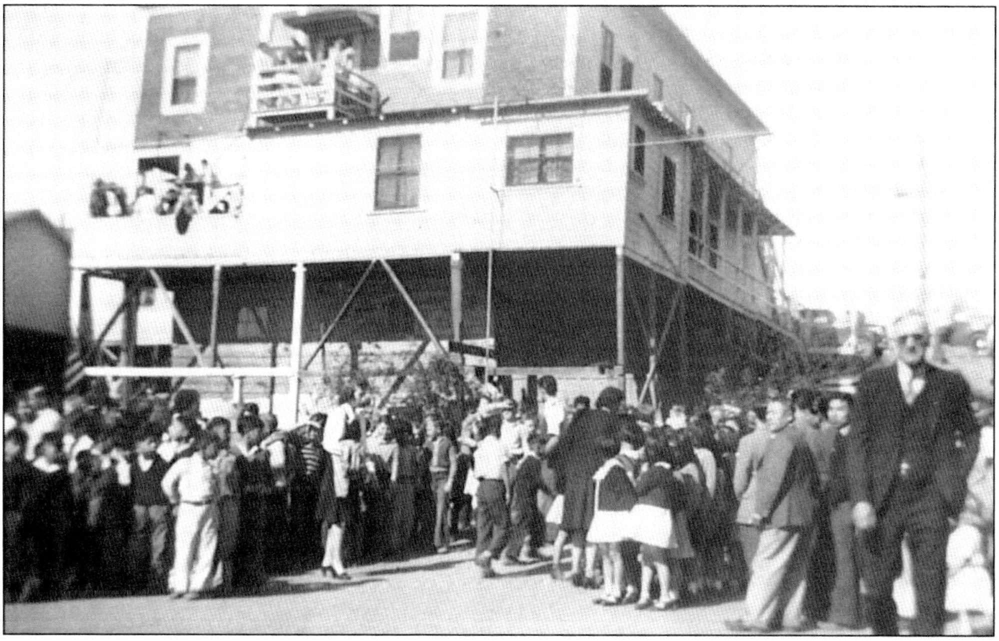

The old Red & White store was originally built for the IDES as a meeting hall. Like so many historical wooden buildings, it was destroyed by fire in 1984 while in the process of being renovated into a private residence. Both of the photographs on this page were taken on March 11, 1941. (SRDHS.)

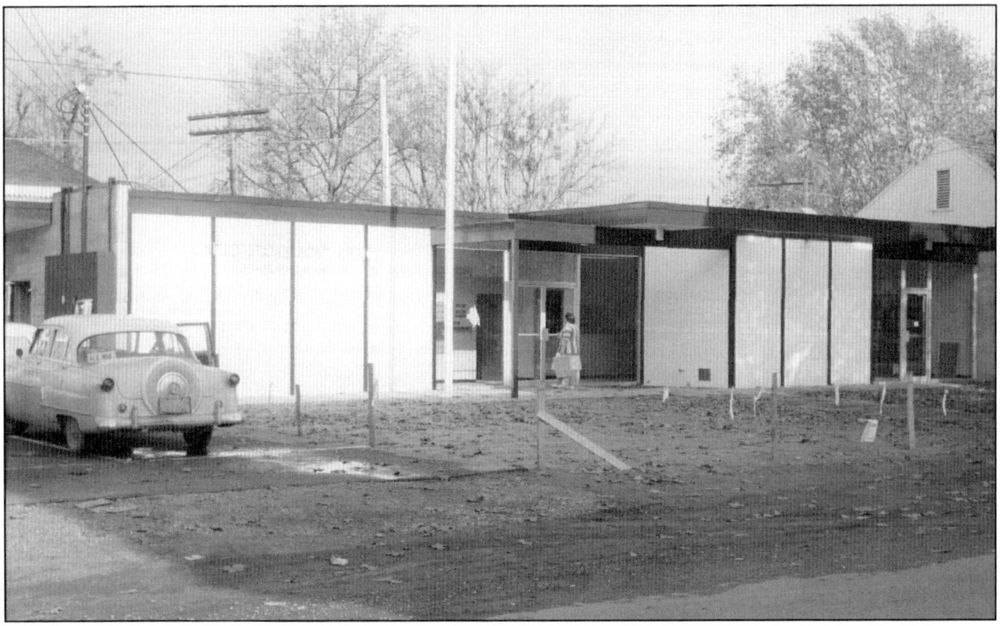

The original post office was established in Onsibo in the 1860s. Eventually, the post office was moved to Courtland, into the building next to Bauer, Miller & Newbert's general merchandise store. In the late 1800s and the early 1900s, mail arrived daily on the steamships *Apache* and *Modoc*. This photograph shows the existing post office shortly after it was built. (SRDHS.)

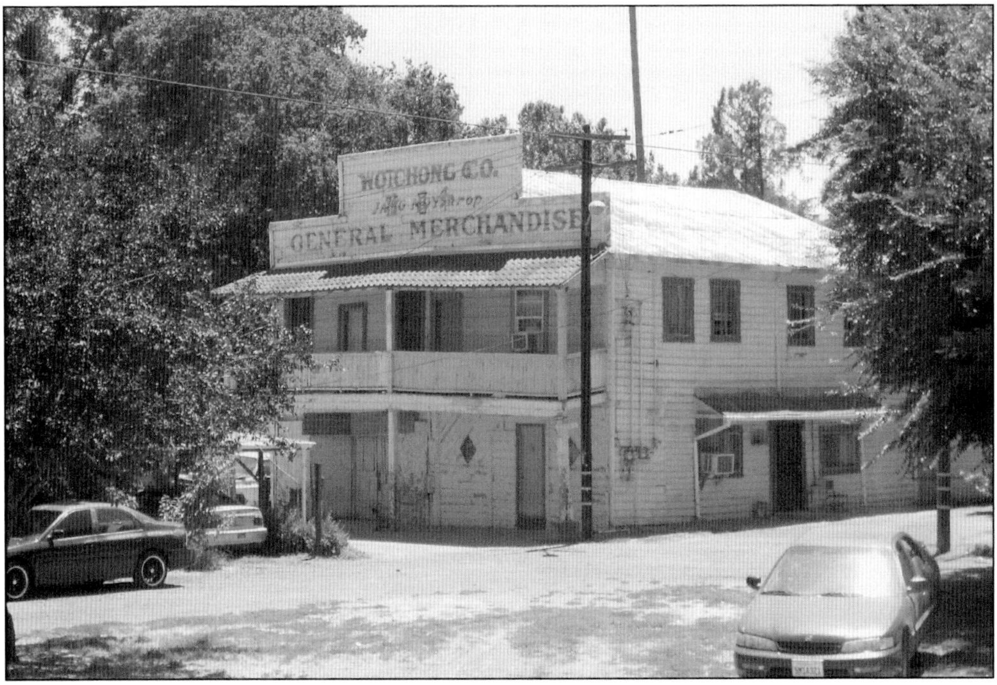

A new Chinatown was constructed in Courtland, only to be destroyed by fire again in 1906. The third Chinatown was built on property owned by Deming L. Winters and J.W. Houston. All that remains of the Chinese section of Courtland are the Wotchong Co. store building (seen here), the Nishihara Grocery Company, and a handful of houses. (Author's collection.)

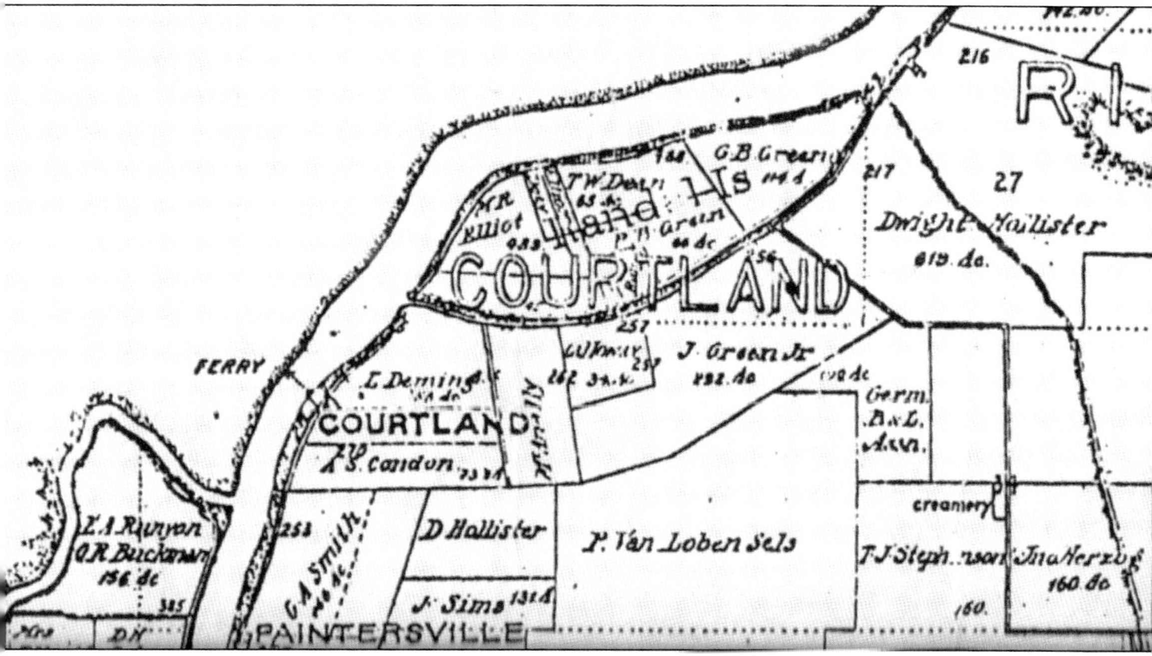

This enlarged section of a 1903 map shows the location of the Chinese community known as Elliot's Village, which was on D.J. Elliott's land near Courtland. The Chinatown overhung the river on the levee upstream from the Courtland wharf. That first Chinese community was destroyed by fire on December 24, 1879. Between 1870 and 1915, there were Chinese communities in Rio Vista, Isleton, Walnut Grove, Locke, Vordon, Paintersville, Courtland, and Elliott Village. (RVM.)

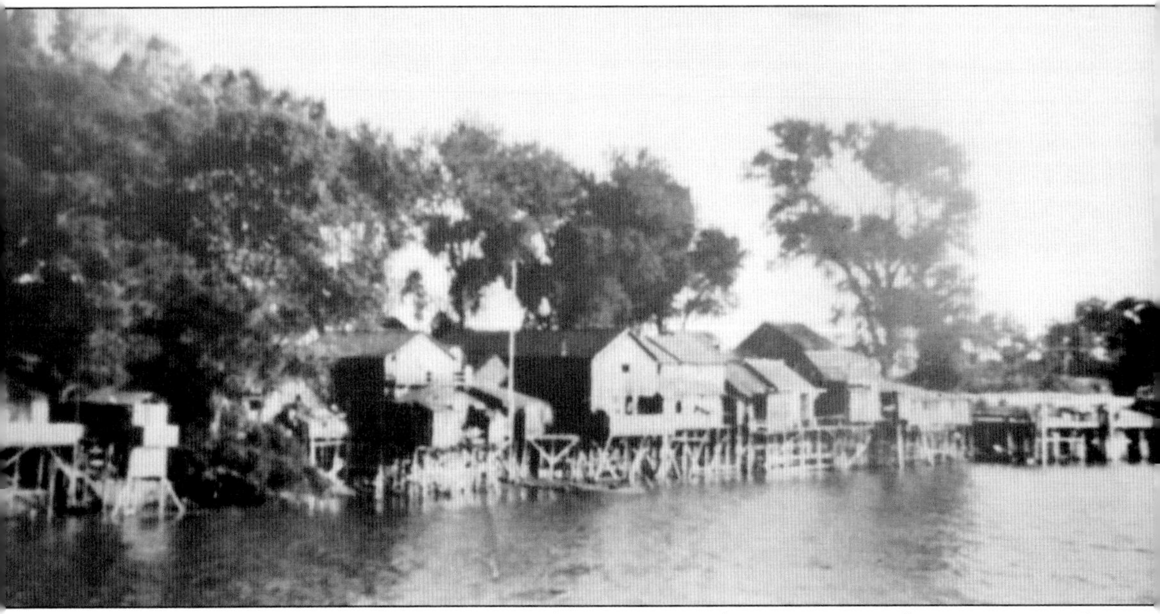

The date and location of this photograph are contested. Some sources list it as an 1885 photograph of Elliott Village Chinatown, while other list it as a 1910 photograph of Courtland's Chinatown. Many locals recall the stories of Elliott Village. James F. Elliott is reported to have moved to the delta around 1890 to work for David Osborn, a local rancher. Upon his death, Osborn left property to his niece Marth Rebecca Osborn, who married Elliott in 1895. Thus the settlement may have been either originally on Osborn's property or, at a later date, after the property changed hands to Elliott. (SRDHS.)

Eight

Hood

Originally established as Richland in 1860, the settlement became a shipping point for grain. As the population grew, a schoolhouse and several other buildings were constructed. By 1880, all that remained of the community was the schoolhouse, which was used for church services by the Methodists.

In 1909, the settlement was named Hood, in honor of Southern Pacific Railroad engineer and Civil War veteran William Hood (1846–1926). Since the village was established primarily as a railroad town, a name synonymous with the railroad seemed fitting. Unfortunately, more information is known about the man than about the town named after him.

The site that the community of Hood is located on was purchased from the Johnson and Edinger families. At the time, the property was comprised mostly of orchards. The Hood train station was constructed just south of what would become the town of Hood, on Franklin Road. A spur went to the wharf, where a large packing shed was constructed. Through the years, the shed was maintained by the California Fruit Exchange, Stillwater Orchards, and David J. Elliott and Son. The American Fruit Growers had a shed near Hood junction until 1943, when it was dismantled and moved to Walnut Grove.

In July 1976, the Southern Pacific Railroad filed to abandon the line to Hood and the use of Hood junction. Although the railroad received protests from the Del Monte Corporation, the Interstate Commerce Commission (ICC) approved the abandonment. Southern Pacific was told by the ICC to keep the right-of-way intact, just in case the California Department of Parks and Recreation had any interest in acquiring it. The railroad continued to operate until 1978, when the last Southern Pacific train arrived at the Hood junction on October 10 that year.

Looking at Hood today, it is hard to believe that during its heyday, Hood not only had packing sheds and a train station but also boasted a hotel, grocery store, café, hardware store, church, and post office.

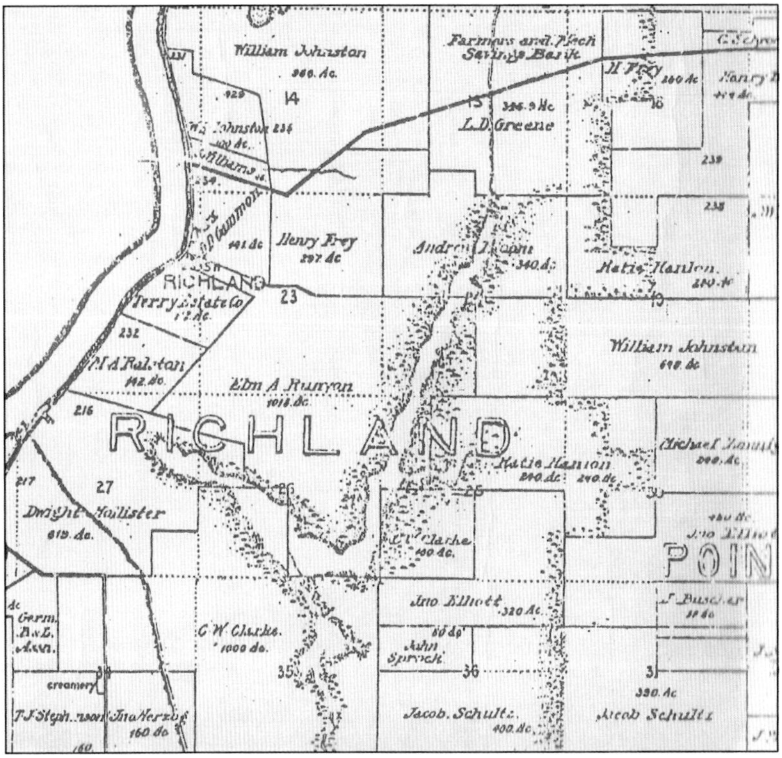

This enlarged section of a 1903 map of the delta shows the Richland district and the community of Richland, which was renamed Hood in 1909. It also shows all property division lines and the names of the property owners. (RVM.)

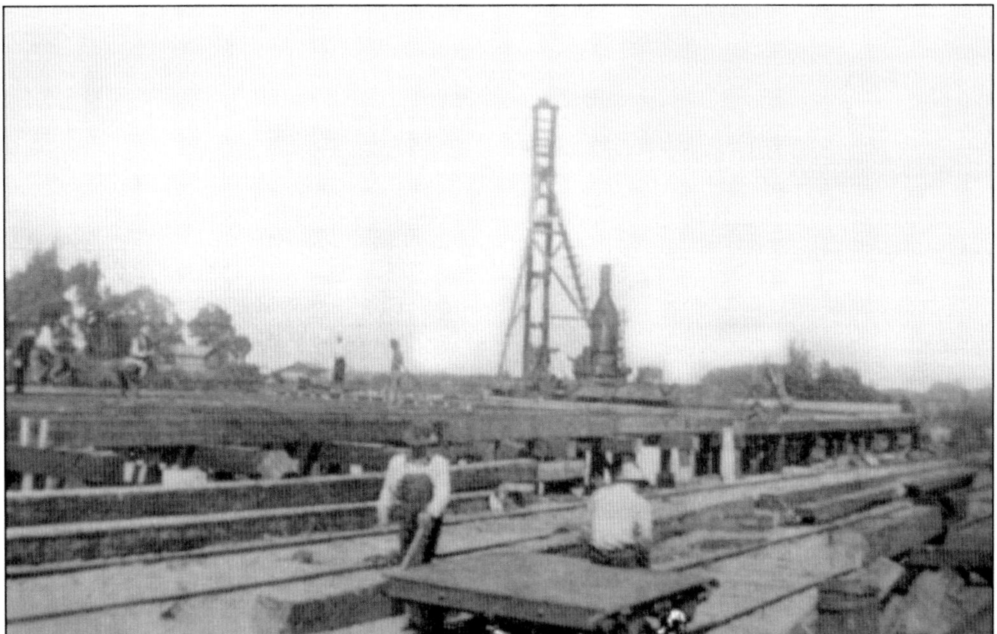

This image shows the construction of the Hood wharf, which was built by the Southern Pacific Railroad but not used exclusively by it. The wharf was open to all river travelers and transportation, no matter what company. The Hood junction was built just south of Hood-Franklin Road, and a spur went from it to the wharf. (SRDHS.)

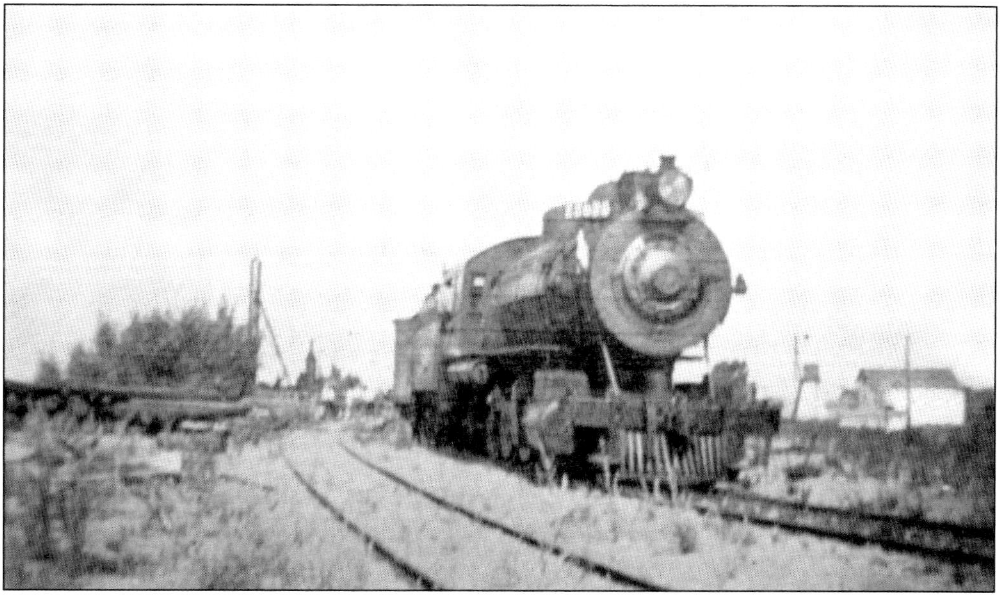

Since Hood was primarily a railroad community, many of the historical photographs that have survived are railroad-related, such as this image of a Southern Pacific steam locomotive pulling into town. (SRDHS.)

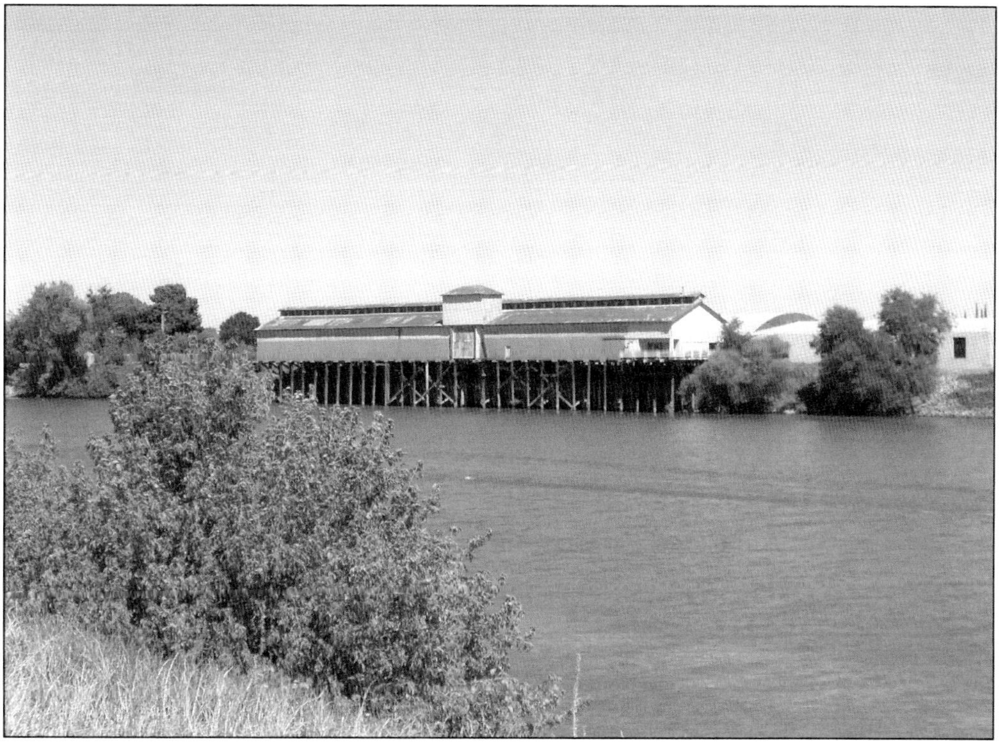

A large packing shed was built next to the wharf, with a spur from the Southern Pacific Railroad to it. Through the years, the shed was used by the California Fruit Exchange, Stillwater Orchards, and David J. Elliott and Son. This 2012 image, taken from across the river, shows that the shed design resembled the sheds built in Locke and Isleton. (Photograph by Christina Pezzaglia.)

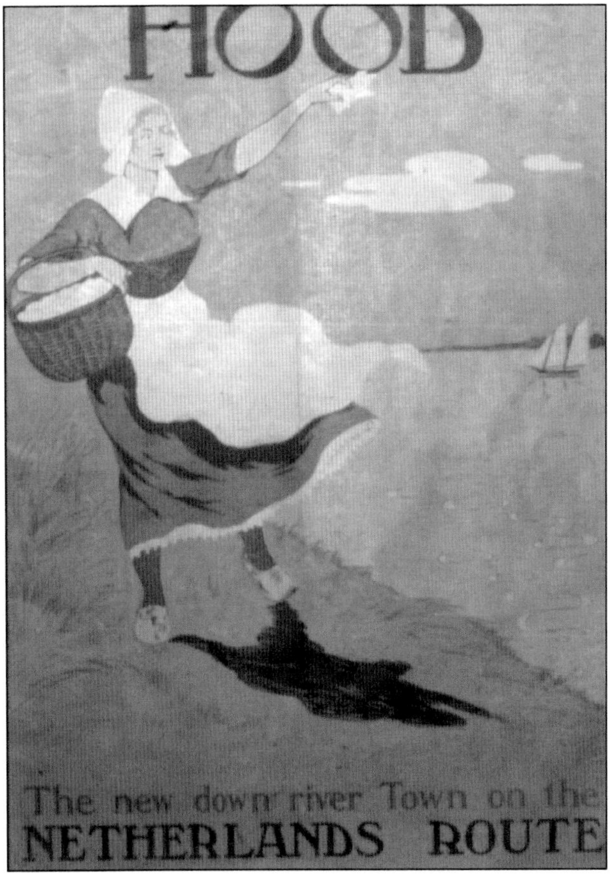

This 1920s advertisement—"Hood, the new down river Town on the Netherlands Route"—shows that the Southern Pacific Railroad tried hard to market Hood as both a vacation destination and a real estate venture. F.E. Batturs, a Southern Pacific assistant passenger traffic manager, has been credited with labeling the Sacramento River delta the "Netherlands of America" because of the levees and the agriculture activity taking place behind them. (SRDHS.)

With its Dutch-inspired architecture, the Hood Hotel, later renamed the Hood River Inn and at one time named Hotel Netherlands, was another fine hotel that looked slightly out of place in the delta. Its architecture rivaled that of the Boon-Dox in Walnut Grove, and its size that of the Hotel Ryde and the Hotel Rio Vista. The Hood Hotel burned down in the early 1950s. (SRDHS.)

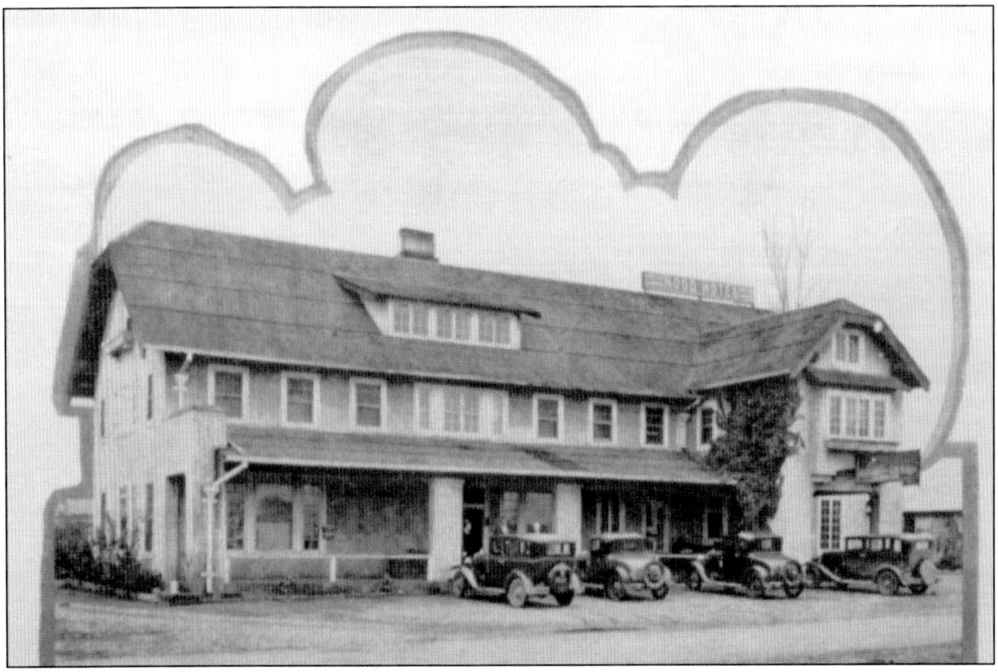

Nine

CLARKSBURG

The settlement of Clarksburg was established by Judge Robert Christopher Clark in 1849 (some accounts say 1856) under the original name of Clarksburgh. That spelling lasted for several years, but the *h* was dropped in 1893. The community is located at the tip of Yolo County, between Sutter and Elk Sloughs, straddling the natural levee adjacent to the west with a swamp. Because of this unique location, early settlers were often referred to as "rim landers" or "rim farmers." Even though the community was named after him, Judge Clark and his wife only resided there until 1869, when they moved to Sacramento.

Similar to its counterparts downriver, the community started with a few structures and a wharf. Once the wharf was constructed, the town became a stop for the earliest travelers who journeyed from San Francisco to Sacramento by steamship and sailing vessels. Before long, a schoolhouse, a general store, a blacksmith shop, and a post office were established to meet the needs of the young community. In 1878, Daniel Grant Webber established a store on the wharf, which was then renamed Webber's Landing.

Due to the lack of levees, many of the earliest homes were built on stilts and many residents lived on houseboats. The community did not grow nearly as fast as the other delta towns that followed, but growth began to occur in 1911 when the Netherlands Farm Company started buying up land and formed Reclamation District 999. In 1916, the Holland Land Company was formed, under the supervision of J.V. Mendenhall, and purchased all stock and land from the Netherlands Farm Company. By 1920, the New Holland Land Company had subdivided the tracts, selling some 80 units out of the 15,000 acres for a total of more than $4.25 million. After that, Clarksburg was formally established as an unincorporated community.

There are still disagreements about the boundaries of Clarksburg. Some accounts state that the portion of Sacramento County directly across the Sacramento River was at one time considered to be part of the community because a ferry crossing existed there from 1920 until 1930. Some still consider that area part of Clarksburg.

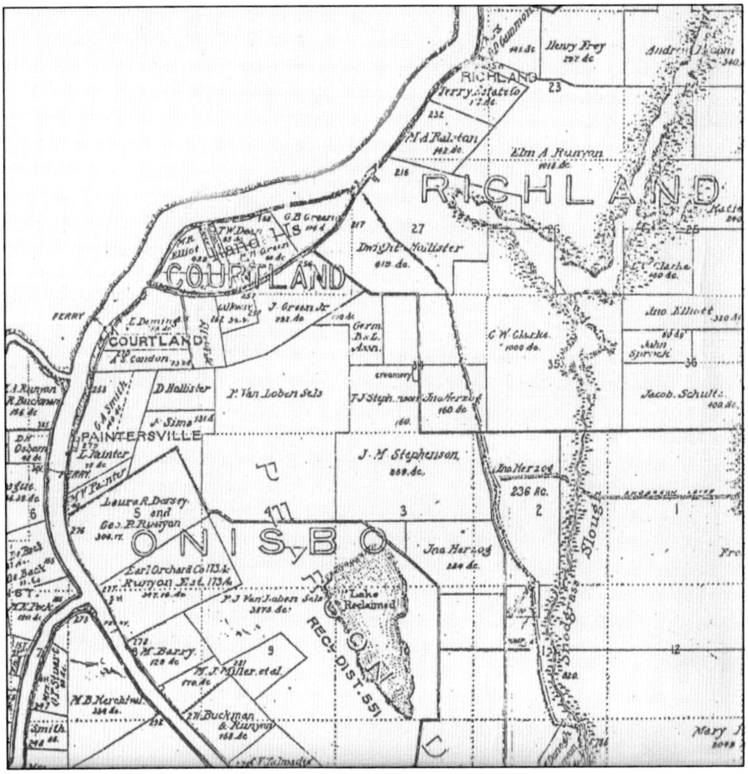

This 1903 map shows Paintersville, Courtland, and Richland. Although Richland was established in 1860, by 1880, there was little left of the community but the schoolhouse. The settlement ceased to exist, only to be reborn and renamed Hood in 1909. Many of the descendants of the property owners listed on this map still remain in the delta, farming the same land their ancestors did. (RVM.)

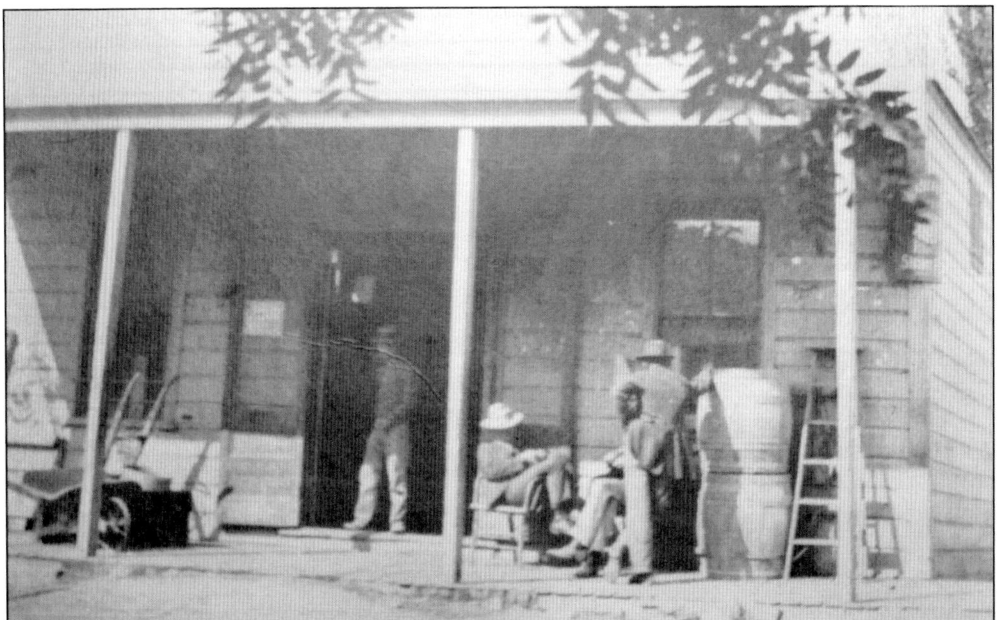

One of the first businesses built in any town was a general merchandise store. Unfortunately, the name of the owner of this particular Clarksburg establishment is unknown. The store looks very similar in its architectural design to many of the other general stores scattered throughout the delta towns. (SRDHS.)

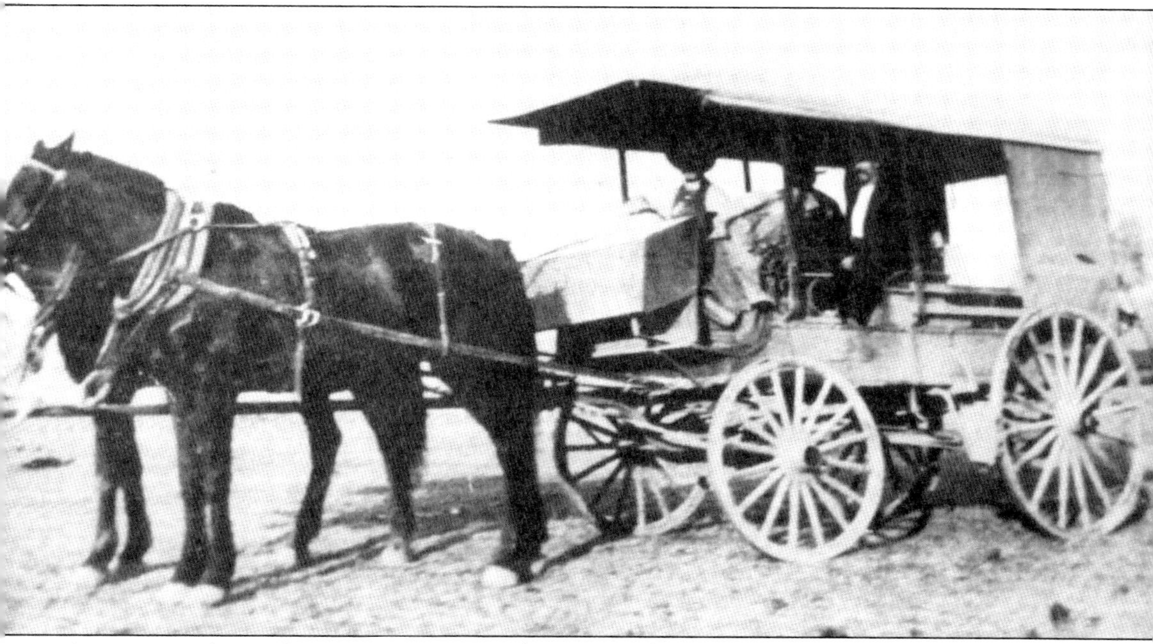

At one time, horse-drawn carriages were the means of transportation throughout the delta, traveling the levee roads from Clarksburg to Rio Vista. Before area bridges were built, ferries were put into operation where needed. After the flood of 1902, the community received government aid from both state and federal agencies. The Federal Reclamation Act of June 17, 1902, and the Harbor Act of March 1917 helped to provide for flood control in the delta. (SRDHS.)

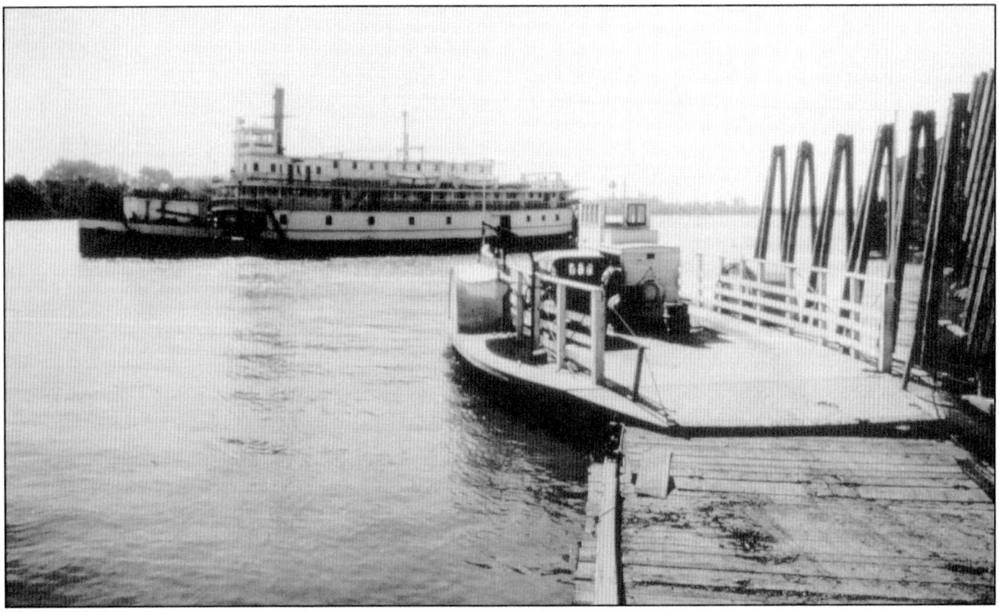

The first ferry linking Clarksburg with the east bank of the river was owned by Jack Foster and put into operation in 1855. The ferry in this photograph, christened *Mary Ann*, was placed into service in Clarksburg in 1920 and was designed by Nunes Brothers of Clarksburg. It could carry six trucks, or the equivalent, and was advertised as the "largest, best, and fastest" boat on the Sacramento River. (SRDHS.)

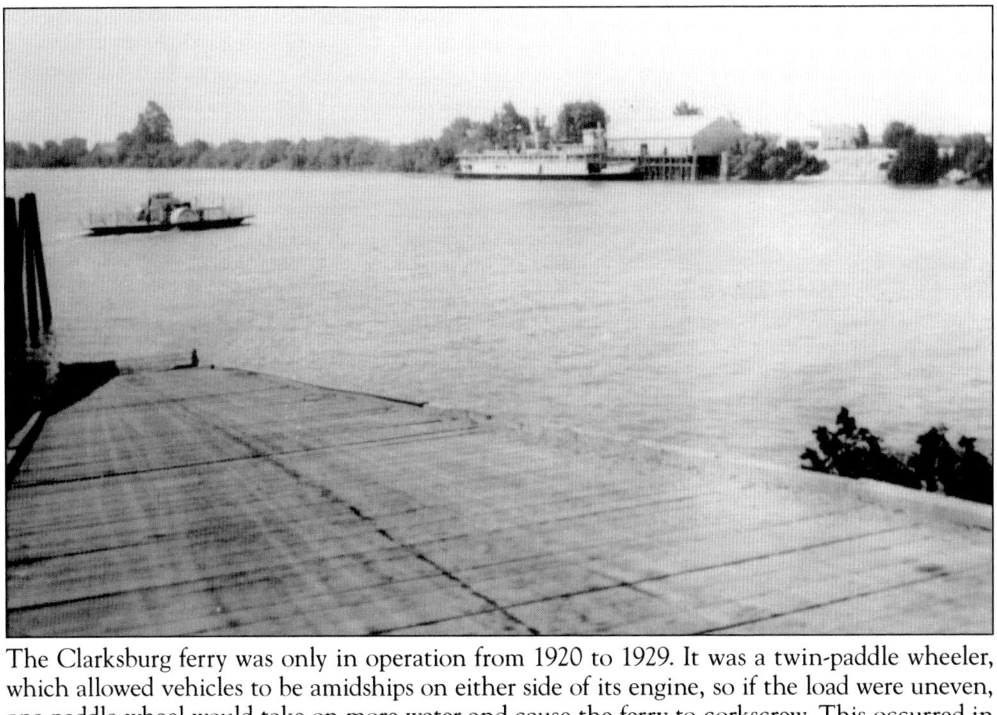

The Clarksburg ferry was only in operation from 1920 to 1929. It was a twin-paddle wheeler, which allowed vehicles to be amidships on either side of its engine, so if the load were uneven, one paddle wheel would take on more water and cause the ferry to corkscrew. This occurred in 1929, when the ferry was overloaded with a shipment of hardwood flooring intended for the new high school. (SRDHS.)

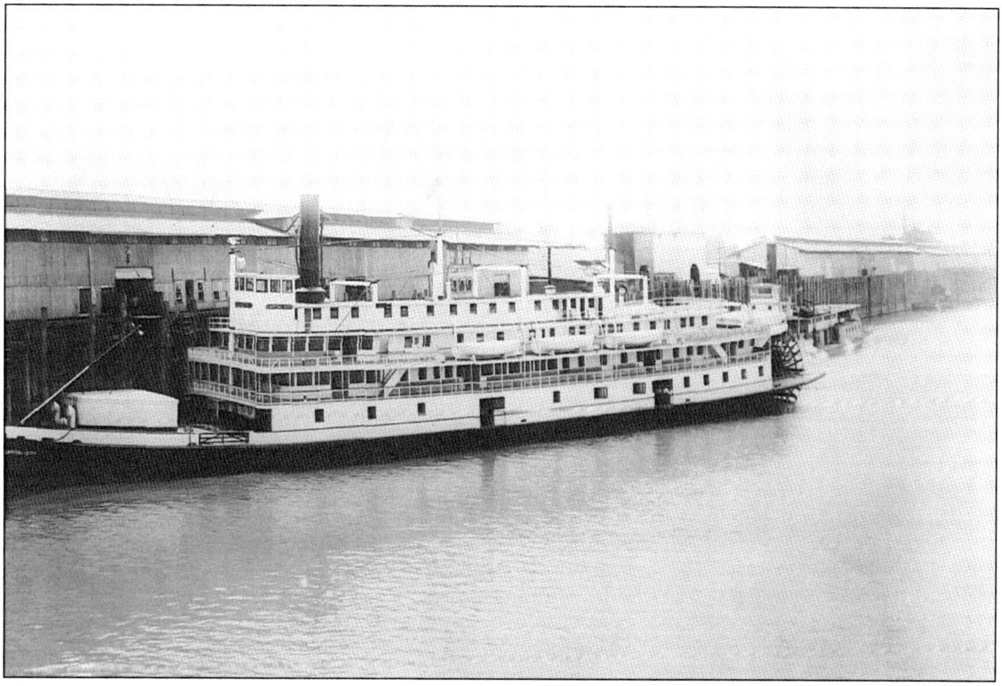

This is a typical scene of a steamship docked at the Clarksburg wharf. The wharf burned three times—in 1909, 1915, and 1941. After the last fire, it was decided not to rebuild. From the time Clarksburg was established, it was always a popular stop for steamships. (SRDHS.)

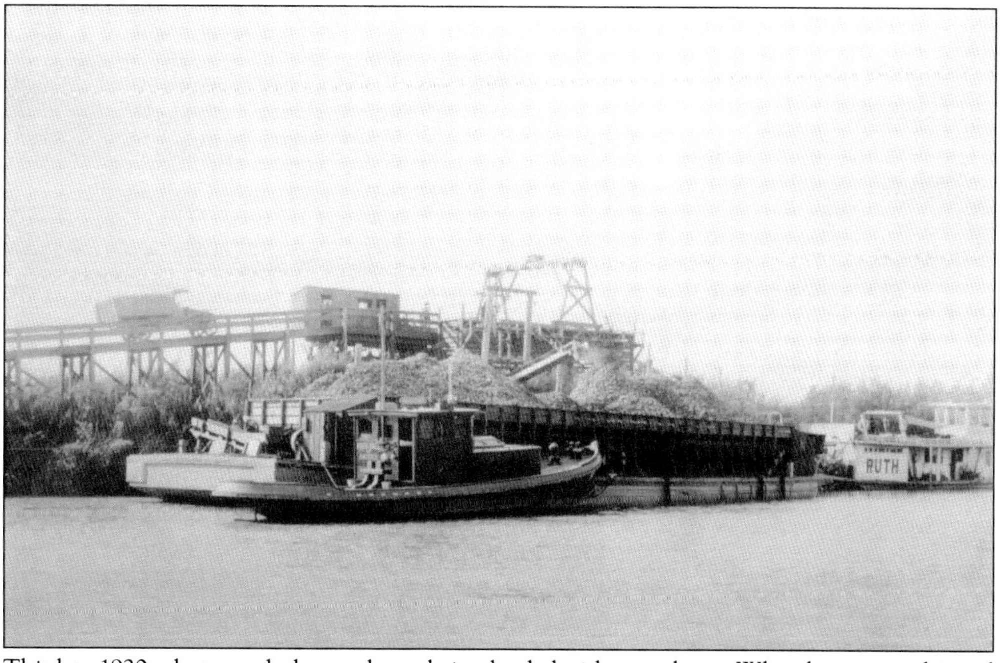

This late-1920s photograph shows a barge being loaded with sugar beets. When beets were shipped out of the area, they were moved by truck to a "beet dump." A bulkhead held the produce until it was time to ship, and the beets were then shoveled onto a conveyer operated by a small engine, which dumped them onto a waiting barge. (SRDHS.)

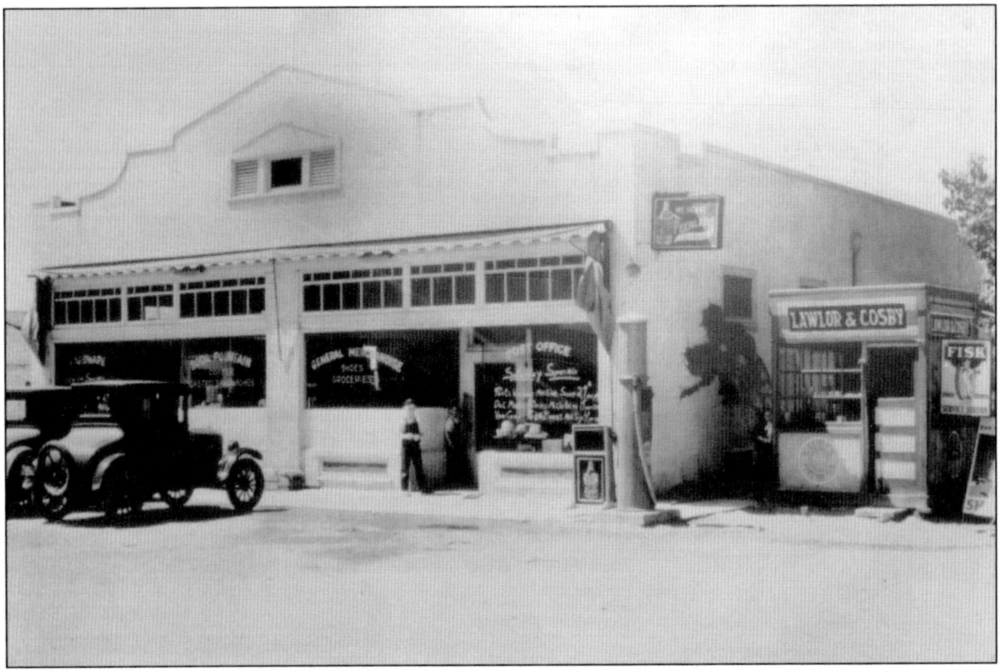

This building on the south end of town is known as Husick's. At the time of this photograph, it served as a soda fountain, a general merchandise store, and a post office. (SRDHS.)

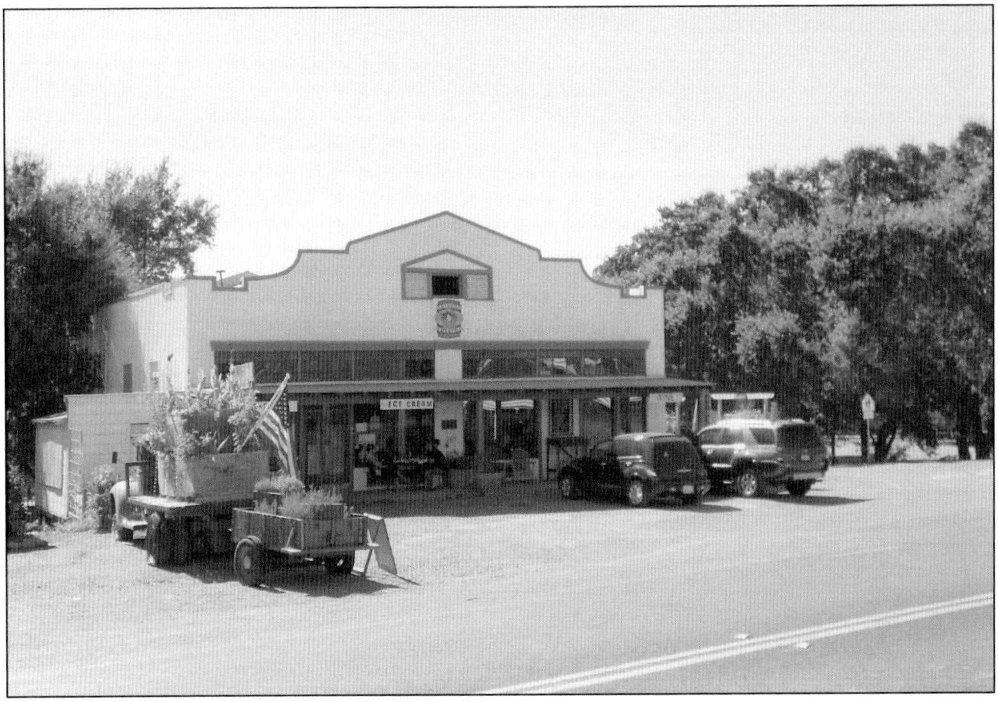

Compare this 2012 photograph with the one above. The exterior appearance has changed little since the days when Frank Husick occupied the building with his inventory of hardware and general merchandise. When Husick, a native of Minnesota, arrived on the riverbank in Clarksburg, he opened a hardware store and an adjacent blacksmith shop. (Author's collection.)

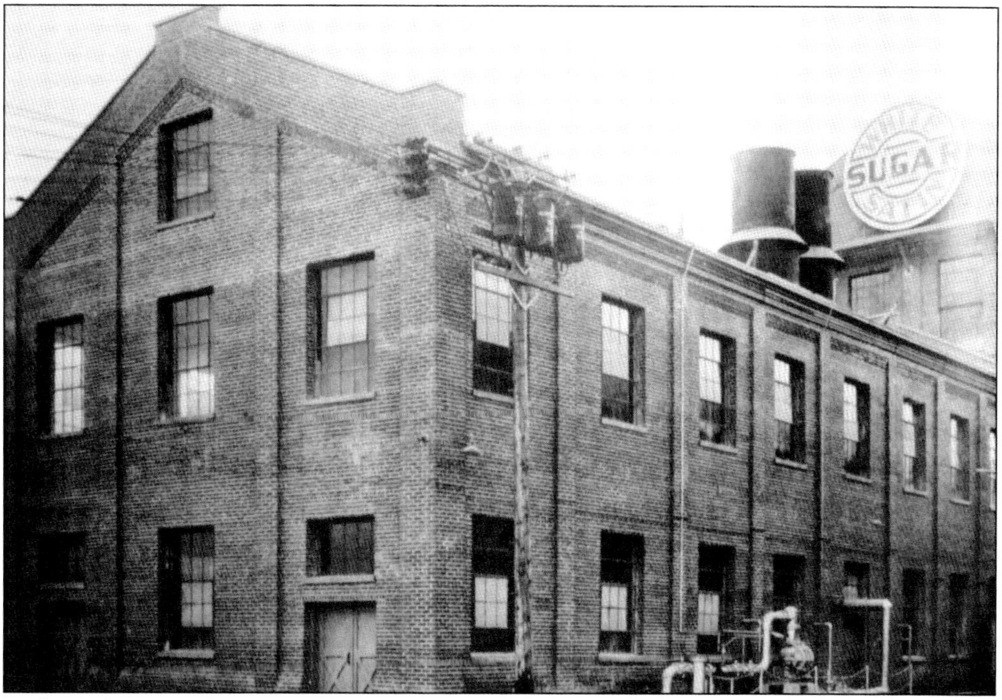

In the early 1920s, the Alameda Sugar Company contracted for the first sugar beets grown in the Holland tract. Shortly thereafter, the company was bought by the Holly Sugar Company, which sold it to the Amalgamated Sugar Company in 1934. It was finally bought by American Crystal Sugar in 1936. The brick plant seen here was constructed between 1934 and 1936. (SRDHS.)

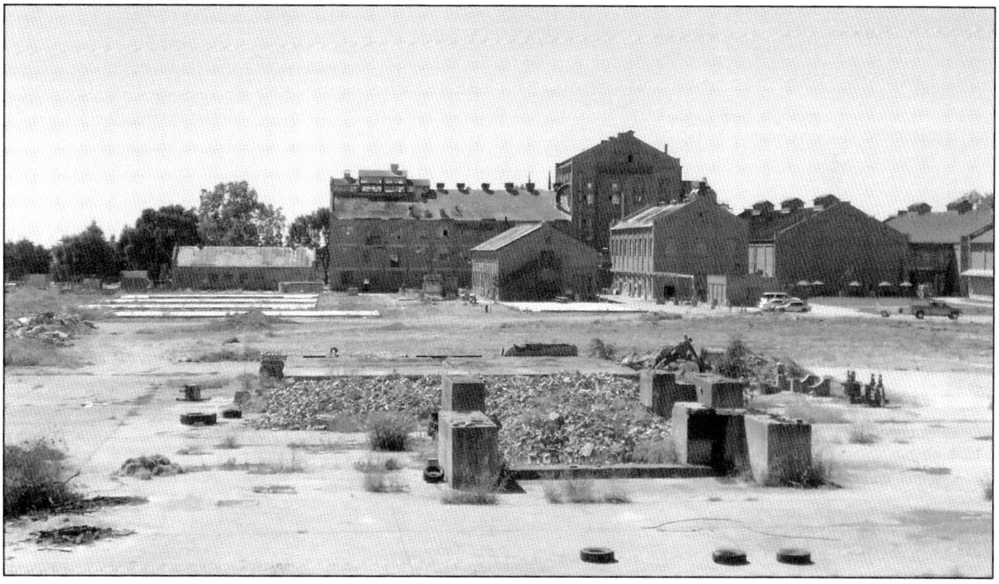

The sugar refinery closed in 1980 and the plant became a cooperative, which closed permanently in 1993. After much renovation, the Old Sugar Mill reopened and is now home to a unique community of six California wineries and their signature wines. This 2012 photograph captures the beauty of the 1930s brick industrial architecture of the plant. It also recalls the community's agricultural and industrial past. (Photograph by Christina Pezzaglia.)

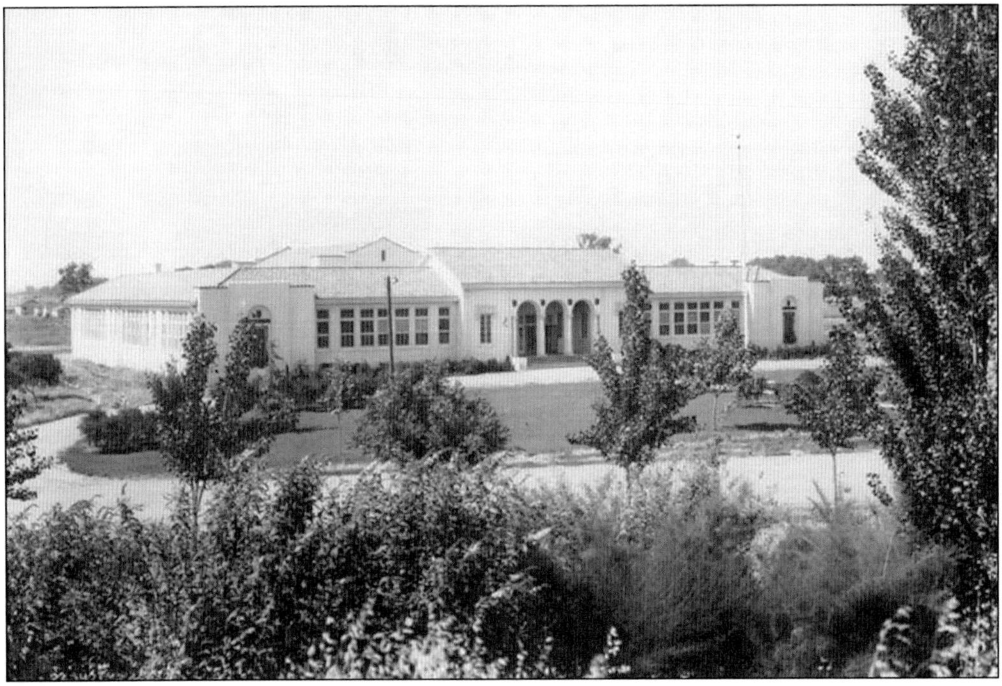

Clarksburg Elementary School opened in 1923 after the consolidation of several neighboring schools, including the Merrit and Lisbon schools, in the Clarksburg School District. Prior to this school's construction, the community had outgrown three schoolhouses, built in 1856, 1879, and 1883. (CSL.)

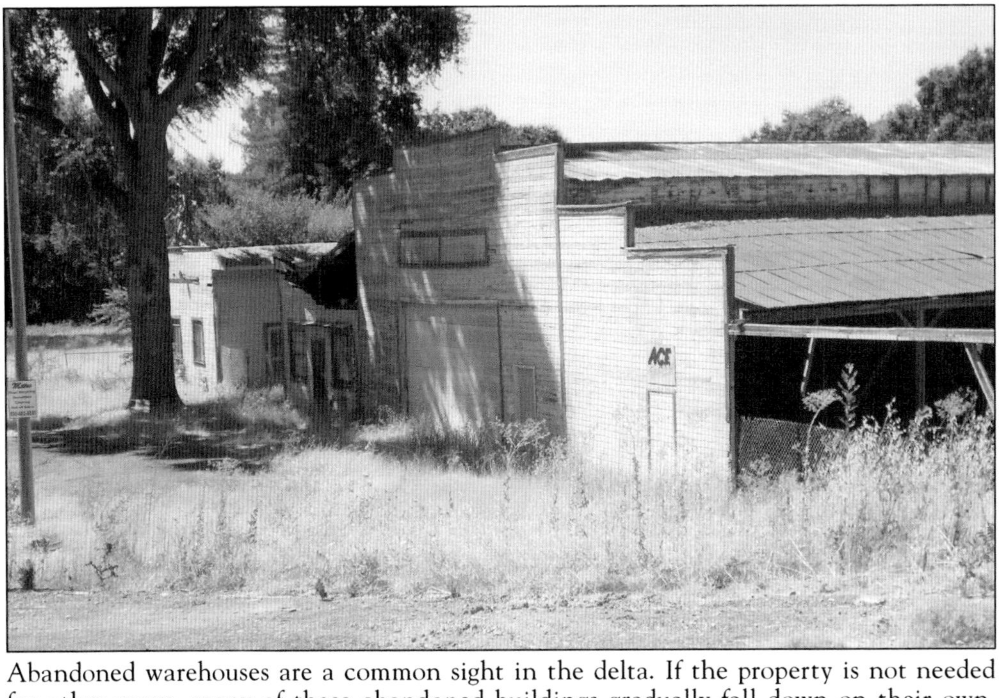

Abandoned warehouses are a common sight in the delta. If the property is not needed for other usage, many of these abandoned buildings gradually fall down on their own. (Photograph by Christina Pezzaglia.)

Ten

FREEPORT

The town of Freeport is on the eastern banks of the Sacramento River in Sacramento County and is one of the oldest communities in the delta. It was established as a railroad town in 1862 or 1863 in an attempt to construct a railway that bypassed Sacramento and connected with the Sacramento Valley Railroad at the midpoint between Sacramento and Folsom—all to avoid the fees imposed at Sacramento's embarcadero for landing both freight and passengers. When a 10-mile short line was constructed from Brighton station, on the Sacramento Valley Railroad, to what would become a free port, the community of Freeport was born.

Because the railroad envisioned that the free docking facilities would divert Folsom and Virginia City traffic from Sacramento to Freeport, the community grew to a population of 400 within the first three years. The Central Pacific Railroad purchased the line in 1865 in order to eliminate competition, and then removed the track in 1866. From that point on, the population of Freeport declined. By 1890, the settlement had become essentially a ferry point, with a general merchandise store containing a post and express office, and a handful of homes.

In the early days of Freeport, the community held an event called "Pole Day," when the liberty flagpole was erected during the Grant-Colfax presidential campaign of 1868. A 130-foot flagpole was erected at the intersection of Freeport Road and the road leading to Freeport Landing, and stayed for many years after. Early Freeport pioneers included Andrew J. Bump, the local grocer, postmaster, and saloonkeeper; Tom Kirkland, a blacksmith; Andy Greer, a boot maker; a Mrs. Eilbach, the proprietor of a hostelry; Jim Lea; and a Mr. Hunt.

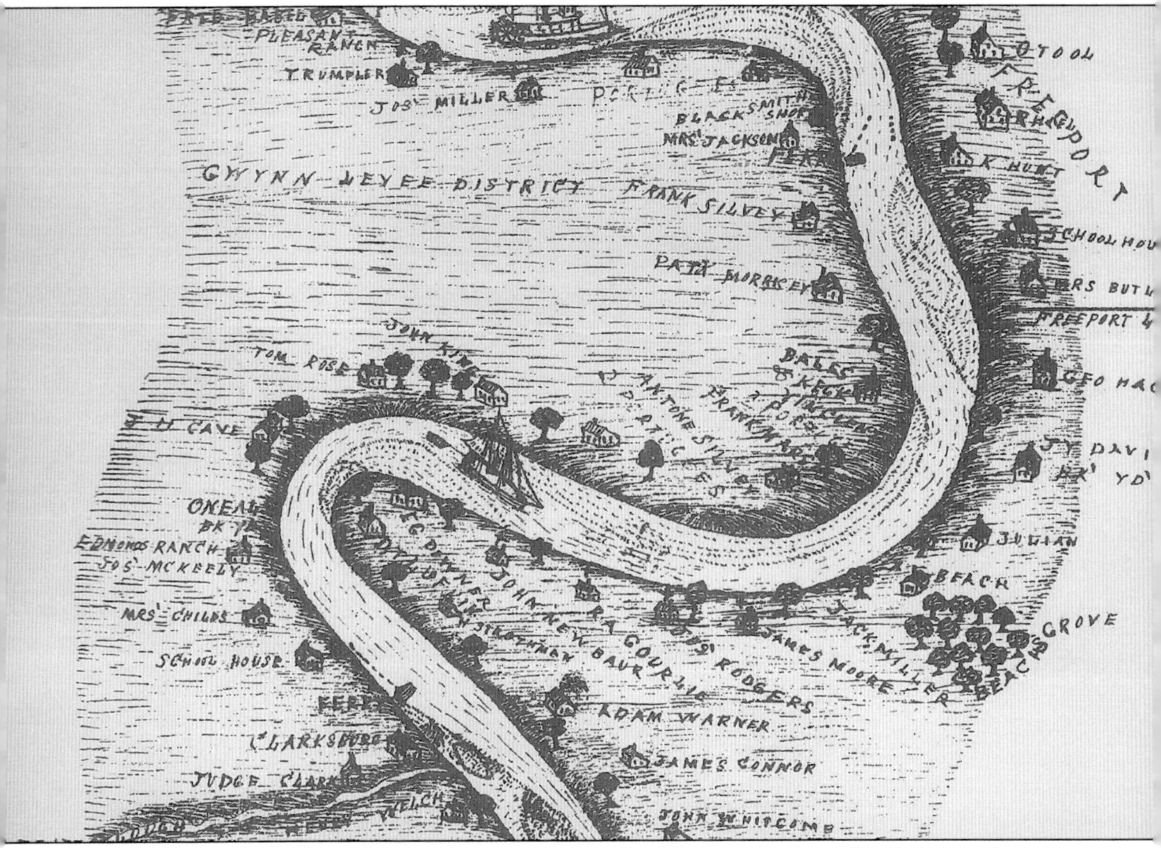

This early map of the delta shows Freeport and Clarksburg as well as all of the ranches along the Sacramento River. Steamship captains used this and similar maps so that they would know the location of not just the settlements but also the individual ranches, where they often made routine stops. Compare this map—and the names of the communities, as well as those of the landowners—with the maps in previous chapters. (RVM.)

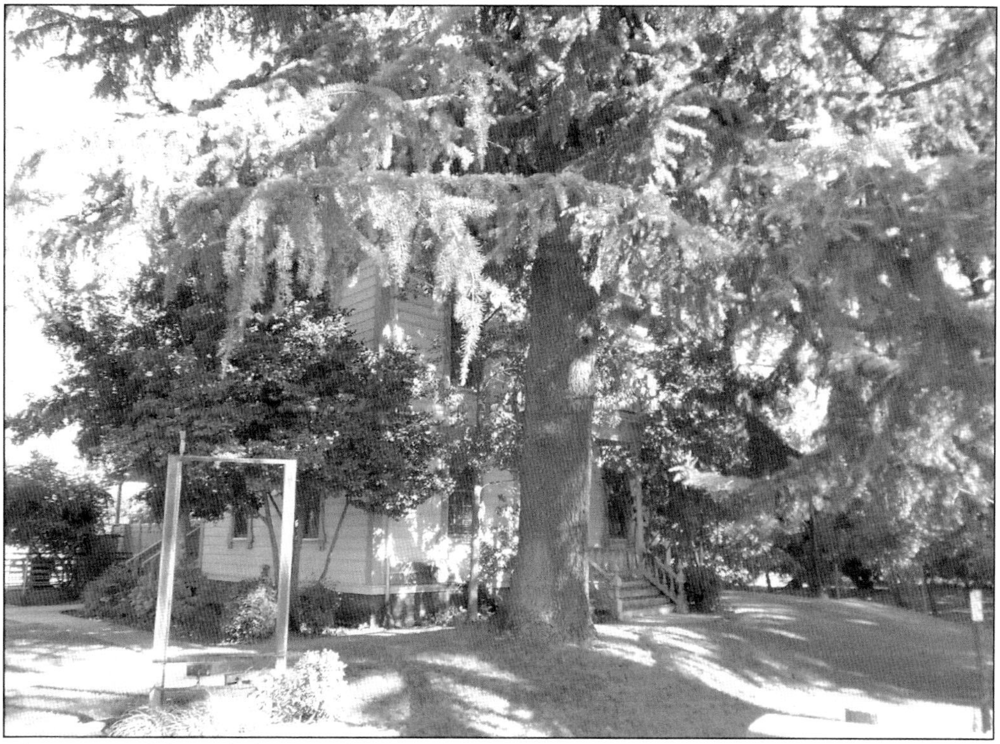

This is one of the only historic homes still standing in Freeport. The local business with the most documentation, but no photograph available, was the Freeport store, operated by Andrew J. Bump, who carried dry goods, wet goods, candy, and games of chance. Bump eventually sold to Daniel Webber, who later sold to Phil Riehl. (Author's collection.)

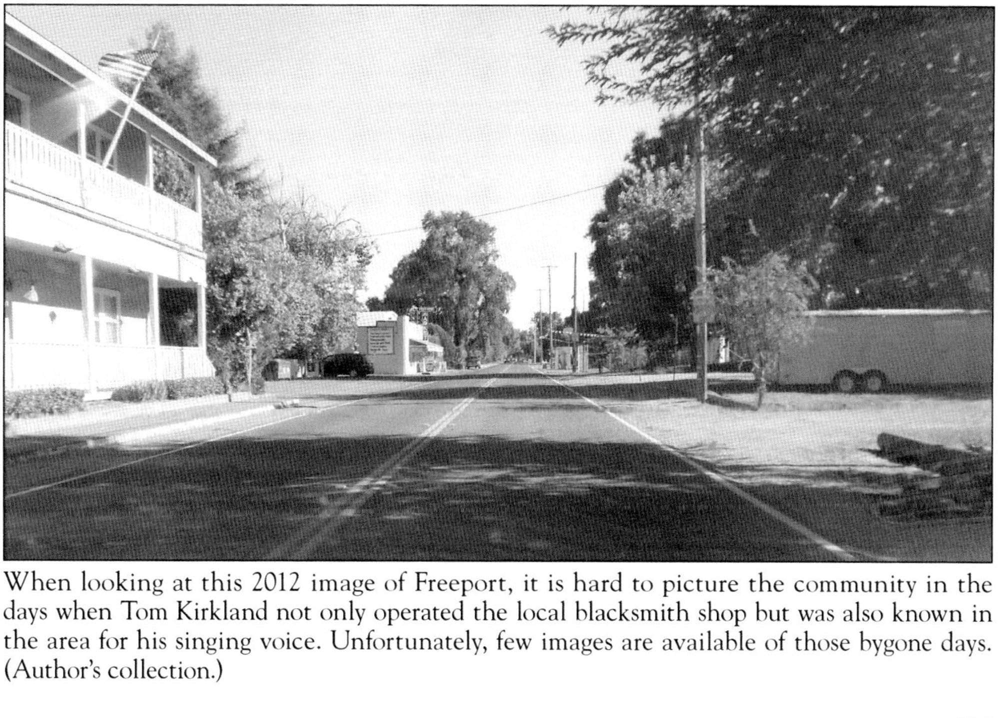

When looking at this 2012 image of Freeport, it is hard to picture the community in the days when Tom Kirkland not only operated the local blacksmith shop but was also known in the area for his singing voice. Unfortunately, few images are available of those bygone days. (Author's collection.)

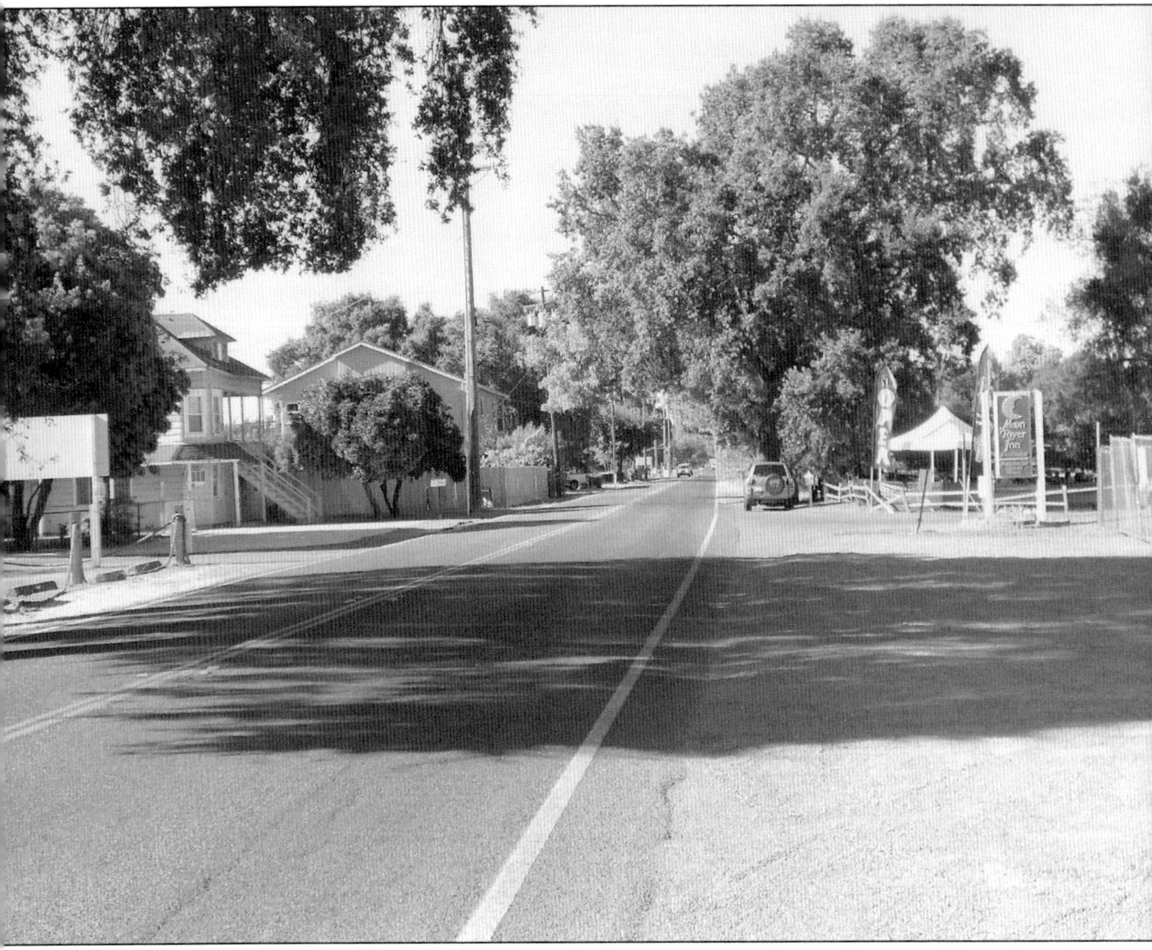

This 2012 view looks up Highway 160 towards Sacramento at the small, peaceful community of Freeport, with a current population of approximately 125. The community contains a handful of houses, three restaurants, two marinas, a market, a bait store, and a golf course. (Author's collection.)

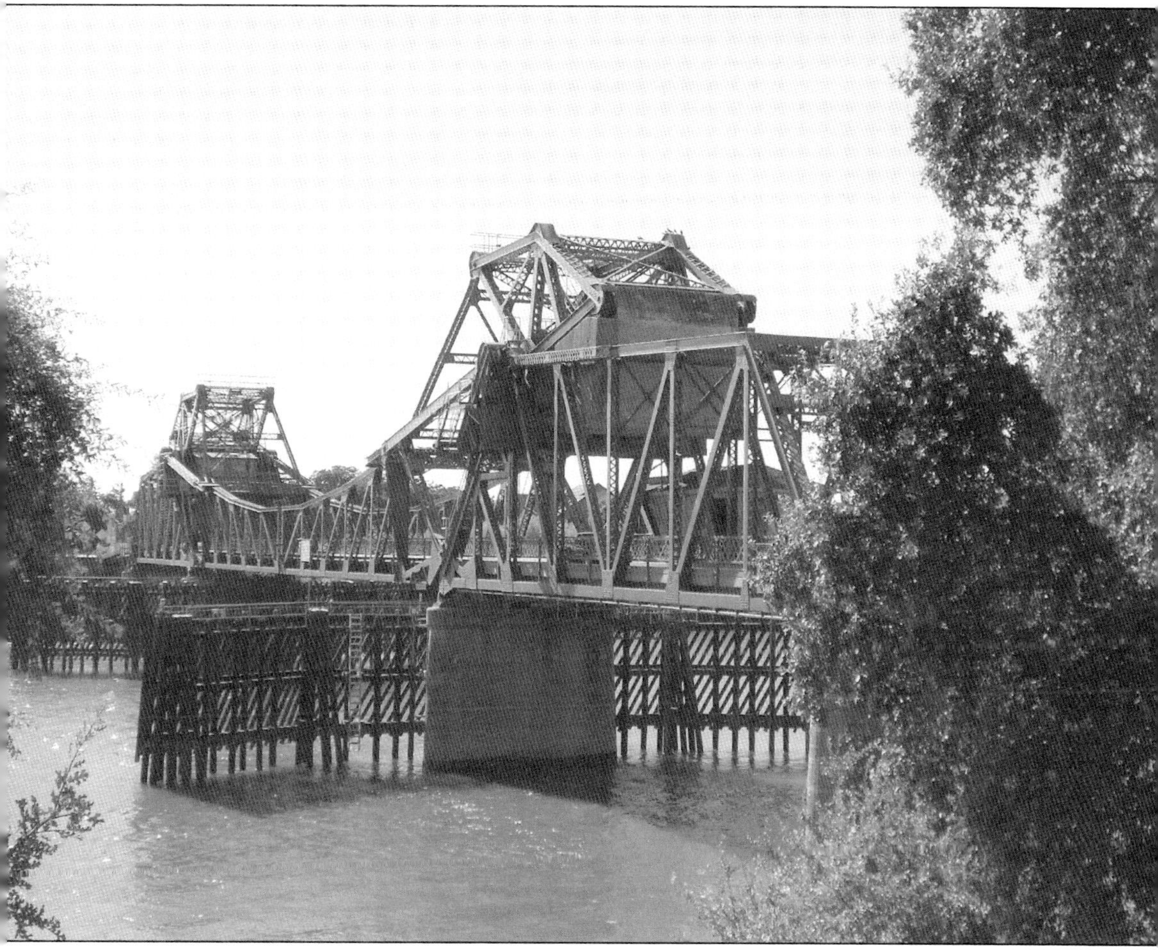

The double-leaf, heel-trunnion bascule bridge in Freeport was prefabricated in 1928 at the Moore Dry Dock Company in Oakland. When fabrication was completed, the bridge superstructure was towed up the Sacramento River on barges. When it arrived at Freeport, it was erected upon recently poured concrete foundations. The 656-foot-long bridge was opened to traffic on January 1, 1930. The bridge underwent a complete overhaul in 1955, and in 1992, the control house was replaced, bridge controls were computerized, and the traffic lights and gates were upgraded. The bridge looks virtually the same today as it did when it was originally constructed in 1928. The span is often described as an almost perfect copy of the Paintersville Bridge. (Author's collection.)

Discover Thousands of Local History Books Featuring Millions of Vintage Images

Arcadia Publishing, the leading local history publisher in the United States, is committed to making history accessible and meaningful through publishing books that celebrate and preserve the heritage of America's people and places.

Find more books like this at
www.arcadiapublishing.com

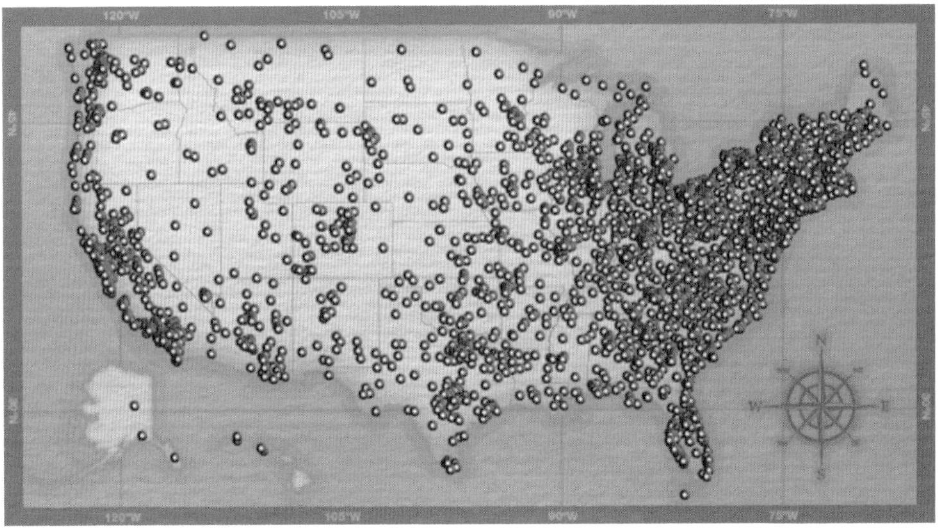

Search for your hometown history, your old stomping grounds, and even your favorite sports team.

Consistent with our mission to preserve history on a local level, this book was printed in South Carolina on American-made paper and manufactured entirely in the United States. Products carrying the accredited Forest Stewardship Council (FSC) label are printed on 100 percent FSC-certified paper.

MADE IN THE USA